**THIRD EDITION**

**4**

# Skills for Success
## READING AND WRITING

Debra Daise | Charl Norloff

**OXFORD**
UNIVERSITY PRESS

OXFORD
UNIVERSITY PRESS

198 Madison Avenue
New York, NY 10016 USA

Great Clarendon Street, Oxford, OX2 6DP, United Kingdom

Oxford University Press is a department of the University of Oxford.
It furthers the University's objective of excellence in research, scholarship,
and education by publishing worldwide. Oxford is a registered trade
mark of Oxford University Press in the UK and in certain other countries

ISBN: 978 0 19 490395 0    Student Book 4 with iQ Online pack
ISBN: 978 0 19 490371 4    Student Book 4 as pack component
ISBN: 978 0 19 490431 5    iQ Online student website

Printed in China
This book is printed on paper from certified and well-managed sources

ACKNOWLEDGMENTS

*Back cover photograph*: Oxford University Press building/David Fisher
*Illustrations by*: 5W Infographics p.215; Mark Duffin pp.95–96, 103.

*The Publishers would like to thank the following for their kind permission to
reproduce photographs and other copyright material*: 123rf: pp.103 (desert
plant/Oleksandr Petrunovskyi), 125 (woman shopping/Antonio Diaz),
131 (berry cheesecake/rawpixel), 134 (scientist with test tubes/scanrail),
144 (feet on scales/George Tsartsianidis), 181 (graduation ceremony/
dolgachov); Alamy: pp.14 (girl drinking water/Jake Lyell), 17 (meals
on wheel volunteer/Tina Manley), 18 (free meal event/roger parkes),
21 (runner crossing finishing line/Hero Images Inc.), 23 (goals notepad/
ALLASH), 31 (school in India/ephotocorp), 41 (leaving feedback rating/
Anna Berkut), 62 (students bowing to parents/Xinhua), 78 (child walking
off baseball field/Juice Images), 83 (cup and saucer/Nick Young), 88 (empty
wallet/Chris Pancewicz), 107 (irrigation channel Africa/Mike Goldwater),
113 (Otto Lilienthal/INTERFOTO), (Wright brothers/World History
Archive), 126 (schoolchildren on allotment/Paula Solloway), 152 (students
in computer class/imageBROKER), 182 (wildlife on coral reef/SeaTops),
185 (coldwater coral/Frank Hecker), 194–195 (Bristol Bay scenic/Design Pics
Inc), 205 (underwater submersible/david gregs), 236 (reservoir dam/Dimitar
Todorov); AP: p.92 (girl using i-limb/Patrick Record); Getty: pp.cover (close-
up of Crassulaceae plants/Johner Images), 6 (father constructing camp fire/
Hero Images), 12 (community house building project/AFP Contributor),
32 (teen passing advertising hoarding/SOPA Images), 35 (generation z/Tara
Moore), 43 (boy on phone/Eternity in an Instant), 55 (weekend warrior/
Elli Thor Magnusson), 61 (Times Square/Jack Berman), 66 (students
checking noticeboard/Hero Images), 74 (father and daughter fishing/Hero
Images), 91 (group of girls walking/Klaus Vedfelt), 121 (man blowing into
respiratory machine/The AGE), 122 (germinating seeds/LOIC VENANCE),
137 (colorful food/Maximilian Stock Ltd.), 151 (cubed ingredients/Martin
Kreppel/EyeEm), 163 (businessman/Hero Images), 168 (people in art gallery/
JGI/Tom Grill), 169 (analyzing graphs/Wutthichai Luemuang/EyeEm),
(analyst discussing graphs/Ariel Skelley), 175 (woman looking at notice
board/Hero Images), 176 (woman shaking hand/laflor), 178 (decision
tick boxes/jayk7), 193 (salmon fisherman/Jeff Rotman), 206 (urban park/
Vicki Jauron, Babylon and Beyond Photography), 211 (cruise shop on
ocean/Daniel Piraino/EyeEm), 212 (instructing bridge/Construction
Photography/Avalon), 230 (Chernobyl nuclear power station/Wojtek
Laski), 233 (students working together/Westend61), 242 (aerial view of
roads/anucha sirivisansuwan); Oxford University Press: pp.73 (sunset
over sea/Shutterstock; S–F), 108 (ouds/Galyna Andrushko/shutterstock.
com), 146 (citrus fruits/Shutterstock/Studio Dagdagaz), 199 (wind farm/
Shutterstock); Shutterstock: pp.2 (firefighter/Tithi Luadthong), 48 (data
mining/Paul Fleet), 52 (interior of restaurant/Koksharov Dmitry), 58 (female
influencer taking selfie/mentatdgt), 72 (alarm clock/MK photograp.55),
115 (petri dish with mold/grebcha), 139 (pill containing food/Lightspring),
141 (science museum/cowardlion), 142 (lazy man/txking), 155 (frustrated
employee/fizkes), 186 (map of Zealandia/Crystal Eye Studio), 225 (engineer
and apprentices/goodluz); Third party: p.44 (laptop with note/emc design).

*The authors and publisher are grateful to those who have given permission to
reproduce the following extracts and adaptations of copyright material*: p.12
Excerpt from Interview with Katrina fried, author of Everyday Heroes:
50 Americans Changing the World One Nonprofit at a Time. Copyright
© 2012 Katrina Fried, Published by Welcome Books. p.35 Adapted extract
from 'Your Guide to Generation Z The Frugal, Brand-Wary, Determined
Anti-Millennials' by Elizabeth Segran, 8 September 2016. Used with
permission of Fast Company Copyright © 2018. All rights reserved. p.43
Adapted extract from 'This is why you're addicted to your phone' by Nick
Arnold, 12 October 2017, www.bbc.co.uk. © 2019 BBC. Reproduced by
permission. p.73 Adapted extract from '10 Life Lessons I Learned from
my Dad in 23 years' by Katie Hurley, 10 June 2014, www.huffingtonpost.
com. Reproduced by permission of Katie Hurley, LCSW, author of No
More Mean Girls and The Happy Kid Handbook. p.95 Adapted extract
from 'Five Innovative Technologies That Bring Energy to the Developing
World' by Joseph Stromberg, 2 May 2013, www.smithsonian.com. © 2019
Smithsonian Institution. Reprinted with permission from Smithsonian
Enterprises. All rights reserved. Reproduction in any medium is strictly
prohibited without permission from Smithsonian Institution. p.103
Adapted extract from 'This Device Pulls Water Out of Desert Air' by Emily
Matchar, 20 June 2018, www.smithsonian.com. © 2019 Smithsonian
Institution. Reprinted with permission from Smithsonian Enterprises. All
rights reserved. Reproduction in any medium is strictly prohibited without
permission from Smithsonian Institution. p.134 From 'A Personalized
Nutrition Company Will Use Your DNA To Tell You What To Eat' by Claire
Maldarelli, 25 October 2016, popularscience.com. Used with permission
of PopularScience.com. Copyright © 2018. All rights reserved. p.163
From 'Making My First Post-College Decision' by Devin Reams, www.
employeeevolution.com. Reproduced by permission. p.194 Extract from
'Is Alaska's Pebble Mine the Next Keystone XL?' by Svati Kirsten Narula, 14
March 2014, www.theatlantic.com. © Svati Kirsten Narula. Reproduced by
permission. p.224 Adapted extract from 'How to … design a student project
that benefits the developing world' by Keith Pullen, 24 January 2014,
www.theguardian.com. © Copyright Guardian News & Media Ltd 2018.
Reprinted by permission.

# ACKNOWLEDGMENTS

We would like to acknowledge the teachers from all over the world who participated in the development process and review of *Q: Skills for Success* Third Edition.

## USA

Kate Austin, Avila University, MO; **Sydney Bassett**, Auburn Global University, AL; **Michael Beamer**, USC, CA; **Renae Betten**, CBU, CA; **Pepper Boyer**, Auburn Global University, AL; **Marina Broeder**, Mission College, CA; **Thomas Brynmore**, Auburn Global University, AL; **Britta Burton**, Mission College, CA; **Kathleen Castello**, Mission College, CA; **Teresa Cheung**, North Shore Communtiy College, MA; **Shantall Colebrooke**, Auburn Global University, AL; **Kyle Cooper**, Troy University, AL; **Elizabeth Cox**, Auburn Global University, AL; **Ashley Ekers**, Auburn Global University, AL; **Rhonda Farley**, Los Rios Community College, CA; **Marcus Frame**, Troy University, AL; **Lora Glaser**, Mission College, CA; **Hala Hamka**, Henry Ford College, MI; **Shelley A. Harrington**, Henry Ford College, MI; **Barrett J. Heusch**, Troy University, AL; **Beth Hill**, St. Charles Community College, MO; **Patty Jones**, Troy University, AL; **Tom Justice**, North Shore Community College, MA; **Robert Klein**, Troy University, AL; **Wheeler Loreley**, North Shore Communtiy College, MA; **Patrick Maestas**, Auburn Global University, AL; **Elizabeth Merchant**, Auburn Global University, AL; **Rosemary Miketa**, Henry Ford College, MI; **Myo Myint**, Mission College, CA; **Lance Noe**, Troy University, AL; **Irene Pannatier**, Auburn Global University, AL; **Annie Percy**, Troy University, AL; **Erin Robinson**, Troy University, AL; **Juliane Rosner**, Mission College, CA; **Mary Stevens**, North Shore Communtiy College, MA; **Pamela Stewart**, Henry Ford College, MI; **Karen Tucker**, Georgia Tech, GA; **Amanda Wilcox**, Auburn Global University, AL; **Heike Williams**, Auburn Global University, AL

## Canada

**Angelika Brunel**, Collège Ahuntsic, QC; **David Butler**, English Language Institute, BC; **Paul Edwards**, Kwantlen Polytechnic University, BC; **Cody Hawver**, University of British Columbia, BC; **Olivera Jovovic**, Kwantlen Polytechnic University, BC; **Tami Moffatt**, Univeristy of British Columbia, BC; **Dana Pynn**, Vancouver Island University, BC

## Latin America

**Georgette Barreda**, SENATI, Peru; **Claudia Cecilia Díaz Romero**, Colegio América, Mexico; **Jeferson Ferro**, Uninter, Brazil; **Mayda Hernández**, English Center, Mexico; **Jose Ixtaccihusatl**, Tecnologico de Tecomatlan, Mexico; **Andreas Paulus Pabst**, CBA Idiomas, Brazil; **Amanda Carla Pas**, Instituição de Ensino Santa Izildinha, Brazil; **Allen Quesada Pacheco**, University of Costa Rica, Costa Rica; **Rolando Sánchez**, Escuela Normal de Tecámac, Mexico; **Luis Vasquez**, CESNO, Mexico

## Asia

**Asami Atsuko**, Women's University, Japan; **Rene Bouchard**, Chinzei Keiai Gakuenj, Japan; **Francis Brannen**, Sangmyoung University, South Korea; **Haeyun Cho**, Songang University, South Korea; **Daniel Craig**, Sangmyoung University, South Korea; **Thomas Cuming**, Royal Melbourne Institute of Technology, Vietnam; **Jissen Joshi Daigaku**, Women's University, Japan; **Nguyen Duc Dat**, OISP, Vietnam; **Wayne Devitte**, Tokai University, Japan; **James D. Dunn**, Tokai University, Japan; **Fergus Hann**, Tokai University, Japan; **Michael Hood**, Nihon University College of Commerce, Japan; **Hideyuki Kashimoto**, Shijonawate High School, Japan; **David Kennedy**, Nihon University, Japan; **Anna Youngna Kim**, Songang University, South Korea; **Jae Phil Kim**, Songang University, South Korea; **Jaganathan Krishnasamy**, GB Academy, Malaysia; **Peter Laver**, Incheon National University, South Korea; **Hung Hoang Le**, Ho Chi Minh City University of Technology, Vietnam; **Hyon Sook Lee**, Songang University, South Korea; **Ji-seon Lee**, Iruda English Institute, South Korea; **Joo Young Lee**, Songang University, South Korea; **Phung Tu Luc**, Ho Chi Minh City University of Technology, Vietnam; **Richard Mansbridge**, Hoa Sen University, Vietnam; **Kahoko Matsumoto**, Tokai University, Japan; **Elizabeth May**, Sangmyoung University, South Korea; **Naoyuki Naganuma**, Tokai University, Japan; **Hiroko Nishikage**, Taisho University, Japan; **Yongjun Park**, Sangji University, South Korea; **Paul Rogers**, Dongguk University, South Korea; **Scott Schafer**, Inha University, South Korea; **Michael Schvaudner**, Tokai University, Japan; **Brendan Smith**, RMIT University, School of Languages and English, Vietnam; **Peter Snashall**, Huachiew Chalermprakiat University, Thailand; **Makoto Takeda**, Sendai Third Senior High School, Japan; **Peter Talley**, Mahidol University, Faculty of ICT, Thailand; **Byron Thigpen**, Songang University, South Korea; **Junko Yamaai**, Tokai University, Japan; **Junji Yamada**, Taisho University, Japan; **Sayoko Yamashita**, Women's University, Japan; **Masami Yukimori**, Taisho University, Japan

## Middle East and North Africa

**Sajjad Ahmad**, Taibah University, Saudi Arabia; **Basma Alansari**, Taibah University, Saudi Arabia; **Marwa Al-ashqar**, Taibah University, Saudi Arabia; **Dr. Rashid Al-Khawaldeh**, Taibah University, Saudi Arabia; **Mohamed Almohamed**, Taibah University, Saudi Arabia; **Dr Musaad Alrahaili**, Taibah University, Saudi Arabia; **Hala Al Sammar**, Kuwait University, Kuwait; **Ahmed Alshammari**, Taibah University, Saudi Arabia; **Ahmed Alshamy**, Taibah University, Saudi Arabia; **Doniazad sultan AlShraideh**, Taibah University, Saudi Arabia; **Sahar Amer**, Taibah University, Saudi Arabia; **Nabeela Azam**, Taibah University, Saudi Arabia; **Hassan Bashir**, Edex, Saudi Arabia; **Rachel Batchilder**, College of the North Atlantic, Qatar; **Nicole Cuddie**, Community College of Qatar, Qatar; **Mahdi Duris**, King Saud University, Saudi Arabia; **Ahmed Ege**, Institute of Public Administration, Saudi Arabia; **Magda Fadle**, Victoria College, Egypt; **Mohammed Hassan**, Taibah University, Saudi Arabia; **Tom Hodgson**, Community College of Qatar, Qatar; **Ayub Agbar Khan**, Taibah University, Saudi Arabia; **Cynthia Le Joncour**, Taibah University, Saudi Arabia; **Ruari Alexander MacLeod**, Community College of Qatar, Qatar; **Nasir Mahmood**, Taibah University, Saudi Arabia; **Duria Salih Mahmoud**, Taibah University, Saudi Arabia; **Ameera McKoy**, Taibah University, Saudi Arabia; **Chaker Mhamdi**, Buraimi University College, Oman; **Baraa Shiekh Mohamed**, Community College of Qatar, Qatar; **Abduleelah Mohammed**, Taibah University, Saudi Arabia; **Shumaila Nasir**, Taibah University, Saudi Arabia; **Kevin Onwordi**, Taibah University, Saudi Arabia; **Dr. Navid Rahmani**, Community College of Qatar, Qatar; **Dr. Sabah Salman Sabbah**, Community College of Qatar, Qatar; **Salih**, Taibah University, Saudi Arabia; **Verna Santos-Nafrada**, King Saud University, Saudi Arabia; **Gamal Abdelfattah Shehata**, Taibah University, Saudi Arabia; **Ron Stefan**, Institute of Public Administration, Saudi Arabia; **Dr. Saad Torki**, Imam Abdulrahman Bin Faisal University, Dammam, Saudi Arabia; **Silvia Yafai**, Applied Technology High School/Secondary Technical School, UAE; **Mahmood Zar**, Taibah University, Saudi Arabia; **Thouraya Zheni**, Taibah University, Saudi Arabia

## Turkey

**Sema Babacan**, Istanbul Medipol University; **Bilge Çöllüoğlu Yakar**, Bilkent University; **Liana Corniel**, Koc University; **Savas Geylanioglu**, Izmir Bahcesehir Science and Technology College; **Öznur Güler**, Giresun University; **Selen Bilginer Halefoğlu**, Maltepe University; **Ahmet Konukoğlu**, Hasan Kalyoncu University; **Mehmet Salih Yoğun**, Gaziantep Hasan Kalyoncu University; **Fatih Yücel**, Beykent University

## Europe

**Amina Al Hashamia**, University of Exeter, UK; **Irina Gerasimova**, Saint-Petersburg Mining University, Russia; **Jodi**, Las Dominicas, Spain; **Marina Khanykova**, School 179, Russia; **Oksana Postnikova**, Lingua Practica, Russia; **Nina Vasilchenko**, Soho-Bridge Language School, Russia

# CRITICAL THINKING

The unique critical thinking approach of the *Q: Skills for Success* series has been further enhanced in the Third Edition. New features help you analyze, synthesize, and develop your ideas.

### Unit question
The thought-provoking unit questions engage you with the topic and provide a critical thinking framework for the unit.

UNIT QUESTION

## What makes someone admirable?

**A.** Discuss these questions with your classmates.

1. Why do we like to read stories about admirable people?
2. Who do you admire? Why do you admire this person?
3. Look at the photo. What makes this person admirable?

### Analysis
You can discuss your opinion of each reading text and analyze how it changes your perspective on the unit question.

**WRITE WHAT YOU THINK**

**A. DISCUSS** Discuss the questions in a group.

1. Do athletes make good role models? Why or why not?
2. Who are you a role model for?
3. Imagine yourself 20 years from now. What would you like to hear people saying about you? What can you do between now and then so that people will say that?

**B. SYNTHESIZE** Choose one of the questions from Activity A and write a paragraph of 5–7 sentences in response. Look back at your Quick Write on page 5 as you think about what you learned.

**NEW!** Critical Thinking Strategy with video
Each unit includes a Critical Thinking Strategy with activities to give you step-by-step guidance in critical analysis of texts. An accompanying instructional video (available on iQ Online) provides extra support and examples.

**NEW!** Bloom's Taxonomy
Pink activity headings integrate verbs from Bloom's Taxonomy to help you see how each activity develops critical thinking skills.

**CRITICAL THINKING STRATEGY**

**Analyzing texts for cause and effect relationships**

Some texts clearly describe cause and effect relationships. In other texts, the reader must analyze the information in the text to understand potential cause and effect between the events or elements presented.

An example of this can be found in Reading 1, Exercise F (p. 129). There you completed a chart on the benefits of an urban garden. To do this, you had to analyze the connection between causes and effects to determine whether they are related.

**Cause**: Food doesn't have to be brought to supermarkets.

**Effect**: Food is fresher. (Because it doesn't have to go to the supermarket, it can be eaten sooner after it is picked.)

**Not an effect**: Children learn how to plant and grow vegetables. (This is true for programs aimed toward children, but it is not an effect of food not going to supermarkets. The two are not directly related.)

**iQ** PRACTICE Go online to watch the Critical Thinking Skill Video and check your comprehension. *Practice > Unit 5 > Activity 6*

**C. ANALYZE** Reread paragraphs 6, 7, and 8 of Reading 1. Consider the causes and the possible effects. Check *yes* (✓) if they are related and *no* (✓) if they are not. Use the information in the article and your own experience. Then compare answers with a partner and give reasons.

1. **Paragraph 6** Cause: shopping at a small local farmers' market instead of a large supermarket
   a. ☐ yes ☐ no  Effect: eating fresher food
   b. ☐ yes ☐ no  Effect: saving money
   c. ☐ yes ☐ no  Effect: sharing a meal with others
2. **Paragraph 7** Cause: learning to cook
   a. ☐ yes ☐ no  Effect: improving physical fitness
   b. ☐ yes ☐ no  Effect: eating well

# THREE TYPES OF VIDEO

## UNIT VIDEO

The unit videos include high-interest documentaries and reports on a wide variety of subjects, all linked to the unit topic and question. All videos are from authentic sources.

**NEW!** "Work with the Video" pages guide you in watching, understanding, and discussing the unit videos. The activities help you see the connection to the Unit Question and the other texts in the unit.

## CRITICAL THINKING VIDEO

**NEW!** Narrated by the Q series authors, these short videos give you further instruction into the Critical Thinking Strategy of each unit using engaging images and graphics. You can use them to get a deeper understanding of the Critical Thinking Strategy.

## SKILLS VIDEO

**NEW!** These instructional videos provide illustrated explanations of skills and grammar points in the Student Book. They can be viewed in class or assigned for a flipped classroom, for homework, or for review. One skill video is available for every unit.

Easily access all videos in the Resources section of iQ Online.

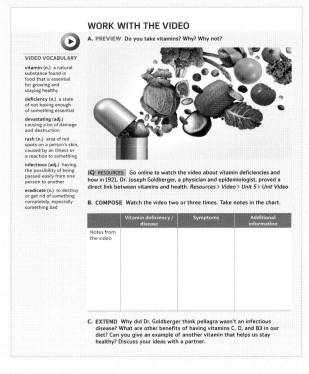

**WORK WITH THE VIDEO**

**A. PREVIEW** Do you take vitamins? Why? Why not?

**VIDEO VOCABULARY**

**vitamin (n.)** a natural substance found in food that is essential for growing and staying healthy

**deficiency (n.)** a state of not having enough of something essential

**devastating (adj.)** causing a lot of damage and destruction

**rash (n.)** area of red spots on a person's skin, caused by an illness or a reaction to something

**infectious (adj.)** having the possibility of being passed easily from one person to another

**eradicate (v.)** to destroy or get rid of something completely, especially something bad

**iQ RESOURCES** Go online to watch the video about vitamin deficiencies and how in 1921, Dr. Joseph Goldberger, a physician and epidemiologist, proved a direct link between vitamins and health. *Resources > Video > Unit 5 > Unit Video*

**B. COMPOSE** Watch the video two or three times. Take notes in the chart.

| | Vitamin deficiency / disease | Symptoms | Additional information |
|---|---|---|---|
| Notes from the video | | | |

**C. EXTEND** Why did Dr. Goldberger think pellagra wasn't an infectious disease? What are other benefits of having vitamins C, D, and B3 in our diet? Can you give an example of another vitamin that helps us stay healthy? Discuss your ideas with a partner.

How to compare and contrast

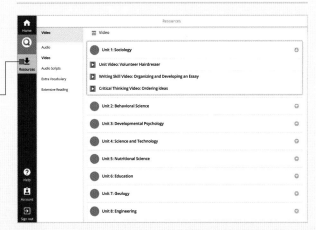

v

# VOCABULARY

A research-based vocabulary program focuses on the words you need to know academically and professionally.

The vocabulary syllabus in *Q: Skills for Success* is correlated to the CEFR (see page 244) and linked to two word lists: the Oxford 5000 and the OPAL (Oxford Phrasal Academic Lexicon).

## ꭍ+ OXFORD 5000

The Oxford 5000 is an expanded core word list for advanced learners of English. As well as the Oxford 3000 core list, the Oxford 5000 includes an additional 2,000 words, guiding learners at B2-C1 level on the most useful high-level words to learn.

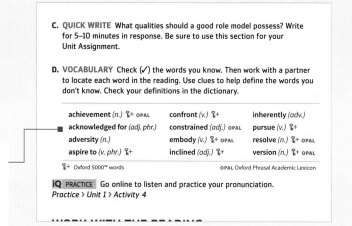

C. **QUICK WRITE**  What qualities should a good role model possess? Write for 5–10 minutes in response. Be sure to use this section for your Unit Assignment.

D. **VOCABULARY**  Check (✓) the words you know. Then work with a partner to locate each word in the reading. Use clues to help define the words you don't know. Check your definitions in the dictionary.

| | | |
|---|---|---|
| achievement *(n.)* ꭍ+ OPAL | confront *(v.)* ꭍ+ | inherently *(adv.)* |
| acknowledged for *(adj. phr.)* | constrained *(adj.)* OPAL | pursue *(v.)* ꭍ+ |
| adversity *(n.)* | embody *(v.)* ꭍ+ OPAL | resolve *(n.)* ꭍ+ OPAL |
| aspire to *(v. phr.)* ꭍ+ | inclined *(adj.)* ꭍ+ | version *(n.)* ꭍ+ OPAL |

ꭍ+ Oxford 5000™ words          OPAL Oxford Phrasal Academic Lexicon

**iQ** PRACTICE  Go online to listen and practice your pronunciation. *Practice › Unit 1 › Activity 4*

**Vocabulary Key**
In vocabulary activities, ꭍ+ shows you the word is in the Oxford 5000 and **OPAL** shows you the word or phrase is in the OPAL.

## OPAL
## OXFORD PHRASAL ACADEMIC LEXICON

**NEW!** The OPAL is a collection of four word lists that provide an essential guide to the most important words and phrases to know for academic English. The word lists are based on the Oxford Corpus of Academic English and the British Academic Spoken English corpus. The OPAL includes both spoken and written academic English and both individual words and longer phrases.

Academic Language tips in the Student Book give information about how words and phrases from the OPAL are used and offer help with features such as collocations and phrasal verbs.

**ACADEMIC LANGUAGE**
The corpus shows that *in contrast* and *in contrast to* are often used in academic writing.
. . . *In contrast, ammonia is* . . .
. . . *In contrast to penicillin, ammonia is* . . .

─────────── OPAL
Oxford Phrasal Academic Lexicon

A. **IDENTIFY**  Read each sentence. Underline the wo a comparison or a contrast. Then write *CP* (comp

____  1. The GravityLight and the SOCCKET each use though they use different types of motion.

____  2. The Berkeley-Darfur Stove helps users directly reducing the amount of smoke inhaled. Simila shortening the amount time spent gathering

____  3. Each of the innovative technologies described energy simply and safely. Nonetheless, some than others.

____  4. While the Window Socket uses solar energy to uses the heat produced by a charcoal- or wood

____  5. The electricity produced by VOTO can power can even charge a spare battery.

# EXTENSIVE READING

**NEW!** Extensive Reading is a program of reading for pleasure at a level that matches your language ability.

There are many benefits to Extensive Reading:

- It helps you to become a better reader in general.
- It helps to increase your reading speed.
- It can improve your reading comprehension.
- It increases your vocabulary range.
- It can improve your grammar and writing skills.
- It's great for motivation—reading something that is interesting for its own sake.

Each unit of *Q: Skills for Success* Third Edition has been aligned to an Oxford Graded Reader based on the appropriate topic and level of language proficiency. The first chapter of each recommended graded reader can be downloaded from iQ Online Resources.

UNIT 1

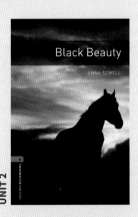

UNIT 2

UNIT 3

UNIT 4

UNIT 5

UNIT 6

UNIT 7

UNIT 8

# What is iQ ONLINE?

## iQ ONLINE extends your learning beyond the classroom.

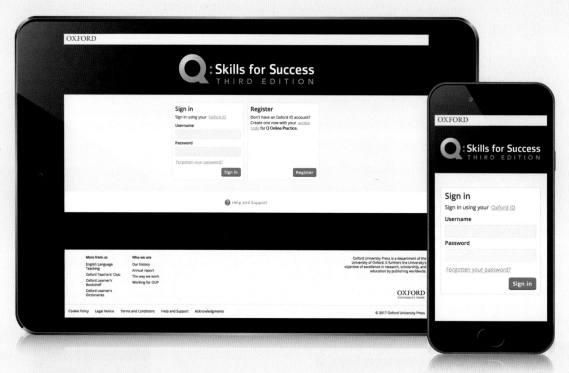

- Practice activities provide essential skills practice and support.
- Automatic grading and progress reports show you what you have mastered and where you still need more practice.
- Discussion Board to discuss the Unit Questions helps you develop your critical thinking.
- Writing Tutor helps you practice your academic writing skills.
- Essential resources such as audio and video are easy to access anytime.

## NEW TO THE THIRD EDITION

- Site is optimized for mobile use so you can use it on your phone.
- An updated interface allows easy navigation around the activities, tests, resources, and scores.
- New Critical Thinking Videos expand on the Critical Thinking Strategies in the Student Book.
- Extensive Reading program helps you improve your vocabulary and reading skills.

# How to use
# iQ ONLINE

Go to **Practice** to find additional practice and support to complement your learning in the classroom.

Go to **Resources** to find
- All Student Book video
- All Student Book audio
- Critical Thinking videos
- Skills videos
- Extensive Reading

Go to **Messages** and **Discussion Board** to communicate with your teacher and classmates.

Progress bar shows you how many activities you have completed.

View your scores for all activities.

Online tests assigned by your teacher help you assess your progress and see where you still need more practice.

# CONTENTS

# Sociology

**1**

| READING | previewing and predicting |
| CRITICAL THINKING | using the dictionary |
| WRITING | organizing and developing an essay |
| CRITICAL THINKING | ordering ideas |
| GRAMMAR | restrictive relative clauses |

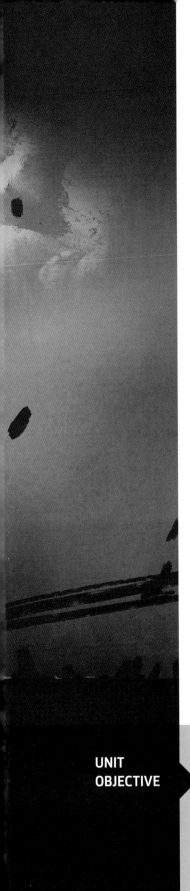

# What makes someone admirable?

**A.** Discuss these questions with your classmates.

1. Why do we like to read stories about admirable people?

2. Who do you admire? Why do you admire this person?

3. Look at the photo. What makes this person admirable?

**B.** Listen to *The Q Classroom* online. Then answer these questions.

1. Marcus says admirable people are brave and sacrifice themselves. What two examples does he give? Yuna says regular people can also be admirable. What example does she give? What do you think makes someone admirable?

2. What qualities of an admirable person do Felix and Sophy discuss? Which qualities are most important, in your opinion?

**iQ** PRACTICE   Go to the online discussion board to discuss the Unit Question with your classmates. *Practice > Unit 1 > Activity 1*

**UNIT OBJECTIVE**

Read an essay and a newspaper interview. Gather information and ideas to write an analysis essay about what makes someone admirable.

# We All Need a Role Model

You are going to read an essay about role models. Use the essay to gather information and ideas for your Unit Assignment.

## PREVIEW THE READING

**READING SKILL** Previewing and predicting

When you **preview** a text, you look through it quickly to learn general information. To preview:

• Read the title of the text.

• Look at any charts, graphs, pictures, or captions.

• Skim the text for paragraph headings. These indicate important ideas that will be developed in the text.

Previewing will help you **predict** what the text is about and prepare you to better understand it.

**TIP FOR SUCCESS**
When you write a research paper, you need to get information from a variety of sources. Previewing many books and articles will help you decide which ones are important for your research.

**A. PREVIEW** Read the title and look at the picture on page 6. Write two things you think the essay might be about.

1. _____

2. _____

**B. IDENTIFY** Skim the essay and read the paragraph headings. Then look at the pairs of ideas below. Check (✓) one idea in each pair that you think might be developed in the essay.

1. ☐ the qualities of role models        ☐ a description of a specific role model

2. ☐ how people become role models      ☐ which people may be role models

3. ☐ how role models can inspire us      ☐ how we can inspire others

4. ☐ why role models do wrong things     ☐ how role models learn from mistakes

**iQ** PRACTICE  Go online for more practice with previewing and predicting. *Practice > Unit 1 > Activity 2*

C. **QUICK WRITE** What qualities should a good role model possess? Write for 5–10 minutes in response. Be sure to use this section for your Unit Assignment.

D. **VOCABULARY** Check (✓) the words you know. Then work with a partner to locate each word in the reading. Use clues to help define the words you don't know. Check your definitions in the dictionary.

| | | |
|---|---|---|
| achievement *(n.)* 🎓+ OPAL | confront *(v.)* 🎓+ | inherently *(adv.)* |
| acknowledged for *(adj. phr.)* | constrained *(adj.)* OPAL | pursue *(v.)* 🎓+ |
| adversity *(n.)* | embody *(v.)* 🎓+ OPAL | resolve *(n.)* 🎓+ OPAL |
| aspire to *(v. phr.)* 🎓+ | inclined *(adj.)* 🎓+ | version *(n.)* 🎓+ OPAL |

🎓+ Oxford 5000™ words          OPAL Oxford Phrasal Academic Lexicon

**iQ** PRACTICE Go online to listen and practice your pronunciation.
*Practice > Unit 1 > Activity 4*

## WORK WITH THE READING

A. **INVESTIGATE** Read the essay and gather information about what makes someone admirable.

# We All Need a Role Model

1   Who do you turn to when you have a problem or don't know how to do something? If you have someone to help you, you are lucky. If you have someone who takes a personal interest in helping you, you are luckier still. You have a role model.

**ACADEMIC LANGUAGE**
The phrase *not necessarily* is often used in academic writing to express contrast.

⎯⎯⎯⎯⎯⎯⎯⎯ OPAL
Oxford Phrasal Academic Lexicon

### ⭐ Definition of a Role Model

2   Just what is a role model? First, let's recognize what it is not. It is not necessarily the smartest, strongest, or most successful person you know—although it could be. A role model is a person who has the characteristics you want for yourself and who can help you develop those traits. In other words, a role model both **embodies** positive qualities and teaches others directly or through example.

### ⭐ Who Can Be a Role Model?

3   For most of us, our parents are our first role models. From when we are young children, they help us learn how to interact with other people— how to share, how to ask for what we need, and how to disagree without hurting someone. They are **inherently** interested in us and want us to do well. Furthermore, our parents teach us how to be adults in our society. A mother demonstrates to her daughters how to be a daughter, a woman, a wife, and a

mother. Lessons learned from our parents will stay with us throughout our lives.

4    Other family members also serve as role models. Grandparents, uncles and aunts, cousins, and even siblings can show us how to manage our daily lives. Other obvious candidates include teachers and community leaders.

5    Sometimes we find role models in unexpected places. A family story might inspire us to have the same generosity as our grandfather had. We might see a young child fall, pick herself up, fall again, and pick herself up again. Her **resolve** might inspire us to continue in our own struggles, just as she learns to stand, keep her balance, and take a step. We might even find a model within ourselves, remembering back to a time when we were brave, or imagining a different **version** of ourselves who has the quality we desire.

## ★ What Role Models Do

6    Besides showing us how to do different things, a good role model also inspires us to **pursue** our dreams and **achievements**. A wise lawyer may inspire one person to

study law, while a competent, compassionate physician may lead another person to the medical profession. Role models should empower others to become good parents, leaders, and members of society, and to internalize the qualities that they value. Therefore, role models must do the right thing, even when no one is watching, even when they won't be **acknowledged for** what they have done.

## ★ When Things Go Wrong

7    It is easy to be a role model when everything is going well, but it is perhaps more important to be a role model when things go wrong. A role model can show us how to handle **adversity**. For instance, we all make mistakes, but what do we do when we realize that we have made one? Do we try to hide it or pretend that it never happened? Are we **inclined** to look for someone to blame? Do we get angry?

8    A role model can show us how to deal with mistakes. A parent or teacher can help us repair any damage that was done or soothe any feelings that were hurt. He or she can listen to us, advise us on alternative courses

A role model shows us how to do different things and how to handle adversity.

of action, and support us as we make amends. The example of a community leader might serve to guide us toward appropriate action, encouraging us to imagine what he would do in our circumstances.

9   Other situations that we might find ourselves in include dealing with stress, illness, or other misfortunes. **Confronting** these predicaments and overcoming them is made easier by the knowledge that people we admire and respect have faced similar conditions. Asking ourselves what they would do might help us be brave for a little while longer or figure out how to deal with life when we feel **constrained** by difficulties.

10   We need role models throughout our lives, and we only need to look around us to find someone who has experienced what we are going through, who has faced difficult decisions, or who has accomplished something we **aspire to** do. Sometimes we only have to look as far as the mirror to see a role model for our children, our neighbors, or even ourselves. Who is your role model? Maybe it is time to say thank you.

**B. VOCABULARY** Here are some words and phrases from Reading 1. Read the sentences. Then write each bold word next to the correct definition. You may need to change the form of some of the words.

**VOCABULARY SKILL REVIEW**

Remember to read the whole sentence and consider the *context*. This can help you identify the correct meaning of a word.

1.  My father **embodies** the quality of honesty; he never tells a lie.

2.  The best athletes have the **resolve** to keep trying even when everything looks hopeless.

3.  I will **pursue** my goal to be an engineer even though it will be difficult.

4.  Winning the competition was an incredible **achievement** for such a young player.

5.  When you set goals, don't be **constrained** by your present situation. If you can dream it, you can do it.

6.  The athlete is suffering from a long-term injury, but he still **aspires to** race at the Olympics.

7.  Skydiving is an **inherently** dangerous sport.

8.  We all want to be **acknowledged for** our good deeds and the things we do to help others.

9.  He had a hard life, but the **adversity** and challenges he faced made him a stronger person.

10. She had to **confront** the problem even though she was frightened.

11. I prefer my usual routine and am not **inclined** to try new things.

12. The first witness's **version** of the accident was quite different from what the second witness described.

    a. _____ *(adj.)* recognized or shown appreciation for something

    b. _____ *(n.)* a strong determination to do something

c. _____ (adv.) being a basic part of something that cannot be removed

d. _____ (v. phr.) to have a strong desire to do or become something

e. _____ (adj.) limited by something or someone

f. _____ (n.) a form of something that is different from another form of the same thing

g. _____ (n.) something that has been done successfully, especially through hard work or skill

h. _____ (v.) to deal with a problem or difficult situation

i. _embody_____ (v.) to represent an idea or quality

j. _____ (adj.) wanting to do something

k. _____ (n.) a difficult or unpleasant situation

l. _____ (v.) to try to achieve something over a period of time

**iQ PRACTICE** Go online for more practice with the vocabulary.
*Practice > Unit 1 > Activity 5*

**C. RESTATE** Answer these questions.

1. What is the main idea of the essay? Write it in a complete sentence.

   _____

2. The main idea is found in two places. Where did you find the main idea?

   _____

**D. IDENTIFY** Read the sentences. Number the main ideas in the order they are developed in the essay. (Use the headings in the essay to help you.)

____ a. Role models can show us how to deal with mistakes.

____ b. Role models can show us how to deal with problems.

_1_ c. A role model is a person with qualities that other people want to have.

____ d. Role models inspire us to develop our talents and abilities.

____ e. Many different kinds of people are role models.

**E. EXPLAIN** Answer these questions.

1. Who are some of the people that can be role models? _____

_____

2. How can a lawyer or doctor serve as a role model? _____

_____

3. How can a role model help us deal with mistakes? _____

_____

_____

4. When is another time role models might help us? _____

_____

_____

**F. CATEGORIZE** Read the statements. Write *T* (true) or *F* (false) and the paragraph number where the answer is found. Then correct each false statement to make it true according to the essay.

____ 1. A role model is sometimes the most successful person you know. (paragraph ____)

_____

____ 2. A teacher is usually our first role model. (paragraph ____)

_____

____ 3. A young child can be a role model. (paragraph ____)

_____

____ 4. You can be your own role model. (paragraph ____)

_____

____ 5. A role model is supposed to do the right thing. (paragraph ____)

_____

____ 6. A role model never makes mistakes. (paragraph ____)

_____

____ 7. We need role models only when we confront adversity. (paragraph ____)

_____

____ 8. It's hard to find a role model. (paragraph ____)

_____

**G. CATEGORIZE** Complete the chart with two more people the essay identified as role models and what they can teach us.

| Role models | What they can teach us |
|---|---|
| 1. parents | 1. how to interact with other people:<br>    -how to share<br>    -how to ask for what we need<br>    -how to disagree without hurting<br>      someone<br>2. how to be adults in our society |
| 2. | |
| 3. | |

**H. SYNTHESIZE** Look back at your Quick Write on page 5. What qualities should a good role model possess? Add any new ideas or information you learned from the reading.

**iQ** PRACTICE   Go online for additional reading and comprehension.
*Practice > Unit 1 > Activity 3*

# WRITE WHAT YOU THINK

**A. DISCUSS** Discuss the questions in a group.

1. Do athletes make good role models? Why or why not?

2. Who are you a role model for?

3. Imagine yourself 20 years from now. What would you like to hear people saying about you? What can you do between now and then so that people will say that?

**B. SYNTHESIZE** Choose one of the questions from Activity A and write a paragraph of 5–7 sentences in response. Look back at your Quick Write on page 5 as you think about what you learned.

**Everyday Heroes**

OBJECTIVE ▶

You are going to read an interview with Katrina Fried, the author of *Everyday Heroes: 50 Americans Changing the World One Nonprofit at a Time*. Use the interview to gather information and ideas for your Unit Assignment.

# PREVIEW THE READING

**A. PREVIEW** Answer the questions.

1. Read the title of the article and skim the first three paragraphs. Which of the two definitions is better for the title "Everyday Heroes"?

   a. special people who are heroes all the time

   b. common, normal people who do something special with their lives

   What information from the article helped you find the answer?

   _____

2. Read the question that comes before paragraph 4. What are two answers to that question? Where did you find the answers?

   _____

   _____

3. There are many people's names in the interview, such as Roger Egger, Rebecca Onie, and Adam Braun. Why are these people named in the interview?

   _____

**B. QUICK WRITE** If you could do something to make your community better, what would you do? What would you need in order to accomplish this? Write for 5–10 minutes in response. Be sure to use this section for your Unit Assignment.

**C. VOCABULARY** Check (✓) the words you know. Use a dictionary to define any new or unknown words. Then discuss with a partner how the words will relate to the unit.

| | | |
|---|---|---|
| advocate *(n.)* 🔑+ | empower *(v.)* 🔑+ OPAL | humility *(n.)* |
| authenticity *(n.)* | exponential *(adj.)* | perceive *(v.)* 🔑+ OPAL |
| cause *(n.)* 🔑+ OPAL | funding *(n.)* 🔑+ OPAL | personify *(v.)* |
| diverse *(adj.)* 🔑+ OPAL | humanitarian *(adj.)* 🔑+ | phenomenon *(n.)* 🔑+ OPAL |

🔑+ Oxford 5000™ words          OPAL Oxford Phrasal Academic Lexicon

**iQ PRACTICE** Go online to listen and practice your pronunciation.
*Practice ▸ Unit 1 ▸ Activity 6*

# WORK WITH THE READING

 **A. INVESTIGATE** Read the interview and gather information about what makes someone admirable.

# EVERYDAY HEROES
## AN INTERVIEW WITH WRITER KATRINA FRIED

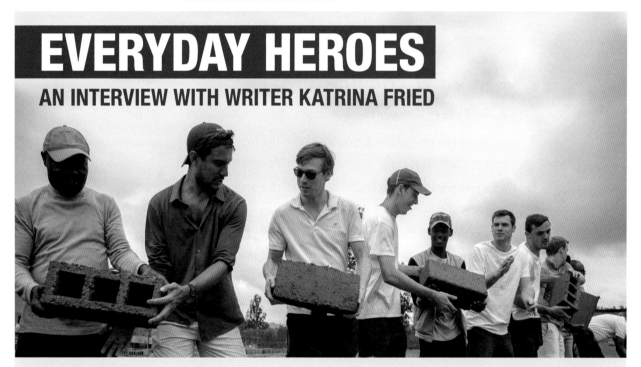

**Q:** *What makes an everyday hero?*

1 **A:** In this book, "everyday heroes" are not those that **personify** physical bravery. Though heroes such as firefighters are by no means less praiseworthy, I chose to feature passionate promoters of social justice and equality. Their work is **humanitarian** in nature. They are founders or leaders of successful nonprofits[1], representing a **diverse** range of **causes** and people. Nearly all self-identify as social entrepreneurs[2].

**Q:** *Some readers might **perceive** a contradiction in the phrase "everyday heroes." Is heroism an everyday **phenomenon**? Can the everyday be heroic? What did you mean by the title?*

2 **A:** Many people think heroism is a quality reserved for an exceptional few, such as Nobel Peace Prize winners or famous leaders.

These are heroes. But these heroes should be idealized and looked to for guidance, like the North Star—a moral compass, not a literal road map[3]. The more I read in researching and creating this book—and learned, and listened—the more obvious it became. The heroes of today are anything but rare. They are everywhere.

**Q:** *Do you think that we, as a society, do enough to recognize and reward heroism, and thus to encourage it?*

3 **A:** Everyday heroes are standing beside you in the elevator and sitting across from you on the subway; they're your next-door neighbors and your college roommates; they're teachers, doctors, lawyers, inventors, and orphans. There are quiet heroes among us—

---

[1] **nonprofit:** a business, such as a charity, that does not intend to make money for its owners
[2] **social entrepreneur:** a person who starts businesses to help deal with social problems
[3] **a moral compass, not a literal road map:** an example of an ethical way of living, not a list of rules

ordinary men and women who have devoted themselves to uplifting the lives of others. And it is precisely their ordinariness that makes them extraordinary.

**Q:** *What do you think we learn from reading the stories of these heroes?*

## OUT WITH CHARITY, IN WITH PARTNERSHIP.

4 **A:** Today, there is a shift in the relationship between the giver and the receiver. The handout has been replaced by the handshake. Today's nonprofit reformers are interested in creating meaningful equal partnerships to **empower** communities and individuals to raise themselves out of poverty.

5 Robert Egger founded DC Central Kitchen, which trains people for jobs, distributes meals, and supports local food systems. Doing these things strengthens community and builds long-term solutions to the interconnected problems of poverty, hunger, poor health, and homelessness. Egger said, "A great nonprofit doesn't try to solve the problem; it tries to reveal the power we have as a community to solve the problem."

## YOU'RE NEVER TOO YOUNG.

6 The growing group of young social entrepreneurs proves that experience is not necessary for leadership.

7 Rebecca Onie was a sophomore at Harvard when she founded Health Leads, which connects low-income families with the basic resources they need to be healthy.

8 Adam Braun founded Pencils of Promise when he was 25 with a modest $25 deposit. It has raised more than $3 million to build schools in poor developing countries.

## YOU'RE NEVER TOO OLD.

9 Roy Prosterman of Landesa, now in his seventies, is the world's leading expert on democratic land reform and a fierce **advocate** for the rights of the rural poor. Through Landesa, formerly known as the Rural Development Institute, he has helped secure land rights for more than 105 million families in 45 developing countries. Prosterman, who continues to work, says, "I'm not tired at all. In fact, it energizes me."

## ENTREPRENEURS ARE BORN, NOT MADE.

10 I think that every entrepreneur I interviewed would agree this is true. Most have walked to the beat of their own drum[4] since they took their first uncertain steps as toddlers and have never been satisfied in a conventional professional setting. All believe that risking failure is fundamental. It takes a healthy dose of confidence, courage, and determination to be responsible for others day in and day out.

## YOU CAN'T RELY ON THE KINDNESS OF STRANGERS.

11 Because of the growing number of nonprofits, it is harder to get **funding**. Today's social entrepreneurs realize that the surest way to survival is self-sustainability[5].

12 Chuck Slaughter, founder and CEO of Living Goods, has two driving passions: global travel and solving social problems. Living Goods empowers entrepreneurs to deliver life-changing products to the doorsteps of the poor. Slaughter's goal is to make Living Goods a completely self-sustaining business that "fights poverty and disease with profitability."

---

[4] **walk to the beat of their own drum:** to do things the way they want to, not how most people did them
[5] **self-sustainability:** ability to raise enough money to pay for expenses without depending on donations

## GO BIG OR GO HOME.

13 Take a small idea and make it huge. The potential for **exponential** growth is practically a necessity for the new social entrepreneurs.

14 Jill Vialet of Playworks, which has helped ensure safe recreational time for 130,000 kids in 300 schools in 23 cities across the U.S., said she spends a lot of time thinking about how Playworks is going to grow enough to change the system. Her ultimate vision is that one day every kid in America will have access to safe, healthy play every day. And she feels it's doable!

## TRUE HEROES NEVER CONSIDER THEMSELVES HEROES.

15 If I had a dollar for every time one of these charitable leaders said to me, "You know, the true heroes are the *[blank]*, not me," I'd be $50 richer. They all possess a sense of **humility** and **authenticity** that I've come to realize is essential to the achievement of their visions. The basic fact remains: none of these nonprofits would have succeeded so well without the profound sacrifices of their dedicated founders and CEOs.

16 Eugene Cho, founder and president of One Day's Wages, found the courage to give up one year's wages in the name of service. One Day's Wages has raised more than a million dollars and supports many projects around the world to improve education, deliver clean water, and end poverty.

**Q:** *How did you find these everyday heroes?*

17 **A:** There were thousands of worthy candidates who deserve to be recognized and celebrated—how to choose just 50? With each hero's story there is yet another example of generosity all around us. There is no contribution too small or insignificant. Whether you choose to show kindness to a loved one or a neighbor, to volunteer, to donate, or to build your own movement—you are helping to grow a culture of giving.

18 Jill Vialet summed it up best, "Believing in the idea that everyone can be an everyday hero is essential to our future as a society. And it's the everyday-ness of it that's more important than the heroism."

**B. VOCABULARY** Here are some words from Reading 2. Read the word and the three definitions in each row. Two of the definitions are similar and correct. A third is incorrect. Cross out the incorrect definition.

| | | | |
|---|---|---|---|
| 1. **personify** *(v.)* | a. to be a good example of | b. to change someone | c. to represent |
| 2. **humanitarian** *(adj.)* | a. belonging to people | b. caring about people | c. wanting to improve the way people live |
| 3. **diverse** *(adj.)* | a. backward | b. having many differences | c. varied |
| 4. **cause** *(n.)* | a. belief that people fight for | b. organization that people support | c. belief in something that isn't true |
| 5. **perceive** *(v.)* | a. to get from someone | b. to notice | c. to see |
| 6. **phenomenon** *(n.)* | a. someone or something special | b. someone or something difficult | c. someone or something very different or unusual |
| 7. **empower** *(v.)* | a. to calm someone down | b. to encourage someone | c. to give power to someone |
| 8. **advocate** *(n.)* | a. supporter | b. banker | c. promoter |
| 9. **funding** *(n.)* | a. savings in a bank | b. money for a specific purpose | c. financial support for an organization |
| 10. **exponential** *(adj.)* | a. increasing quickly | b. becoming more and more | c. bringing things together |
| 11. **humility** *(n.)* | a. modesty | b. sadness | c. quality of not feeling more important than others |
| 12. **authenticity** *(n.)* | a. quality of being easy to work with | b. quality of being real | c. quality of being what someone seems to be |

**iQ** PRACTICE Go online for more practice with the vocabulary.
*Practice > Unit 1 > Activity 7*

**C. CATEGORIZE** Read the statements. Write *T* (true) or *F* (false). Then correct each false statement to make it true according to the interview.

_____ 1. Everyday heroes are ordinary people who help other people.

_____ 2. The social entrepreneurs in the book all have the same goals.

_____ 3. The nonprofits in the book are focused on giving away money.

_____ 4. All nonprofits rely on people to donate money so that the business can continue.

_____ 5. At least one nonprofit leader believes that people need to help themselves.

_____ 6. The heroes in the book seem to be satisfied with helping a small number of people.

**D. CATEGORIZE** Complete the chart with information about the heroes from the article.

| Person | Business | What the business does | Local, national, or international |
|---|---|---|---|
| Roger Egger | | trains people for jobs, distributes meals, and supports local food systems | |
| | Health Leads | | |
| Adam Braun | | builds schools in poor developing countries | |
| | Landesa | | international |
| | | fights poverty and disease | international |
| | Playworks | ensures safe recreational time for kids | |
| Eugene Cho | One Day's Wages | | |

**E. CATEGORIZE** Using the information in the chart on page 16, put the name of each hero in the column (or columns) that describes the focus of his or her company.

| Education and training | Health and safety | Legal help |
| --- | --- | --- |
| Roger Egger | Roger Egger | |

**F. EXPLAIN** Answer these questions. Discuss your answers with a partner.

1. In paragraph 3, what does the author mean when she says, "… it is precisely their ordinariness that makes them extraordinary"?

_____

2. Using your own words, what is the main idea of paragraph 10?

_____

3. Can someone who doesn't fit the description in paragraph 10 still be a hero? Why or why not? _____

_____

# WORK WITH THE VIDEO

**A. PREVIEW** Do you volunteer in your community? Why? Why not?

**iQ** RESOURCES  Go online to watch the video about a volunteer hairdresser.
*Resources > Video > Unit 1 > Unit Video*

**B. COMPOSE** Watch the video two or three times. How do the volunteers help people? Who do they help? Take notes in the first part of the chart.

|  | Josh Coombes | Jade | Both |
|---|---|---|---|
| Notes from the video |  |  |  |
| My ideas |  |  |  |

**C. EXTEND** What makes Josh and Jade admirable? Write your ideas in the chart above. The video ends by asking if there is something you can give to your community. Can you think of examples of others who could use their skills to help in their community? Discuss your ideas with a partner.

# WRITE WHAT YOU THINK

**SYNTHESIZE** Think about Reading 1, Reading 2, and the unit video as you discuss the questions. Then choose one question and write a paragraph of 5–7 sentences in response.

1. Have you ever volunteered to do something to help your community? If so, describe your experience.

2. Firefighters are often seen as admirable. What other people are seen as admirable because of their profession? Why?

3. Think of someone in the news who is a real-life role model. What makes this person a role model?

## VOCABULARY SKILL  Using the dictionary

When you look up a word in the dictionary, you will find the definition and other information about the word and how it is used. Different dictionaries may include slightly different information, but they are generally organized in a similar way. Notice the different parts of this dictionary entry from the *Oxford Advanced American Dictionary for learners of English*.

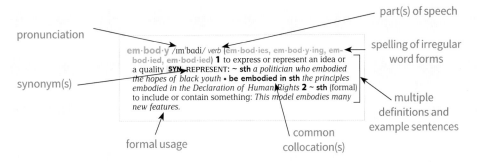

All dictionary entries adapted from the *Oxford Advanced American Dictionary for learners of English* © Oxford University 2011.

**A. IDENTIFY** Look at the dictionary entry for *mentality*. Check (✓) the information that this entry has.

men·tal·i·ty /mɛnˈtæləʈi/ *noun* [usually sing.] (*pl.* men·tal·i·ties) the particular attitude or way of thinking of a person or group **SYN** MINDSET: *I cannot understand the mentality of video gamers.* • *a criminal/ghetto mentality*

☐ pronunciation        ☐ example sentence

☐ part(s) of speech       ☐ formal usage

☐ spelling of irregular word forms    ☐ synonym(s)

☐ multiple definitions       ☐ common collocation(s)

The abbreviations *-sth* and *-sb* mean "something" and "somebody." They show you whether a verb is followed by a noun for a thing (*-sth*), a person (*-sb*), or both.

**B. IDENTIFY** Look at the dictionary entries. Answer the questions. Then compare answers with a partner.

---

**con·front** ⚏+ /kənˈfrʌnt/ *verb*
**1** ~ **sb/sth** (of problems or a difficult situation) to appear and need to be dealt with by someone: *the economic problems confronting the country* • *The government found itself confronted by massive opposition.* **2** ~ **sth** to deal with a problem or difficult situation **SYN** FACE UP TO: *She knew that she had to confront her fears.* **3** ~ **sb** to face someone so that they cannot avoid seeing and hearing you, especially in an unfriendly or dangerous situation: *This was the first time he had confronted an armed robber.* **4** ~ **sb with sb/sth** to make someone face or deal with an unpleasant or difficult person or situation: *He confronted her with a choice between her career or their relationship.* **5** **be confronted with sth** to have something in front of you that you have to deal with or react to: *When confronted with a bear, stop and stay calm.*

---

1. How many definitions does *confront* have? ____

2. What synonym is given for *confront*? _____

3. What common expression is given that uses *confront*?

   _____

---

**in·her·ent** ⚏+ **Ⓦ** /ɪnˈhɪrənt; -ˈhɛr-/ *adj.* ~ **(in sb/sth)** that is a basic or permanent part of someone or something and that cannot be removed **SYN** INTRINSIC: *the difficulties inherent in a study of this type* ◆ *Violence is inherent in our society.* ◆ *an inherent weakness in the design of the machine* ▸ **in·her·ent·ly** *adv.*: *an inherently unworkable system*

---

4. What part of speech is *inherent*? _____

   *Inherently*? _____

5. What synonym is given for *inherent*? _____

---

**con·strain** **Ⓦ** /kənˈstreɪn/ *verb* (*formal*) **1** [usually passive] ~ **sb to do sth** to force someone to do something or behave in a particular way: *The evidence was so compelling that he felt constrained to accept it.* **2** [often passive] to restrict or limit someone or something: ~ **sth** *Research has been constrained by a lack of funds.* ◆ ~ **sb (from doing sth)** *She felt constrained from continuing by the threat of losing her job.*

---

6. In what form is *constrain* usually used? _____

7. How many example sentences are given for *constrain*? ____

8. What words often follow *constrain*? _____

**a·chieve·ment** ⓘ Ⓦ /əˈtʃiːvmənt/ *noun*
**1** [C] a thing that someone has done successfully, especially using their own effort and skill: *the greatest scientific achievement of the decade* ◆ *It was a remarkable achievement for such a young player.* ◆ *They were proud of their children's achievements.* **2** [U] the act or process of achieving something: *the need to raise standards of achievement in education* ◆ *Even a small success gives you a* ***sense of achievement*** (= a feeling of pride).

9. How many definitions does *achievement* have? ____

10. What common collocation is given that uses *achievement*?

    _____

**C. EXTEND** Work with a partner. Look up words from Readings 1 and 2 in your dictionary. Take turns asking questions like the ones in Activity B.

**iQ** PRACTICE   Go online for more practice with using the dictionary.
*Practice > Unit 1 > Activity 8*

# WRITING

**OBJECTIVE ▶** At the end of this unit, you will write an analysis essay about the qualities that make someone admirable. This essay will include specific information from the readings, the unit video, and your own ideas.

## WRITING SKILL  Organizing and developing an essay

An **analysis essay** examines a topic by breaking it down into smaller parts. Remember that an essay includes an **introduction**, one or more **body paragraphs**, and a **conclusion**.

### Introduction

This paragraph should make the reader interested in your topic. It usually includes a "hook" to catch the reader's attention. It also provides background information or general statements about the topic. Within the introduction paragraph, include a **thesis statement**. The thesis statement contains the topic and the **controlling idea** (a specific idea or an opinion about the topic) of the essay. It tells the reader the purpose of the essay.

        topic                  controlling idea

☐ **Thesis statement:** A role model inspires people to do their best.

### Body paragraphs

For each body paragraph, include a **topic sentence** that states the topic of the paragraph and the controlling idea. Add supporting sentences that provide as much detail as possible to fully develop your thesis. Use supporting sentences that all relate to or develop the topic to create **unity**. Organize the supporting sentences in a logical way, so there is a clear connection between the ideas to create **coherence**. Often **transition words** like *first*, *in addition*, and *for example* are used to show the relationship between supporting ideas.

### Conclusion

The conclusion brings the essay to a close. This paragraph may restate the thesis statement in different words, summarize the main points, or do both. Write sentences that remind the reader of why he or she is reading the essay. You can also use the conclusion to help your reader look beyond the essay or think about further ideas that relate to your topic.

**iQ** RESOURCES  Go online to watch the Writing Skill Video.
*Resources ▶ Video ▶ Unit 1 ▶ Writing Skill Video*

**A. WRITING MODEL** Read the model essay. Then follow the steps below.

## Successful People

1    Are fame and fortune in your future? Do you dream of becoming a billionaire or a famous actor? For most of us, that is not too likely. Even though we may never see our picture on the cover of a glossy magazine, we all want to make something of ourselves and have a good life. We all want to succeed, and identifying what qualities make someone successful can help us to achieve that goal.

2    Successful people share three common qualities that allow them to stand out. First, people who are successful are organized. They don't waste time, and they work in ways that maximize their efficiency. They also work longer hours. Second, they are focused and single-minded. They can see where they want to go, and they only do the things that will get them there. For example, when they are working on something, they don't get lost in the details or overwhelmed by the tasks they need to do. Finally, people who are successful must be able to set and accomplish goals. Knowing what they want helps them stay both organized and focused.

3    If you want to be successful, you need to get organized, stay focused, and set and accomplish goals. Not many people succeed without these qualities, but don't despair. These behaviors can be learned and improved, and anyone can stand out if he or she develops organization, focus, and goals.

1. Read the introduction again. Circle the hook.

2. Find the thesis statement in the introductory paragraph. Underline the topic once. Underline the controlling idea twice.

3. Underline the topic sentence of the body paragraph.

4. One sentence in the body doesn't contribute to the unity of the essay, because it doesn't develop the topic. Draw a line through it.

5. Circle the transition words that contribute to the coherence of the body paragraph.

6. Read the conclusion again. Circle the answer that best describes what the conclusion does.

   a. It restates the thesis statement and suggests further examination of the topic.

   b. It summarizes the main points and suggests ways to be successful.

   c. It restates the thesis statement and summarizes the main points.

**B. CREATE** In the chart, list two people you consider successful, the qualities you believe contributed to their success, and their accomplishments. List one family member or friend and a famous or well-known person.

| Successful people | Qualities | Accomplishments |
|---|---|---|
| my mother | hardworking, organized, caring | worked as a nurse while raising my sisters and me |
| | | |
| | | |

 **CRITICAL THINKING STRATEGY**

### Ordering ideas

To **order your ideas** is to decide which idea should come first, second, third, etc. The order can inform your reader of the relative importance of each point. Transition words can help the reader see not only the order of those points, but also logical connections between the points and explanations or examples you choose to include.

> Successful people share several basic qualities. **First**, they are organized. **Second**, they are focused and single-minded. **For example**, when they are working on something, they don't get lost in the details or overwhelmed by the tasks they need to do. **Finally**, they are goal oriented: they set and accomplish goals.

**iQ** PRACTICE  Go online to watch the Critical Thinking Video and check your comprehension. *Practice > Unit 1 > Activity 9*

**C. ANALYZE** Work with a partner. Read the sentences and number them to make a logically ordered body paragraph. First, identify the topic sentence. Then order the supporting sentences to create unity and coherence. Then write the whole paragraph in order and check for unity and coherence. Compare your order with a partner and discuss any differences.

_____ a. First, role models have a well-developed set of skills or qualities, but they may be unwilling or unable to help others develop them.

_____ b. Mentors, on the other hand, may have the same skills or qualities, but they make it a point to train or teach others on a personal basis.

_____ c. There are two important differences between role models and mentors.

__3__ d. For example, a research scientist may be great in the lab but not in the classroom.

_____ e. Role models may or may not pay personal attention to those they inspire and may affect a large number of people at once, but mentors always have a few special people they work with individually.

_____ f. A role model can inspire many people just by his or her actions, while a mentor is limited to inspiring a few people at a time.

_____ g. This is because of the time it takes to work with someone individually.

_____ h. A second factor is the number of people a role model or mentor can influence at one time.

**D. CREATE** The paragraph in Activity C is the body paragraph for an essay about role models and mentors. Answer the questions.

1. List some possible hooks for an introduction to this paragraph.

_____

_____

2. Choose the best thesis statement for the essay.

   a. We all need both role models and mentors.

   b. Role models and mentors are both admirable, but their effect on our lives will be very different.

   c. Both role models and mentors are admirable.

3. What is the best way to conclude this essay?

_____

**iQ** PRACTICE   Go online for more practice with organizing and developing an essay. _Practice > Unit 1 > Activity 10_

1. **Restrictive relative clauses**\* describe or identify nouns. Usually, they directly follow nouns, noun phrases, or indefinite pronouns (*something*, *everyone*, etc.).

pronoun / noun | restrictive relative clause (adjective clause)

A role model is <u>someone</u> **who makes a difference in people's lives.**
Role models face <u>questions</u> **that we may also face.**

2. Most relative clauses begin with a relative pronoun.

   • Use *who* or *that* after nouns for people.

   Role models are <u>people</u> **who may volunteer in their communities.**
   <u>Ordinary people</u> **that we each know** can be role models.

   • Use *that* or *which* after nouns for things. (*Which* usually sounds more formal.)

   <u>Biographies</u> **that tell stories of successful people** are very popular.
   Role models do <u>things</u> **that we would like to do.**
   Sarah works for a <u>company</u> **which helps the homeless.**

3. You can think of a sentence with a relative clause as a combination of two sentences about the same noun.

   • In a **subject relative clause**, the relative pronoun stands for the subject of the clause. It is followed by a verb.

   A role model is someone. + ~~He or she~~ makes a difference in people's lives. =

   subject + verb

   A role model is <u>someone</u> **who makes a difference in people's lives.**

   • In an **object relative clause**, the relative pronoun stands for the object of the clause. The relative pronoun is followed by a subject + verb.

   Role models face questions. + We may also face ~~the questions~~. =

   object + subject + verb

   Role models face <u>questions</u> **that we may also face.**

4. In object relative clauses, the relative pronoun can be omitted.

   <u>Ordinary people</u> ~~that~~ **we each know can be role models.**
   Role models do <u>things</u> ~~that~~ **we would like to do.**

\*also called *identifying adjective clauses*

**A. IDENTIFY** Underline the restrictive relative clause in each sentence. Circle the noun, noun phrase, or indefinite pronoun it identifies.

1. Not every (person) who makes his or her community a better place is acknowledged for it.

2. They do the things that they do because they want to make their communities better.

3. At 19, Ahmed borrowed a book that changed his life forever.

4. His father was an illiterate cattle merchant who insisted that his son have an education.

5. She reads storybooks to children who have no access to television.

6. Maryam started a youth environmental group which is trying to clean up the city.

7. The trash Maryam's group collects is carried away by bicycles.

**B. COMPOSE** Combine each pair of sentences using a restrictive relative clause with *who*, *that*, or *which*. Use the words in bold to help you.

1. We all aspire to do **something**. Other people will respect **it**.

    We all aspire to do something that other people will respect.

2. Role models may inspire us to help **people**. **They** cannot help themselves.

    _____

3. Role models have **qualities**. We would like to have **them**.

    _____

4. To me, **a person** is a role model. **He** inspires others to do good deeds.

    _____

5. Reading novels gives students **something**. They cannot get **it** in textbooks.

    _____

6. Caring for the environment is **something**. We can all do **it**.

    _____

7. **Someone** is a generous person. **He or she** donates money to charity.

    _____

**C. IDENTIFY** Which sentences in Activity B can omit the relative pronoun? Cross out the relative pronoun if it can be omitted.

iQ PRACTICE Go online for more practice with restrictive relative clauses.
*Practice > Unit 1 > Activities 11–12*

**UNIT ASSIGNMENT**   Write an analysis essay

**OBJECTIVE ▶**

In this assignment, you are going to write a three-paragraph analysis essay. As you prepare your essay, think about the Unit Question, "What makes someone admirable?" Use information from Reading 1, Reading 2, the unit video, and your work in this unit to support your essay. Refer to the Self-Assessment checklist on page 30.

**iQ** PRACTICE   Go online to the Writing Tutor to read a model three-paragraph analysis essay. *Practice > Unit 1 > Activity 13*

# PLAN AND WRITE

**A. BRAINSTORM** Follow these steps to help you organize your ideas.

1. In the chart, list three people who you think are admirable. Describe the qualities that they possess and give an example of their accomplishments.

| Person | Qualities | Accomplishments |
|---|---|---|
| 1. | | |
| 2. | | |
| 3. | | |

2. Compare the people in your chart. What qualities do they share? How are their accomplishments similar or different?

| Similarities | Differences |
|---|---|
| | |

**WRITING TIP**
Outlines help you put your ideas in order. Often when you write an outline for an essay, you include the thesis statement, notes about supporting ideas for your body paragraphs, and notes for the concluding paragraph.

**B. PLAN** Follow these steps to plan your essay.

1. Write a topic for your essay.

2. Write an opinion or a specific idea about the topic above. This will be your controlling idea for your thesis statement.

3. Now combine your topic from 1 and your controlling idea from 2 to form your thesis statement.

**iQ** RESOURCES  Go online to download and complete the outline for your analysis essay. *Resources > Writing Tools > Unit 1 > Outline*

**TIP FOR SUCCESS**
The writer is responsible for producing text that others can understand. Write on one topic (unity) in a logical way (coherence).

**C. WRITE** Use your planning notes to write your essay.

1. Write your analysis essay about the qualities that make a person admirable. Be sure to have an introduction, a body paragraph, and a conclusion. Include restrictive relative clauses where appropriate. You may also use transition words from the box to help connect your ideas.

| | | | |
|---|---|---|---|
| In addition, | For example, | First, | Finally, |
| Also, | For instance, | Second, | Most importantly, |

2. Look at the Self-Assessment checklist below to guide your writing.

**iQ** PRACTICE  Go online to the Writing Tutor to write your assignment.
*Practice > Unit 1 > Activity 14*

# REVISE AND EDIT

**iQ** RESOURCES  Go online to download the peer review worksheet.
*Resources > Writing Tools > Unit 1 > Peer Review Worksheet*

**A. PEER REVIEW** Read your partner's essay. Then use the peer review worksheet. Discuss the review with your partner.

**B. REWRITE** Based on your partner's review, revise and rewrite your essay.

**C. EDIT** Complete the Self-Assessment checklist as you prepare to write the final draft of your essay. Be prepared to hand in your work or discuss it in class.

| SELF-ASSESSMENT | Yes | No |
|---|---|---|
| Does the essay have an introduction with a hook and thesis statement? | ☐ | ☐ |
| Are there enough details in the body paragraph to support the topic sentence? | ☐ | ☐ |
| If transition words are included, are they used appropriately? | ☐ | ☐ |
| Are restrictive relative clauses used correctly? | ☐ | ☐ |
| Does the essay include vocabulary from the unit? | ☐ | ☐ |
| Did you check the essay for punctuation, spelling, and grammar? | ☐ | ☐ |

**D. REFLECT** Discuss these questions with a partner or group.

1. What is something new you learned in this unit?

2. Look back at the Unit Question—What makes someone admirable? Is your answer different now than when you started the unit? If yes, how is it different? Why?

**iQ** PRACTICE  Go to the online discussion board to discuss the questions.
*Practice > Unit 1 > Activity 15*

# TRACK YOUR SUCCESS

**iQ** PRACTICE  Go online to check the words and phrases you have learned in this unit. *Practice > Unit 1 > Activity 16*

Check (✓) the skills and strategies you learned. If you need more work on a skill, refer to the page(s) in parentheses.

| | |
|---|---|
| READING | ☐ I can preview and predict the content of a text. (p. 4) |
| VOCABULARY | ☐ I can understand the organization of a dictionary entry. (p. 19) |
| WRITING | ☐ I can organize and develop an essay. (p. 22) |
| CRITICAL THINKING | ☐ I can order ideas to indicate their relative importance. (p. 24) |
| GRAMMAR | ☐ I can use restrictive relative clauses. (p. 26) |

---

**OBJECTIVE ▶**  ☐ I can gather information and ideas to write an analysis essay about what makes someone admirable.

---

# 2

## Behavioral Science

READING highlighting and annotating
CRITICAL THINKING discussing ideas
VOCABULARY collocations with nouns
WRITING writing a descriptive essay
GRAMMAR definite and indefinite articles

UNIT QUESTION

# How do marketers get our attention?

**A.** Discuss these questions with your classmates.

1. Where do you get information about products you want to buy?

2. Look at the photo. Is the boy paying attention to the ad? Do you pay attention to ads or ignore them?

**B.** Listen to *The Q Classroom* online. Then answer these questions.

1. Why are appearances important to Sophy when she makes a purchase? Do you share this value? Why or why not?

2. What does Marcus say about packaging and Felix about presentation? Give other examples of how packaging or presentation affects your decision to buy something.

**iQ** PRACTICE  Go to the online discussion board to discuss the Unit Question with your classmates. *Practice > Unit 2 > Activity 1*

UNIT OBJECTIVE

Read the articles. Gather information and ideas to write a descriptive essay about an advertisement for a product, business, or service.

## READING 1

# Your Guide to Generation Z: The Frugal, Brand-Wary, Determined Anti-Millennials

**OBJECTIVE ▶**

You are going to read an article by Elizabeth Segran, PhD, a staff writer at the business magazine *Fast Company*. The article discusses what companies need to know about Generation Z. Use the article to gather information and ideas for your Unit Assignment.

## PREVIEW THE READING

**A. PREVIEW** Read the title. Read the caption under the photograph. Answer the questions.

1. Who is Generation Z? What do you think the title means by *anti-millennials*?

2. The Great Recession was a period of economic decline from the end of 2007 through early 2009 and was started by the failure of the housing market. What effect did the Great Recession have on Gen Z?

**B. QUICK WRITE** How do you decide which product to buy? What influences your decision? Popularity? Quality? Value? Cost? Other factors? What type of information do you look for in advertisements about the product? Write for 5–10 minutes in response. Remember to use this section for your Unit Assignment.

**C. VOCABULARY** Check (✓) the words you know. Then work with a partner to locate each word in the reading. Use clues to help define the words you don't know. Check your definitions in the dictionary.

| | |
|---|---|
| **allure** *(n.)* | **insight** *(n.)* 🔑+ OPAL |
| **assume** *(v.)* 🔑+ OPAL | **obsession** *(n.)* 🔑+ |
| **disclose** *(v.)* 🔑+ | **put a premium on** *(v. phr.)* |
| **distinct** *(adj.)* 🔑+ OPAL | **resistance** *(n.)* 🔑+ OPAL |
| **endorse** *(v.)* 🔑+ | **tolerant** *(adj.)* |
| **exaggerated** *(adj.)* 🔑+ | **transparency** *(n.)* 🔑+ |

🔑+ Oxford 5000™ words          OPAL Oxford Phrasal Academic Lexicon

**iQ** PRACTICE  Go online to listen and practice your pronunciation.
*Practice > Unit 2 > Activity 2*

**A. INVESTIGATE** Read the article and gather information about Generation Z.

# Your Guide to Generation Z:
## The Frugal[1], Brand-Wary, Determined Anti-Millennials[2]

@ by Elizabeth Segran, PhD

The generation forged during the Great Recession

1    For the past several years, the media has been obsessed with millennials, the most studied group ever. But as Generation Z grows up, corporations are paying more attention to these young people, born between 1996 and 2011. At 60 million in the United States, they outnumber millennials by 1 million. It would be easy to **assume** that they are just an **exaggerated** version of the generation that came before them, spending even more of their lives on social media and doing even more shopping online. But Generation Z grew up in a very different historical context than millennials, which has given them a **distinct** outlook on the world.

2    Millennials were Internet pioneers. They invented Facebook, shopped from their smartphones, and smoothly transitioned from satellite TV to Hulu and Netflix. Generation Z, meanwhile, doesn't remember life without these basics of the 21st century. Since many members of Generation Z are just now leaving the nest, it's impossible to draw definitive conclusions about what their habits, lifestyles, and world views will be. But as the oldest start college and careers, we're beginning to see trends emerge.

## The Rejection of Big Brands

3    Marketers have been studying Generation Z for many years now, observing their preferences as children and teenagers. They have found that they have a very different relationship with companies than their elders. "Compared to any generation before, they are less trusting of brands," says Emerson Spartz, CEO of the digital media company Dose. "They have the strongest misinformation filter because they've grown up in an era where information was available at all times."

4    For decades, brands communicated through advertisements. Corporations with the biggest budgets could make the biggest impact through billboard, magazine, TV, and radio ads. But with the Internet, people can learn about what brands really stand for, beyond the photoshopped visions they project. Online reviews, for example, have made shoddy[3] products easy to spot. Gen Zers know this better than anyone. They immediately learn when a company has lied to them.

5    Gen Zers are also less conspicuous consumers than their predecessors. There was a time when young people aspired to wear flashy labels conspicuously[4]: Millennials flocked to[5] Hollister and Abercrombie and Fitch. But kids are now showing **resistance** to serving as walking advertisements. As a

[1] **frugal:** using only as much money as necessary
[2] **millennial:** a member of the generation of people who became adults around 2000
[3] **shoddy:** made badly or with not enough care
[4] **conspicuously:** easy to see or notice; likely to attract attention
[5] **flock to:** to go to in large numbers

result, many of the major apparel companies are doing poorly. "They're less brand-conscious and they are not spending as much as millennials do," says Kyle Andrew, chief marketing officer of American Eagle Outfitters. This is a brand that targets teens, which unlike some brands, has seen sales rise.

6    Still, Gen Z is hardly a lost cause for major companies. Spartz says that brands that can communicate with customers in an open way tend to do better with young people. Everlane and Cuyana, for instance, offer **insight** into how products are made. Warby Parker and Tom's make a point of explaining how they try to promote social good. In turn, these companies seem to have attracted the shopping attention of Gen Z. "Authenticity and **transparency** are two ideals that they value highly," he says.

7    Gen Zers also tend to trust individuals more than big corporations. As a result, many brands focused on them are partnering with social media influencers[6] in an effort to appear more relatable. These influencers—their peers—appear on social media, such as Instagram and YouTube, and are paid to **endorse** products. (Influencers are required by law to **disclose** this.) Nevertheless, it works: if a brand is endorsed by someone Gen Z follows, then Gen Z trusts that brand.

## Careful Spenders

8    Generation Z doesn't just stand out in the way they relate to brands. They're also spending their money differently. Companies have noticed that young adults **put a premium on** getting good value for their money. Spirit Airlines, for instance, is preparing for Gen Z to become the dominant group of travelers. It is rebranding itself as an ultra-low-cost carrier. The airline offers rock-bottom fares, but with zero frills. Spirit has found that this generation, who are buying their own tickets for the first time, is comfortable paying only for what they

are using. Rana Ghosh, an executive at Spirit says. "It's not so much that they are price-conscious; it's about what they are getting for the money they spend."

9    Gen Z also tends to be savvy in their approach to electronics, resisting the **allure** of the latest, priciest products when there is a constant stream of new, inexpensive options. "Technological innovation is no longer an exciting, celebrated thing as much as an expectation," says Sam Paschel, chief commercial officer of the headphone brand Skullcandy. The brand targets younger consumers. "Generation Z relates to technology as a tool, as opposed to an **obsession**," Paschel says. To keep up with the demands of today's teens, the company has invested heavily in scientists and researchers who work to improve the quality of sound. At the same time, Skullcandy has avoided flashy advertising or even charging a premium for its product. Rather, it strives for subtler messaging that speaks to young consumers.

## Ultra-Competitive, But Very Accepting

10    Market research also suggests that while Generation Z is an independent generation, they are also inclusive and **tolerant** of difference. With this knowledge, American Eagle Outfitters has tried to incorporate these ideals into its marketing, including an e-commerce website and ad campaigns that are diverse. Ads feature models from a wide range of ethnicities, with a variety of hair textures and body types. Company CMO Andrew says because teens no longer rely on mass-market brands to help them express their identity, AEO is trying to sell teens on creating their own personal brand.

11    Daunted or not, marketers are trying to keep up with the demands of Generation Z. "The rate of change in society is increasing exponentially," Dose CEO Spartz says. "The world is changing more in ten years now than it used to change in 100 years."

[6] **influencer:** a person who has the power to affect the purchase decisions of others because of his or her real/perceived authority, knowledge, or position

**B. VOCABULARY** Here are some words and phrases from Reading 1. Read the sentences. Circle the answer that best matches the meaning of each bold word.

1. He **assumed** that they would buy the product because others had bought it.

    a. thought          b. proved

**ACADEMIC LANGUAGE**

The corpus shows that *greater than* is often used in academic writing.

_____ **OPAL**
Oxford Phrasal Academic Lexicon

2. The **exaggerated** number made the ad's effectiveness seem greater than it really was.

    a. accurate         b. overstated

3. Her **distinct** appearance meant that people noticed her.

    a. plain            b. different

4. Because of **resistance** to the plan, he changed it.

    a. agreement        b. opposition

5. By sharing our experience, we hoped to provide the company **insight** about the problem.

    a. understanding    b. answers

6. We need the process to have **transparency** by being open to the public.

    a. clarity          b. secrecy

7. I hope they will **endorse** the product.

    a. say they want    b. say they like

8. The company should **disclose** information, so consumers know the risks.

    a. reveal           b. hide

9. Like most consumers, they **put a premium on** a good deal.

    a. value and want   b. accept and pay for

10. The **allure** of the city, including the nightlife, convinced her to accept the job.

    a. attraction       b. size

11. His has an **obsession** with video games. He plays them constantly.

    a. preoccupation    b. fascination

12. They are **tolerant** of his ideas, but they seldom use them.

    a. able to believe  b. able to accept

**iQ** PRACTICE  Go online for more practice with vocabulary.
*Practice › Unit 2 › Activity 3*

**C. EXPLAIN** Answer the questions.

1.  What is the main idea of the article?

    _____

2.  Who is the audience?

    _____

3.  Why are there references to different companies?

    _____

4.  What does Emerson Spartz, CEO of the digital media company Dose, mean by "Authenticity and transparency are two ideals that they value highly"?

    _____

5.  Where does Gen Z find peers who are influencers? What do they trust them to do?

    _____

**D. CATEGORIZE** Read the statements. Check (✓) the statements that are true of Generation Z. Correct each false statement to make it true according to the article. Write the paragraph number where the answer is found.

**Generation Z**

☐ 1. outnumbers millennials. (paragraph ___)

☐ 2. is a younger version of the millennials. (paragraph ___)

☐ 3. grew up in a context similar to that of millennials. (paragraph ___)

☐ 4. is a group of Internet pioneers. (paragraph ___)

☐ 5. doesn't remember a time without technology. (paragraph ___)

☐ 6. has a different relationship with companies than millennials. (paragraph ___)

☐ 7. is trusting of brands. (paragraph ___)

☐ 8. spends more money than millennials. (paragraph ___)

☐ 9. trusts its peers more than companies. (paragraph ___)

☐ 10. is tolerant of difference. (paragraph ___)

**E. IDENTIFY** Match the companies to information from the reading.

____ 1. American Eagle Outfitters    a. promotes social good.

____ 2. Everlane    b. creates ads that are diverse.

____ 3. Tom's    c. knows Gen Z wants value for its money.

____ 4. Spirit Airlines    d. offers insight into how products are made.

____ 5. Skullcandy    e. invests in science and improving quality.

**F. CATEGORIZE** Complete the chart with information about Generation Z and millennials.

| Generation Z | Millennials |
|---|---|
| Born between 1996 and 2011 | |

**G. SYNTHESIZE** Look back at your Quick Write on page 34. How do you decide which product to buy? Add any new ideas or information you learned from the reading.

**iQ** PRACTICE   Go online for additional reading and comprehension.
*Practice > Unit 2 > Activity 4*

# WRITE WHAT YOU THINK

**A. DISCUSS** Discuss the questions in a group. Think about the Unit Question, "How do marketers get our attention?"

1. What are some brands that you trust? Why do you trust them?

2. What makes a company trustworthy? How do you get reliable information about companies and products?

3. If you were asked for advice on how marketers should get your attention, what advice would you give?

B. **SYNTHESIZE** Choose one of the questions from Activity A and write a paragraph of 5–7 sentences in response. Look back at your Quick Write on page 34 as you think about what you learned.

## READING SKILL  Highlighting and annotating

The purpose of **highlighting** and **annotating** is to identify important ideas in a text. Both of these techniques will allow you to quickly find the information later, without having to reread the text.

### Highlighting

Always decide the purpose of your highlighting before you begin. Then highlight, underline, or circle information in a text such as:

- the main idea or topic of a paragraph
- keywords, details, or examples
- phrases that summarize the information

Use different-colored highlighter pens for different types of information. For example, use one color for main ideas and another for details. Or use a graphic system, such as solid lines, dotted lines, circling, etc.

### Annotating

Annotating—writing notes directly on the page of a text—is a useful way to identify and mark important information. First, read a paragraph and decide what is important. Then write brief notes in the margin. You may use abbreviations such as these:

| | | |
|---|---|---|
| T = thesis | S = summary | R = reason |
| MI = main idea | Ex = example | ? = question |

A. **IDENTIFY** Read this paragraph from Reading 1 and look at the highlighting and annotations. Then answer the questions.

grew up when
information available
at all times

  Marketers have been studying Generation Z for many years now, observing their preferences as children and teenagers. They have found that they have a very different relationship with companies than their elders. "Compared to any generation before, they are less trusting of brands," says Emerson Spartz, CEO of the digital media company Dose. "They have the strongest misinformation filter  ?  because they've grown up in an era where information was available at all times."

1. What does the information highlighted in yellow show? _____

2. What does the information highlighted in pink show? _____

3. What is the purpose of each annotation?

_____

_____

**TIP FOR SUCCESS**

After annotating the text, you may want to write out your notes to use as a reference and study tool.

**B. IDENTIFY** Highlight and annotate the following paragraph, taken from Reading 1. Follow these steps. Then compare notes with a partner.

1. Highlight in one color (or circle) the main idea of the paragraph.

2. Highlight in another color (or underline) the key details.

3. Underline an example and write a note in the margin that identifies the specific example.

4. Write a brief note in the margin to summarize the paragraph.

> For decades, brands communicated through advertisements. Corporations with the biggest budgets could make the biggest impact through billboard, magazine, TV, and radio ads. But with the Internet, people can learn about what brands really stand for, beyond the photoshopped visions they project. Online reviews, for example, have made shoddy products easy to spot. Gen Zers know this better than anyone. They immediately learn when a company has lied to them.

iQ PRACTICE  Go online for more practice with highlighting and annotating.
*Practice > Unit 2 > Activity 5*

# This Is Why You're Addicted to Your Phone

You are going to read an article by Nick Arnold for the BBC news service. The article looks at how technology influences our behavior. Use the article to gather information and ideas for your Unit Assignment.

## PREVIEW THE READING

**A. PREVIEW** The article contains a number references to technology and the Internet. Skim the article to find the answers to these questions.

1. What websites and apps are mentioned in the article?

2. Why do you think these names are mentioned?

**B. QUICK WRITE** Think about your activities over the past day or so. What media sources have been vying for your attention (notifications on your phone, TV commercials, marketing emails, etc.)? How have you responded? Write for 5–10 minutes in response. Be sure to use this section for your Unit Assignment.

**C. VOCABULARY** Check (✓) the words you know. Use a dictionary to define any new or unknown words. Then discuss with a partner how the words will relate to the unit.

| | |
|---|---|
| activation *(n.)* 🔑+ | essentially *(adv.)* 🔑+ OPAL |
| align *(v.)* 🔑+ | functional *(adj.)* 🔑+ OPAL |
| broadly speaking *(adv. phr.)* | impulsive *(adj.)* |
| counter *(v.)* 🔑+ | manipulate *(v.)* 🔑+ |
| crave *(v.)* | metric *(n.)* |
| escalate *(v.)* 🔑+ | tactic *(n.)* 🔑+ |

🔑+ Oxford 5000™ words      **OPAL** Oxford Phrasal Academic Lexicon

**iQ** PRACTICE   Go online to listen and practice your pronunciation.
*Practice › Unit 2 › Activity 6*

# WORK WITH THE READING

🔊 **A. INVESTIGATE** Read the article and gather information about how much technology influences our behavior.

# THIS IS WHY YOU'RE ADDICTED TO YOUR PHONE

BY NICK ARNOLD

1   In 2015, Max Stossel, 28, had an awakening. He was a successful social media strategist[1] working with major multinational companies. But that same year, he realized that some of the work he was doing wasn't actually in people's best interests. Stossel has since become a pivotal part of the Time Well Spent movement. It "aims to **align** technology with our human values."

2   Time Well Spent was co-founded by the former Google "product philosopher" Tristan Harris. It is made up of "a group of industry insiders," many of whom have worked for companies like Facebook and Snapchat but have now aligned themselves with the movement in some way. Last year, Ofcom, the UK communications regulator, found that more than half of all Internet users in Britain feel they're addicted to technology. "There's this idea that we're addicted to our phones, and that we've done this to ourselves," says Stossel. "That is just not true."

3   Stossel explains that tech design is increasingly informed by behavioral psychology and neuroscience. Tristan Harris himself studied at Stanford's Persuasive Tech Lab, which describes itself as creating "insight into how computing products can be designed to influence and change human behavior." The Lab's website states, "Technology is being designed to change what we think and do." It gives several examples of this from Facebook, YouTube, and Twitter.

4   "When you understand neuroscience and you understand how to develop apps, you can **essentially** program the brain," Stossel says. "There are thousands of people on the other side of your screens whose job it is to keep you as hooked as possible, and they've gotten very good at it."

5   I ask Stossel just how good these people are. I control my notifications, not vice versa, I tell him. He asks a simple question: "Do you feel at all stressed when your phone is out of reach and it buzzes?" Um. Yes. Figuring out how to capture my attention like that, is, according to Stossel, "the job of everybody in my industry."

6   **Broadly speaking**, tech design seeks to take advantage of our brain's reward system, where dopamine[2] **activation** leads to feelings of satisfaction and pleasure. Our brains are programmed to seek more of whatever gives us this pleasure—so much so that we **crave** it when we don't have it. The same system that

---

[1] **social media strategist:** a person who helps websites or apps succeed   [2] **dopamine:** a chemical produced by nerve cells

makes us crave drugs or certain foods can also make us crave particular apps, games, sites, and devices.

7    But Time Well Spent believes this problem isn't exclusively a tech one. Stossel points out how the ways that content is created—including negative headlines and clickbait[3] **tactics**—can also fit into this type of persuasion. "The problem is that it's everything," he says. "It's all of the life that we live in. Life has become an "attention economy," Stossel explains. "Everybody wants to grab as much of our attention as possible. I was designing notification structures to help take you out of your world and bring you into mine."

8    Stossel argues that users are not the customers of technology, but the products. Our attention is the thing being sold. "We use lots of platforms for free," he says. But advertisers pay the platforms money to get our attention while we're on there. "We're not the ones paying, so the things that matter to us go second to what matters to advertisers," says Stossel.

9    Success in the tech world is often measured using the **metric** of "time spent"—that is, how long we spend using an app, streaming a service, or browsing a website. An example is the way videos auto-play on certain platforms. This keeps more people online for longer. But, Stossel says, "that doesn't mean that they actually want to stay online for longer." Stossel believes that this constant demand for our attention is making us lose focus on the things that are really important.

10    In the days following my conversation with Stossel, I notice how often I get sucked into aimlessly moving through the Instagram stories of people I don't even know. What starts as a mindless scroll through my Facebook feed before bed can easily **escalate** into huge periods of wasted time. I can certainly see the merit of what Time Well Spent is campaigning for. But the sheer scale of change needed leaves me wondering if their fight might be impossibly idealistic.

11    "It is absolutely possible," Stossel **counters**. "The challenge is getting consumers to demand it." He believes technology will **manipulate** our attention in ever more effective ways. "The future will be so good at this. That's why we need to demand this change now." Until that change comes, Time Well Spent co-founder Harris adheres to certain lifestyle changes the movement has designed for living better in the attention economy:

- He's turned off almost all notifications on his phone and has customized the vibration for text messages. Now he can feel the difference between an automated alert and a human's.

- He's made the first screen of his phone almost empty, with only **functional** apps like Uber and Google Maps. He can't get sucked into spending hours on these.

- He's put any apps he's inclined to waste time on, or any apps with colorful, attention-grabbing icons, inside folders on the second page of his phone. To open an app, he types its name into the phone's search bar—which reduces **impulsive** clicks.

- He also has a sticky note on his laptop. What does it say? "Do not open without intention."

---

[3] **clickbait:** material put on the Internet in order to attract attention and encourage visitors to click on a link to a particular web page

**B. VOCABULARY** Complete each sentence with the vocabulary from Reading 2. You may need to change the form of some of the words.

| | | |
|---|---|---|
| activation *(n.)* | crave *(v.)* | impulsive *(adj.)* |
| align *(v.)* | escalate *(v.)* | manipulate *(v.)* |
| broadly speaking *(adv. phr.)* | essentially *(adv.)* | metric *(n.)* |
| counter *(v.)* | functional *(adj.)* | tactic *(n.)* |

1. When I heard her argument, I wasn't sure how to _____ it with a better one.

2. The _____ we used to measure success in our business was whether we made any money.

3. That desk doesn't _____ with the others in that row; its position is wrong.

4. The business methods that my company uses are based on ethical practices; they are moral _____.

5. Smartphones aren't purely _____: they are also fashion items and people care about what they look like as well as what they can do.

6. _____, web designers want to keep you looking at their websites.

7. My sudden decision to buy these clothes was _____.

8. Playing computer games can quickly _____ from fun to a serious problem.

9. In a sentence, the job of advertisers is _____ to persuade us to buy a product or service.

10. A successful website can _____ us into staying online even if we don't want to.

11. When I get up in the morning, I _____ a cup of hot coffee; I really want one.

12. I could use that website as soon as I signed up: _____ was immediate.

**iQ PRACTICE** Go online for more practice with the vocabulary.
*Practice > Unit 2 > Activity 7*

**C. INTERPRET** Choose an answer. Then explain your answer to a partner.

1. What is the main idea of the article?

   a. We are addicted to our phones, and we have done this to ourselves.

   b. We are addicted to our phones, but tech professionals are trained to addict us.

   c. We are not really addicted to our phones; that idea comes from advertisers.

2. Who is the audience for this article?

   a. website designers

   b. anyone who accesses the Internet

   c. only teenagers

3. What is the purpose of the article?

   a. to inform readers about how they are being manipulated

   b. to tell website and app designers how to make better apps

   c. to encourage readers to stay online

4. What is the purpose of paragraph 3?

   a. to support the idea that we are responsible for our addictions to our phones

   b. to support the idea that advertisers pay for us to stay online

   c. to support the idea that technology is designed to be addictive

5. What is the purpose of paragraph 5?

   a. to demonstrate to tech workers that their tactics work

   b. to demonstrate to the author that he is addicted to his phone

   c. to demonstrate to Stossel that his argument is correct

**D. EXPLAIN** Answer these questions about the article.

1. According to the article, the Time Well Spent movement "aims to align technology with our human values." What might one of those values be?

   _____

2. Many of the people working with Time Well Spent used to work at social media and tech companies. Why do you think they no longer work for these companies?

   _____

3. When Stossel says, "There are thousands of people on the other side of your screens whose job it is to keep you as hooked as possible," what does he mean?

   _____

4. What is the "attention economy"? Why is it a problem?

   _____

**E. RESTATE** The article describes changes that Tristan Harris has made. Fill in the chart with information from the article.

| What he did | Reason |
|---|---|
| 1. He has turned off almost all notifications . . . | so his phone doesn't bother him |
| 2. He set two different vibrations for text messages . . . | |
| 3. | so he can get to "functional" apps but can't see more attractive apps |
| 4. He put attractive icons inside folders on his phone . . . | |
| 5. | to remind him to open apps intentionally |

**F. DISCUSS** Why has Harris done these things? Discuss with a partner.

 **CRITICAL THINKING STRATEGY**

**Discussing ideas**

Many questions require you to discuss your ideas. **Discussion** is the exchange of ideas and opinions about a topic. In Activity F, you shared your ideas about Tristan Harris. Listening to your partner's ideas may have provided other ideas. Through discussion, you can clarify your understanding of new material, which will help you remember it better. Listening to others can provide different perspectives.

**iQ** PRACTICE   Go online to watch the Critical Thinking Skill Video and check your comprehension. *Practice › Unit 2 › Activity 8*

**G. APPLY** Read the ideas for having a good discussion. Check (✓) the ideas that you agree with and make notes about why. Give an example of each point using ideas from this unit. Then discuss your answers with a partner.

☐ 1. prepare what to say ahead of time

☐ 2. refer back to the text to support your ideas

☐ 3. actively follow what others are saying

☐ 4. wait for someone to invite you to speak

☐ 5. take notes on what others say

☐ 6. ask information questions

☐ 7. make the discussion a competition

☐ 8. ask for clarification

☐ 9. restate information to make it clearer

# WORK WITH THE VIDEO

**A. PREVIEW** Do you want companies to gather data about you for marketing purposes? Why? Why not?

## VIDEO VOCABULARY

**data mining (n.)** looking at large amounts of information that has been collected on a computer and using it to provide new information

**data set (n.)** a collection of data which is treated as a single unit by a computer

**instantaneously (adv.)** immediately

**simultaneously (adv.)** at the same time as something else

**iQ RESOURCES** Go online to watch the video about predictive advertising.
*Resources > Video > Unit 2 > Unit Video*

**B. COMPOSE** Watch the video two or three times. Take notes in the chart.

|  | Data mining | How used in advertising |
|---|---|---|
| Notes from the video |  |  |

**C. EXTEND** What are some advantages and disadvantages of personalized advertising? Discuss your ideas with a partner.

# WRITE WHAT YOU THINK

**SYNTHESIZE** Think about Reading 1, Reading 2, and the unit video as you discuss these questions. Then choose one question and write a paragraph of 5–7 sentences in response.

1. Do you trust a company more when it gives you a lot of product information? Why? Why not?

2. What makes you look at an online advertisement?

3. Marketers use sound (e.g., notifications and auto-play ads) and visuals (e.g., color or motion) to grab our attention. Which do you think affects you more?

## VOCABULARY SKILL  Collocations with nouns

**Collocations** are words that often occur together. While there are no rules to help you learn collocations, it is important to pay attention to the patterns of words in a text. These patterns are clues that show you which words collocate. There are several common collocation patterns with nouns.

### Adjective + noun

- Millennials spend much of their lives on **social media**.
- Tech design seeks to take advantage of our brain's **reward system**.

### Verb + noun/noun phrase

- Corporations **are paying more attention to** these young people.
- We **lose focus** on the things that are really important.

### Preposition + noun/noun phrase

- **As a result,** many brands are partnering with social media influencers.
- Some of the work he was doing wasn't actually **in people's best interests**.

**TIP FOR SUCCESS**

Some collocations are idioms. This means that when the words are combined, they take on a unique meaning. Some examples of idioms are *put a premium on* and *pay attention to.*

**A. APPLY** Circle the word that usually goes together with the bold noun in each sentence. Look back at Reading 1 (R1) and Reading 2 (R2) to check your answers.

1. It's impossible to *get / draw* definitive **conclusions** about what their habits, lifestyles, and world views will be. (R1, paragraph 2)

2. *Online / E-based* **reviews** . . . have made shoddy products easy to spot. (R1, paragraph 4)

3. *By / In* **turn**, these companies seem to have attracted the shopping attention of Gen Z. (R1, paragraph 6)

4. The company **has invested** heavily *in / on* scientists and researchers who work to improve the quality of sound. (R1, paragraph 9)

5. The headphone brand Skullcandy. . . *targets / marks* younger **consumers**.
   (R1, paragraph 11)

6. **The rate** *for / of* **change** in society is increasing exponentially.
   (R1, paragraph 11)

7. He was . . . working with major *multination / multinational* **companies**.
   (R2, paragraph 1)

8. [They] have now aligned themselves with the movement *at / in* **some way**.
   (R2, paragraph 2)

9. Products can be designed to influence and change *human / person* **behavior**.
   (R2, paragraph 3)

10. There are thousands of people *in / on* **the other side** of your screens.
    (R2, paragraph 4)

11. Figuring out how to *capture / imprison* **my attention** . . . is . . . "the job of
    everybody in my industry." (R2, paragraph 5)

12. Tristan Harris adheres to certain *lifestyle / way of life* **changes**.
    (R2, paragraph 11)

**B. CREATE** Look at these collocations from Readings 1 and 2. Write sentences
using six of the collocations.

**Reading 1:**

offer insight into

social media influencers

show resistance to

personal brand

see trends emerge

price-conscious

social good

good value

**Reading 2:**

a person's best interest

grab our attention

use an app

stream a service

browse a website

scroll through a Facebook feed

turn off notifications

**iQ PRACTICE** Go online for more practice with collocations with nouns.
*Practice > Unit 2 > Activity 9*

# WRITING

**OBJECTIVE ▶**

At the end of this unit, you will write a descriptive essay about an advertisement for a product, business, or service. This essay will include specific information from the readings, the unit video, and your own ideas.

## WRITING SKILL  Writing a descriptive essay

A **descriptive essay** describes a person, place, or thing in a way that gives the reader a clear mental picture of the subject of the essay.

### Organization

- The **introduction** should make the reader interested in what you are describing. It should include a **thesis statement** that tells why the person, place, or thing is your focus.
- Write one or more **body paragraphs** that contain the details of your description.
- Finish with a **conclusion** that gives your final thoughts or opinion about what you are describing.

### Descriptive language

A good descriptive essay gives a clear mental picture of the subject of the essay. The reader should be able to imagine that he or she is with the person described, at the place described, etc. Include strong **imagery** (language that helps create these mental pictures) in your body paragraphs.

**Not descriptive**

She walked into the room.

He was dressed formally.

The street was filled with people selling food.

**Descriptive**

She walked **slowly** and **nervously** into the **dark** room.
(with adjectives and adverbs)

He wore **a light suit, a silk tie, and shiny shoes**.
(with details and specific language)

The street was filled with **loud men shouting out orders above the smoky smell of grilling meat**.
(with sensory language related to sounds, smells, etc.)

**A. WRITING MODEL** Read the model descriptive essay. Then follow the steps below.

## My Favorite Restaurant

1    One of my favorite restaurants is Ben's Diner on Fourth Street because it's perfect for a casual, delicious meal. Ben's is a family business that has been serving the local community for over 60 years. Look for the red neon sign with its flashing knife and fork. When you see it, you know you can expect good food that was cooked with fresh, local ingredients.

2    As soon as you step through the door at Ben's, you'll be glad you came. The restaurant is brightly lit and spotlessly clean, with gleaming tables and sparkling floors. You'll get a warm welcome from one of the staff, who will take you to a comfortable seat. I like the soft red leather seats in the booths, or sometimes I sit at the smooth marble counter. The pleasant noise of conversation and the soothing clatter of dishes will surround you. If you're not already hungry, the rich smell of homemade chicken soup coming from the kitchen will get you ready to eat.

3    Ben's menu has some old favorites and some unexpected surprises. The perfectly grilled burger is made of 100 percent prime beef. Served on a soft toasted bun, it's crunchy on the outside and moist and peppery inside. Add some sharp cheddar cheese for a satisfying treat. The Greek salad is famous for its fresh ingredients: bright green lettuce leaves, deep red tomatoes, and tangy purple olives. Or how about chicken fajitas, served beside your table in a sizzling skillet, with a spicy aroma I can't resist?

4    So, whether you're looking for somewhere new to get some great food or just passing through, I suggest you head over to Ben's. You'll feel right at home and enjoy some good cooking, too.

1. Underline the thesis statement and the concluding sentence.

2. Find at least two sensory details for each sense.

   a. sight: <u>red neon sign,</u>

   b. sound: _____

   c. taste: _____

   d. smell: _____

   e. touch: _____

**B. RESTATE** Read the sentences. Rewrite them to make them more descriptive. Add adjectives and adverbs, details and specific language, and sensory language. Be creative.

1. The man lived in a house far from the city.

   <u>The old man lived quietly in a small farmhouse far from the busy city.</u>

2. The room was filled with roses, daisies, and lilacs.

   _____

   _____

3. The chicken and potatoes were good.

   _____

   _____

4. We went on a hike though the forest.

   _____

   _____

5. His aunt entered the room.

   _____

   _____

6. I didn't get to watch the soccer game on TV.

   _____

   _____

**C. WRITING MODEL** Read the model descriptive essay. Then answer the questions that follow.

### Adventure Seekers Wanted

1   Do you live for your next escape from your everyday routine? Are you a strong and healthy outdoor person seeking your next great adventure? The Adventurer sport utility vehicle (SUV) is the right vehicle to buy for adventure and outdoor fun if you are a thrill-seeking, athletic person who spends time outdoors. The Adventurer is the best, most reliable SUV to take you, your thrill-seeking friends, and all your gear where you're going, and it will get you there in great comfort and style.

2   Do you spend time climbing snow-capped mountains, rafting through red rock canyons on a raging river, or cruising the rocky shoreline of a vast ocean seeking the perfect wave? If you answered yes to any of these questions, then you know that you need to be driving a powerful, all-wheel-drive vehicle to arrive at your destination. The new Adventurer delivers that power and maneuverability. Don't be fooled by the quiet, comfortable ride. The new Adventurer is the perfect off-road vehicle. It is a powerful, all-wheel-drive vehicle that is as at home on steep, rough dirt roads as it is on a flat, smooth highway. And, as a hybrid, it is the environmentally friendly vehicle you want to drive.

3   Do you plan to take friends and need to carry a lot of gear to your next adventure? There is plenty of room for all the equipment you'll need. The interior of the Adventurer is roomy and comfortable, so you can bring along as many as five fun-loving friends. The seats, of the softest, finest-quality leather, will keep you cool in the heat of the summer and warm in the winter. The climate control air system keeps the interior at a steady, regulated temperature.

4   Each adventure seeker creates his or her own story. Whatever your story, the Adventurer is the means to get you there. You will want the Adventurer because it is the right choice for your healthy, active lifestyle. Test-drive yours today!

1. What is the product?

_____

2. What is the controlling idea about the product?

_____

3. Who is the target customer for the product?

_____

4. What makes the product appealing?

_____

_____

_____

5. What does the conclusion do?

_____

6. Can you form a mental picture of the Adventurer SUV? Explain your answer.

_____

_____

_____

**D. CATEGORIZE** Look at the graphic organizer, a cluster diagram the author used to organize the description of the Adventurer. Complete the cluster diagram with ideas from the essay and your own ideas.

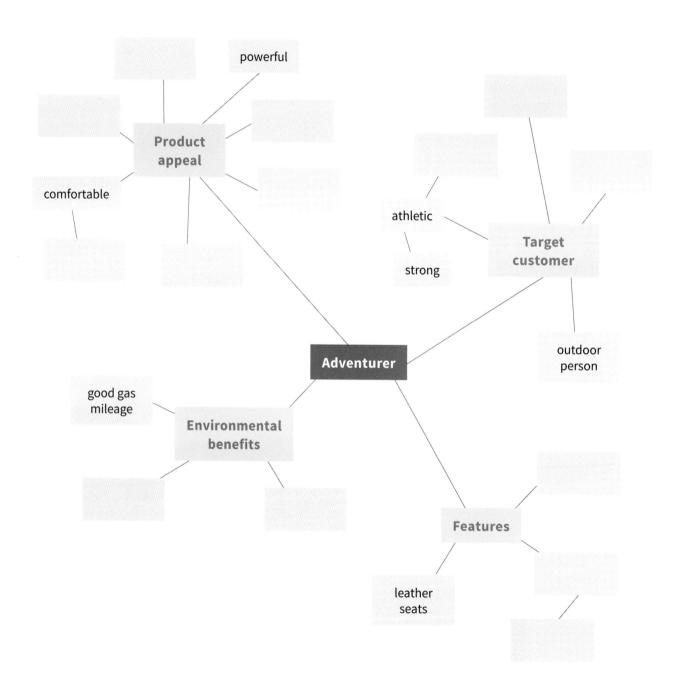

iQ PRACTICE  Go online for more practice writing a descriptive essay.
*Practice > Unit 2 > Activity 10*

A noun (a person, place, thing, or idea) is often introduced by an **article**. Different types of nouns can use different articles. Understanding the context in which a noun occurs will help you use articles correctly.

| Singular count noun | Plural count noun | Noncount noun |
|---|---|---|
| Indefinite article: *a* + consonant sound *an* + vowel sound | No article | No article |
| Definite article: *the* | Definite article: *the* | Definite article: *the* |

### Indefinite article, no article

Use the indefinite article *a/an* when a noun is not specifically identified or is unknown to the reader, for example, on first mention of the noun.

☐  We were excited to have **a new car**.

   (This is the first reference to *a new car*. The reader does not know about it yet.)

Use no article with plural count nouns and noncount nouns to refer to something in general.

☐  **Marketers** have been studying Generation Z for a long time.

   (*Marketers* refers to any marketers, not specific marketers.)

☐  We bought **fish** for dinner.

   (No article is used with noncount nouns.)

### Definite articles

Use *the* when a noun is specifically identified. Both the reader and the writer know the noun because they share information about it. For example:

☐  We were excited to have a new car, but **the car** we chose was terrible!

   (*A new car* was introduced earlier in the sentence.)

☐  Let's go to Ben's Diner. **The owners** are really friendly, and **the soup** is delicious.

   (The reader and writer both know that *the owners* refers to the owners of Ben's Diner, and *the soup* is served at Ben's Diner.)

☐  With **the Internet**, people can learn about what brands really stand for.

   (There is only one Internet. It is unique.)

☐  **The government** should do more about false advertising.

   (You can assume the reader will know which government you are referring to.)

**iQ** RESOURCES  Go online to watch the Grammar Skill Video.
*Resources > Video > Unit 2 > Grammar Skill Video*

**APPLY** Complete the blog. Write the correct articles: *a/an, the,* or Ø for no article.

---

Home         🔍    Sign in 👤

So you want to be _____ social media
             **1**
influencer? _____ job isn't as easy as you
          **2**
might imagine. First, you have to be likable. You
need to seem like _____ person who would
            **3**
be _____ good friend, and like _____
     **4**               **5**
good friend, you should share _____
                 **6**
information freely without thinking about
_____ money you might be making from advertising.
   **7**

     You also have to be interesting. The longer you keep _____
                                                   **8**
attention of your followers, the more likely you are to influence them.
Show _____ curiosity about _____ world around you, and make it
        **9**                   **10**
fun to follow you.

     If you have _____ corporate sponsor, make sure that you and
              **11**
_____ company you represent are compatible. You need to look and
   **12**
sound authentic because today's consumers are savvy about _____
                                                     **13**
social media. Show _____ passion that you have for _____ issue
                 **14**                  **15**
or product you talk about. Speak with _____ honesty, and show
                             **16**
_____ people _____ true reasons for your opinions.
   **17**           **18**

     Follow these guidelines, and you will be on _____ way to
                                                 **19**
becoming _____ influencer.
          **20**

---

**iQ** PRACTICE   Go online for more practice with definite and indefinite articles, and no articles with generic nouns. *Practice ⟩ Unit 2 ⟩ Activities 11–12*

UNIT ASSIGNMENT **Write a descriptive essay**

OBJECTIVE ▶

In this assignment, you are going to write a four-paragraph essay describing an advertisement for a product, business, or service. As you prepare your essay, think about the Unit Question, "How do marketers get our attention?" Use information from Reading 1, Reading 2, the unit video, and your work in this unit to support your essay. Refer to the Self-Assessment checklist on page 60.

**iQ** PRACTICE  Go online to the Writing Tutor to read a model descriptive essay.
*Practice ⟩ Unit 2 ⟩ Activity 13*

# PLAN AND WRITE

**A.** BRAINSTORM  **Follow these steps to help you organize your ideas.**

1. Think of some products, businesses, and services that you trust. These could be things like companies, brands, restaurants, stores, or products like new technology.

2. Browse the Internet or look through magazines for advertisements for these products, businesses, and services.

   a. What features of the advertisements attract your attention? Is there sound? Is there color? Is there movement?

   b. What do you dislike about the advertisement?

   c. How would you describe the advertisements? Think about descriptive language you can use.

3. Choose one product, business, or service advertisement that interests you.

**WRITING TIP**
You can use a **cluster diagram** to help you organize and develop your ideas. See page 56 for an example.

**B.** PLAN  **Follow these steps to plan your essay.**

1. Choose two or three main features or qualities of the ads you found in step 2 of Activity A.

2. Brainstorm some descriptive language to give a clear mental picture of each feature or quality you selected.

**iQ** RESOURCES  Go online to download and complete the outline for your descriptive essay. *Resources ⟩ Writing Tools ⟩ Unit 2 ⟩ Outline*

**C.** WRITE  **Use your planning notes to write your essay.**

1. Write your essay describing an advertisement for a product, business, or service. Be sure to include a thesis statement that tells why it is your focus and body paragraphs that describe the specific features or qualities of the advertisement.

2. Look at the Self-Assessment checklist on page 60 to guide your writing.

**iQ** PRACTICE  Go online to the Writing Tutor to write your assignment.
*Practice ⟩ Unit 2 ⟩ Activity 14*

# REVISE AND EDIT

**iQ** RESOURCES   Go online to download the peer review worksheet.
*Resources > Writing Tools > Unit 2 > Peer Review Worksheet*

**A. PEER REVIEW**  Read your partner's essay. Then use the peer review worksheet. Discuss the review with your partner.

**B. REWRITE**  Based on your partner's review, revise and rewrite your essay.

**C. EDIT**  Complete the Self-Assessment checklist as you prepare to write the final draft of your essay. Be prepared to hand in your work or discuss it in class.

| SELF-ASSESSMENT | Yes | No |
|---|---|---|
| Does the thesis statement have a topic and controlling idea? | ☐ | ☐ |
| Does the essay use descriptive language to create a clear mental picture of the subject? | ☐ | ☐ |
| Are correct articles used? | ☐ | ☐ |
| Did you use collocations from the unit correctly? | ☐ | ☐ |
| Does your essay include vocabulary from the unit? | ☐ | ☐ |
| Did you check the essay for correct punctuation, spelling, and grammar? | ☐ | ☐ |

**D. REFLECT**  Discuss these questions with a partner or group.

1. What is something new you learned in this unit?

2. Look back at the Unit Question—How do marketers get our attention? Is your answer different now than when you started the unit? If yes, how is it different? Why?

**iQ** PRACTICE   Go to the online discussion board to discuss the questions.
*Practice > Unit 2 > Activity 15*

# TRACK YOUR SUCCESS

**iQ** PRACTICE   Go online to check the words and phrases you have learned in this unit. *Practice > Unit 2 > Activity 16*

Check (✓) the skills and strategies you learned. If you need more work on a skill, refer to the page(s) in parentheses.

| | |
|---|---|
| READING | ☐ I can highlight and annotate a text. (p. 40) |
| CRITICAL THINKING | ☐ I can discuss ideas. (p. 47) |
| VOCABULARY | ☐ I can use collocations with nouns. (p. 49) |
| WRITING | ☐ I can write a descriptive essay. (p. 51) |
| GRAMMAR | ☐ I can use definite and indefinite articles. (p. 57) |

OBJECTIVE ▶   ☐ I can gather information and ideas to write a descriptive essay about an advertisement for a product, business, or service.

# Developmental Psychology

**3**

| | |
|---|---|
| CRITICAL THINKING | relating to the reading |
| READING | making inferences |
| VOCABULARY | prefixes and suffixes |
| WRITING | writing a narrative essay and varying sentence patterns |
| GRAMMAR | past perfect and past perfect continuous |

**UNIT QUESTION**

# What important lessons do we learn as young people?

**A.** Discuss these questions with your classmates.

1. Who were your friends when you were growing up? What activities did you participate in?

2. What are some life lessons you learned from your parents?

3. Look at the photo. How do you think the people feel?

**B.** Listen to *The Q Classroom* online. Then answer these questions.

1. What important lessons did Felix, Sophy, and Yuna learn as young people? What is one lesson you learned?

2. What does Marcus say about learning from our parents? Sophy disagrees with Marcus. Who do you agree with? Why?

**iQ** PRACTICE   Go to the online discussion board to discuss the Unit Question with your classmates. *Practice > Unit 3 > Activity 1*

**UNIT OBJECTIVE**   Read a magazine article and a blog post. Gather information and ideas to write a narrative essay about someone or something that influenced you when you were younger.

## READING 1

# The Difference Between Fitting in and Belonging, and Why It Matters

**OBJECTIVE ▶**

You are going to read a magazine article about fitting in and belonging. Use the article to gather information and ideas for your Unit Assignment.

## PREVIEW THE READING

**A. PREVIEW** Read the title. Look at the photograph. What do you think the title means by *fitting in*? What about *belonging*?

**B. QUICK WRITE** What decisions did you make as a young person about your appearance, activities, and time? For example, what did you wear? What activities and groups did you participate in? How did you spend your free time? Write for 5–10 minutes in response. Remember to use this section for your Unit Assignment.

**C. VOCABULARY** Check (✓) the words you know. Use a dictionary to define any new or unknown words. Then discuss with a partner how the words will relate to the unit.

| | |
|---|---|
| anxiety *(n.)* Ⓔ+ OPAL | fit in *(v. phr.)* |
| barrier *(n.)* Ⓔ+ OPAL | foundation *(n.)* Ⓔ+ |
| coping *(n.)* Ⓔ+ | negotiate *(v.)* Ⓔ+ |
| courage *(n.)* Ⓔ+ | self-fulfillment *(n.)* |
| empathy *(n.)* | shame *(n.)* Ⓔ+ |
| extensive *(adj.)* Ⓔ+ OPAL | |

Ⓔ+ Oxford 5000™ words    OPAL Oxford Phrasal Academic Lexicon

**iQ PRACTICE** Go online to listen and practice your pronunciation.
*Practice > Unit 3 > Activity 2*

# WORK WITH THE READING

 **A. INVESTIGATE** Read the article and gather information about the important lessons we learn as young people.

# THE DIFFERENCE BETWEEN FITTING IN AND BELONGING, AND WHY IT MATTERS

1   We all want to **fit in**, don't we? I remember how painful middle school was because my parents couldn't or wouldn't buy me the "cool" clothes for school that the popular kids were wearing. We were much too frugal for that in our family. I was never one of the popular kids. Maybe those clothes would have helped, but in truth, I probably never would have been a popular kid anyway. I made friends and formed connections with kids who didn't care about popularity or cool clothes. Some of those people are still my friends today.

2   Which brings me to the topics of fitting in versus belonging, and how we can get there from here.

## FITTING IN VS. BELONGING

3   We all feel the need to be part of social groups in our communities, and we all make choices that affect the connections we make to others. At a young age, we begin to make decisions about our appearance, our social activities, and our time commitments. We choose how we look—our hair, our clothes, and even what we do to our bodies—who we hang out with, and how we spend our time. In making these choices, we may either be trying to fit in or to belong. Brene Brown, PhD, a social scientist and research professor, has been doing **extensive** research over the past 17 years on what she calls our "inextricable[1] human connections" and on true belonging. "The greatest **barrier** to belonging," she says, "is fitting in." So what are the differences between fitting in and belonging?

4   According to Brown, fitting in is changing ourselves to match the situation. In other words, fitting in is doing what is "cool." For example, it is wearing the right clothes, playing the most popular sport, or hanging out with the "best" social groups. But fitting in may cause feelings of **anxiety** or loneliness. Fitting in is easier in the sense that you don't have to go against the norm. However, according to Brown, it is **shame**-based and sends messages, especially to young people, that they are not good enough. As we work to conform to the expectations of others, we lose the sense of belonging to our real selves. Why? Brown says that we have a deep fear that if we present our authentic selves, we won't be liked. In addition, young people who feel pressured to fit in in ways that aren't healthy to their overall identities may end up participating in unhealthy relationships or going along with the crowd. Worse, they might begin participating in hurtful or mean-spirited behaviors, including bullying.

[1] **inextricable:** too closely linked to be separated

Fitting in or belonging?

5   Belonging is something else. It is letting ourselves be seen and known as we really are—being our true or authentic selves. It is wearing clothing that makes us feel good or that allows us to show our uniqueness, doing activities we enjoy, and spending time with people we can be our authentic selves with. Belonging brings enjoyment, excitement, or **self-fulfillment**. But it doesn't come easy. Being different can make us feel vulnerable—exposed to emotional uncertainty and risk. But, Brown claims, it's this same vulnerability that becomes the **foundation** on which **courage** is built. These findings surprised even Brown. She had assumed that belonging was external—that people **negotiated** with the groups they want to join. Instead, she found that the people with the deepest sense of belonging are those who have the courage to stand alone and risk being disconnected from others.

² **resilient:** able to feel better quickly after something unpleasant such as a shock, injury, etc.

## HOW TO GET FROM HERE TO THERE

6   Belonging matters because it is important to healthy human development. We all need to feel like we are connected to people and groups. We seek love, acceptance, and connection. We want to feel valued, needed, cared for, and appreciated. Humans who belong are more resilient².

7   So how do we get there? Here are three key features of belonging: connecting, caring, and **coping**. Connecting is the experience of having meaningful bonds with others. Caring involves developing **empathy** for others, especially across differences. It helps us deepen connections to others who may also need support in belonging. And coping, according to Kenneth Ginsburg, M.D., a professor of pediatrics, is the act of being resilient in the face of stress, including the pressure to fit in. Developing these three features can help us all find our way along the path to belonging.

**VOCABULARY SKILL REVIEW**

In Unit 2, you learned that there are common collocations with nouns. What three nouns in the Activity B word box can follow *feel?* What verb + noun collocations can you think of?

**B. VOCABULARY** Complete each sentence with the vocabulary from Reading 1.

| | | | |
|---|---|---|---|
| anxiety *(n.)* | courage *(n.)* | fit in *(v. phr.)* | self-fulfillment *(n.)* |
| barrier *(n.)* | empathy *(n.)* | foundation *(n.)* | shame *(n.)* |
| coping *(n.)* | extensive *(adj.)* | negotiate *(v.)* | |

1. They truly understood the feelings of the boy who was being bullied and felt great _____ for him.

2. I wanted to _____ so badly that I was willing to do things I shouldn't have.

3. It's normal to worry and experience _____ when in a new social situation.

4. He found _____ in his work and was satisfied with the career path he had chosen.

5. She showed a lot of _____ when she chose to pursue her dream to write poetry, even though she risked being bullied because of her choice.

6. For the group to reach an agreement, the members had to _____ a decision that was satisfactory to all of them.

7. Because she is an expert, her knowledge is _____.

8. Lack of money is often the _____ that prevents a young person from getting a college education.

9. When he wasn't chosen for the team, he felt _____ that he wasn't good enough.

10. _____ is an important life skill needed to deal with life's challenges.

11. A good friendship is based on a(n) _____ of shared interests.

**iQ** PRACTICE  Go online for more practice with the vocabulary.
*Practice > Unit 3 > Activity 3*

**C. EXPLAIN** Answer the questions.

1. What is the main idea of the reading? _____

_____

2. What is one important difference between fitting in and belonging?

_____

3. Explain one of these ideas: connecting, caring, and coping.

_____

**D. IDENTIFY** Circle the correct answer.

1. What is the purpose of the first paragraph?

    a.  It gives a definition of the topic of the article.

    b.  It gives a solution to the topic of the article.

    c.  It gives an example of the topic of the article.

2. What is the topic of paragraph 3?

    a.  decisions about our appearance

    b.  choices we make

    c.  social groups

3. Fitting in is ____ while belonging is ____.

    a.  changing ourselves / being ourselves

    b.  wanting to be fulfilled / wanting to be accepted

    c.  having courage / feeling uncomfortable

4. What is one possible result of trying to fit in rather than belong?

    a.  We are vulnerable.

    b.  We participate in hurtful activities.

    c.  We are authentic.

5. The audience of this article is probably ____.

    a.  young people experiencing bullying

    b.  researchers specializing in adult anxiety

    c.  readers interested in psychology

6. The conclusion of this reading is: ____.

    a.  We can all belong.

    b.  We have to learn to cope with life.

    c.  It's stressful to fit in.

**E. CATEGORIZE** Read the statements. Write *T* (true) or *F* (false) and the paragraph number where the answer is found. Then correct each false statement to make it true according to the article.

_____ 1. The author didn't make friends in middle school. (paragraph ___)

_____ 2. Fitting in is wearing clothes so others will accept us. (paragraph ___)

_____ 3. Belonging is participating in activities, so we won't be lonely. (paragraph ___)

_____ 4. According to Brene Brown, we change ourselves to belong. (paragraph ___)

_____ 5. Fitting in is hard because we are going with the norm. (paragraph ___)

_____ 6. People who allow themselves to be vulnerable have courage. (paragraph ___)

_____ 7. People with a sense of belonging stay true to what they believe. (paragraph ___)

_____ 8. We should help young people learn how to fit in. (paragraph ___)

**F. CATEGORIZE** Complete the chart with information from the reading. Compare charts with a partner. Discuss where in the reading you found the information and why you have the opinions you do.

|  | Fitting in | Belonging |
|---|---|---|
| is |  |  |
| is doing |  |  |
| is wearing |  |  |
| is being |  |  |
| makes us |  |  |
| in my opinion is |  |  |

**G. SYNTHESIZE** Look back at your Quick Write on page 64. What decisions did you make as a young person about your appearance, activities, and time? Add any new ideas or information you learned from the reading.

**iQ** PRACTICE  Go online for additional reading and comprehension.
*Practice > Unit 3 > Activity 4*

# WRITE WHAT YOU THINK

**A. DISCUSS** Discuss the questions in a group. Think about the Unit Question, "What important lessons do we learn as young people?"

1. Can you think of a time when you were happy to fit in? Can you think of a time when you did not want to just fit it?

2. The article says that "the people with the deepest sense of belonging are those who have the courage to stand alone." What do you think that means?

3. Who are you with when you feel that you really belong? Why is that?

**B. SYNTHESIZE** Choose one of the questions from Activity A and write a paragraph of 5–7 sentences in response. Look back at your Quick Write on page 64 as you think about what you learned.

 CRITICAL THINKING STRATEGY

### Relating to the reading

The following activity asks you to **relate** the information in the article to your own life. When you connect new information to your own experience, you deepen your understanding of it. When you read, ask yourself how the information applies to you.

> **The author says:** We all feel the need to be part of social groups in our communities.
>
> **The reader says:** I am a part of my family, my neighborhood, my group of friends, and my school tennis team.

**iQ PRACTICE** Go online to watch the Critical Thinking Video and check your comprehension. *Practice › Unit 3 › Activity 5*

**C. APPLY** Read these sentences from Reading 1. Write how each relates to you. Use examples from your own experience. Discuss your ideas with a partner.

1. Fitting in is changing ourselves to match the situation.

   _____

2. Belonging . . . is letting ourselves be seen and known as we really are.

   _____

3. Being different can make us feel vulnerable . . . it's this same vulnerability that becomes the foundation on which courage is built.

   _____

4. Young people who feel pressured to fit in . . . may end up participating in unhealthy relationships.

   _____

## READING SKILL Making inferences

Writers don't usually state all their ideas directly. Usually, they expect the reader to **infer** some ideas that the information suggests. Making inferences about a text means that you use your knowledge to make a logical conclusion about the information that is given. Look at this excerpt from Reading 1.

> Brene Brown, PhD, a social scientist and research professor, has been doing extensive research over the past 17 years on what she calls our "inextricable human connections" and on true belonging.

You can infer:

- Brene Brown has the training and the knowledge to conduct and evaluate research.

- She is very interested in human connections and true belonging.

Making inferences helps you improve your comprehension and understand a text more deeply.

**TIP FOR SUCCESS**

Your inferences should always depend on the author's words first and your experience second. Make sure your inferences are not contradicted by statements that are made later in the text.

**A. INTERPRET** Read the paragraph from Reading 1. Check (✓) the statements that can be inferred from the text. Then compare answers with a partner. Explain what information in the paragraph led to the inference.

> We all feel the need to be part of social groups in our communities, and we all make choices that affect the connections we make to others. At a young age, we begin to make decisions about our appearance, our social activities, and our time commitments. We choose how we look—our hair, our clothes, and even what we do to our bodies—who we hang out with, and how we spend our time. In making these choices, we may either be trying to fit in or to belong.

☐ 1. Connecting with others is part of being human.

☐ 2. We continue making decisions about fitting in when we are adults.

☐ 3. We might cut our hair in order to fit in.

☐ 4. The need to be part of a group is not universal.

☐ 5. Our social activities include who we hang out with.

☐ 6. Fitting in and belonging are the same thing.

**B. INTERPRET** Read the paragraph. Make inferences. You may circle *a*, *b*, or both. Then compare answers with a partner. Explain your answers.

> I have always had to struggle to get out of bed in the morning. When I was a young child, the problem wasn't so bad. Because I didn't want to miss anything that my older siblings were doing, I made myself get up. But as each one of them went away to college, I had less and less enthusiasm for getting up in the mornings. After they were all gone, my father used to come to my bedroom door, knock, and say, "It's 6:00. Wake up and get out of bed." I would respond, "One or the other, Dad. One or the other."

1. The writer ____.

   a. had four older siblings          b. was the youngest child

2. The writer ____.

   a. still struggles to get out of bed          b. got out of bed easily as a young child

3. The writer's father ____.

   a. used to get up early          b. would get annoyed

4. The writer's response to the father suggests the writer ____.

   a. has a good sense of humor          b. would get up right away

**iQ** PRACTICE  Go online for more practice making inferences.
*Practice > Unit 3 > Activity 6*

READING 2

# Life Lessons I Learned from My Dad in 23 Years

OBJECTIVE ▶

You are going to read a blog post by Katie Hurley, child and adolescent psychotherapist and author of articles and books on parenting. She writes about the things she learned from her father, who died when she was 23. Use the blog post to gather ideas and information for your Unit Assignment.

## PREVIEW THE READING

**A. PREVIEW** Read the title and answer the first question. Then read the paragraph headings and answer the second question.

1. What life lessons will Katie Hurley discuss? Predict three.

2. Do your predictions match any of the headings?

**B. QUICK WRITE** Who influenced you most as an adult? Write for 5–10 minutes in response. Be sure to use this section for your Unit Assignment.

**C. VOCABULARY** Check (✓) the words you know. Use a dictionary to define any new or unknown words. Then discuss with a partner how the words will relate to the unit.

| | | |
|---|---|---|
| attribute *(v.)* 𝕃+ OPAL | intervention *(n.)* 𝕃+ OPAL | tragic *(adj.)* 𝕃+ |
| encounter *(v.)* 𝕃+ OPAL | petrified *(adj.)* | void *(n.)* |
| hesitation *(n.)* | pitch in *(v. phr.)* | work ethic *(n. phr.)* |
| interaction *(n.)* 𝕃+ OPAL | refrain *(n.)* | wounded *(adj.)* 𝕃+ |

𝕃+ Oxford 5000™ words                                    OPAL Oxford Phrasal Academic Lexicon

**iQ** PRACTICE  Go online to listen and practice your pronunciation.
*Practice* › *Unit 3* › *Activity 7*

# WORK WITH THE READING

**A. INVESTIGATE** Read the blog post and gather information about the important lessons we learn as young people.

Home                                                                     🔍   Sign in 👤

New posts        About                                                         Subscribe

# Life Lessons I Learned from
# My Dad in 23 Years

1   I lost my dad when I was 23 years old. I was days away from completing my first year of graduate school. It was **tragic** and unexpected, as tragedies generally are, and I remember drifting through the days, wondering if I would ever feel whole again.

2   That first year felt impossible. Holidays, birthdays, Father's Day, celebrations, big and small…everything seemed to be missing something. At times, it felt unfair. He would never walk me down the aisle at my wedding. He would never know his grandchildren. He wouldn't be there to guide me through buying a car, buying a house, or countless other "firsts" of adulthood. Had he taught me everything I needed to know?

3   It would be years before I realized that he had. He left me with everything I needed. Time heals, and the best memories come to light as the sadness fades away. Sixteen years later, I think back on the wisdom he imparted over the years and realize that he took the time he had with me to prepare me for almost anything, and his words are forever etched across my soul[1].

[1] **etched across my soul:** made a part of me, so I cannot forget them

### 1 Family consists of the relationships you choose to nurture.

Life is hard, and families can be complicated. My dad's story isn't mine to tell, but his family changed over time. As an adolescent, I questioned him about these changes. Did he miss the people he no longer saw?

His answer was simple: "This is my family. Your family is made up of the people you love, and the people who love you back. That's all you need."

### 2 Kindness counts.

When people recall their memories of my dad they often refer to him as friendly, kind, and generous. They talk about long boat rides and the fact that he was always willing to **pitch in** and lend a hand.

I know he secretly lived in fear that I would bring home every **wounded** bird I **encountered**. I was always trying to help. As much as some might say that can be **attributed** to personality, I like to think that some of it came from my parents. They taught me to be kind and help out when I can, and I teach my children the same.

### 3 Bravery happens when you're ready to be brave.

I was **petrified** of my dad's boat when I was young. It was loud and stinky and made a horrible cracking sound each time he took a wave. My brother loved it. I cried every time they strapped the life jacket on me. For four years, I never even made it out of the lagoon.

I knew his boat was important to him. Kids know things. And I wanted to love that boat just as much as everyone else. So at the end of my fourth summer, I made an announcement: "When I'm five, I'll be brave." For that entire winter following my fifth birthday, I bravely chanted that **refrain**. And when the boat showed up in the garage that spring, the anxiety set in. Sensing my **hesitation**, my dad leaned down and whispered, "You don't have to be brave this year. You can be brave when you're ready."

I never forgot that **interaction**. When I stepped off the dock and onto the boat that summer, I stood tall and smiled. And I loved every second of it.

### 4 Hard work will get you everywhere.

I was always the kind of student who wanted to get straight As and cried when a B+ showed up on my report, so I never needed any **intervention** when it came to school. But my dad noticed my hard work. He frequently complimented my writing and my focus and reminded me that my **work ethic** would help me reach my goals. All of them. As it turns out, he was right.

**12** **5** **It's OK to walk away sometimes.**

There was one summer when my dad was reading the most boring book of all time. It just sat on the coffee table for days at a time. Occasionally, he would pick it up and read a few pages, only to return to the newspaper. I finally asked him about it. "Sometimes things aren't what they seem, Kate. It's important to know when to walk away. I'm walking away from this one."

**13** I'm not a quitter by nature, but I have walked away from a couple of things that weren't as they seemed. And I've never once regretted a decision to leave something behind.

**14** **6** **If you can count your friends on two hands, you're good[2].**

Adolescence was torture at times. I never knew where I fit in. My best friend went off to boarding school, and I couldn't quite fill the **void**. I was sobbing over my outcast status[3] when my dad presented me with this little nugget of wisdom[4] one night. I didn't believe him

at the time, but I've seen the light[5]. I can count my friends on two hands.

**15** **7** **Every sunset has meaning.**

My dad loved a sunset. He was most at peace with himself at our house by the beach, and he never missed a sunset during the summer months. It was the summer before his death that I asked him what he loved about sunsets.

**16** This is what he said: "If you've had a rotten day, a sunset reminds you that another day is ahead. If you've had a great day, a sunset reminds you to soak it in[6]. Either way, it's a win."

**17** **8** **Life is short; make it count.**

Fifty-two years doesn't seem like enough, and yet that's what he had. I believe that my dad did the best that he could with the time he had.

**18** If nothing else, he always encouraged me to just be me. "At the end of the line, you only have who you are. Be the best version of you. People will respect you for it."

---

[2] **you're good:** it's OK; it's a good thing
[3] **outcast status:** not belonging to the group; not having friends
[4] **nugget of wisdom:** piece of important information
[5] **see the light:** to understand
[6] **soak it in:** spend time experiencing and enjoying; like **soak it up:** absorb into your senses

**B. VOCABULARY** Here are some words from Reading 2. Read the sentences. Then write each bold word next to the correct definition on page 76. You may need to change the form of some of the words.

1. We were very sad to hear about the **tragic** accident.

2. If everyone **pitches in**, the work will be done very soon.

3. The **wounded** bicyclist was taken to the hospital to treat his injuries.

4. I **encountered** my neighbors at the community picnic.

5. His success can be **attributed** to his hard work.

6. The young boy was **petrified** by the large angry dog running toward him.

7. He kept repeating the **refrain** over and over to help himself remember it.

8. Her **hesitation** was a result of her feelings of uncertainty.

9. We had a very pleasant **interaction** with them at the meeting.

10. Their quick **intervention** helped save the child from harm.

11. There was nothing there in the **void**.

12. A strong **work ethic** will always help you do well in any job.

a. _____ *(v.)* to say something is the result of a particular thing

b. _____ *(adj.)* extremely frightened

c. _____ *(n.)* the act of being slow to speak or act because you feel uncertain or nervous

d. _____ *(n.)* action taken to improve or help a situation

e. _____ *(v. phr.)* to join in and help with an activity, by doing some of the work

f. _____ *(n.)* a belief in work as a moral good

g. _____ *(n.)* a large empty space

h. _____ *(v.)* to meet, run into

i. _____ *(adj.)* making you feel very sad, usually because someone has died

j. _____ *(n.)* the act of communicating with someone

k. _____ *(n.)* a comment or statement that is often repeated

l. _____ *(adj.)* injured as in an accident

**iQ** PRACTICE  Go online for more practice with the vocabulary.
*Practice › Unit 3 › Activity 8*

**C. IDENTIFY** Each of these sentences gives a main idea of a lesson that Katie Hurley learned from her dad. Write the correct lesson number next to each sentence.

1. Enjoying nature is a good way to end each day. ____

2. When the time is right, you can be brave. ____

3. If something isn't right, it's OK to quit. ____

4. Be kind and help others. ____

5. Be true to yourself. ____

6. Working hard is important. ____

7. Your family is the people you care about. ____

8. A few good friends are enough. ____

**D. EXPLAIN** Answer the questions about Katie Hurley and her father.

1. How old was she when her father died?

   _____

2. What was she doing when her father died?

   _____

3. How much time has passed since her father died?

   _____

4. What has her father missed in her life?

   _____

5. How old was her father when he died?

   _____

6. What time of day did her father like best?

   _____

7. Why did her father quit reading the book?

   _____

8. How do other people remember her father?

   _____

**E. CATEGORIZE** Check (✓) the statements you can infer about Katie Hurley and her father based on the blog post.

| Katie Hurley | Her father |
|---|---|
| ☐ She is successful. | ☐ He was friendly. |
| ☐ She misses her father. | ☐ He had a successful career. |
| ☐ She learned a lot from her father. | ☐ He liked the water. |
| ☐ She was a happy adolescent. | ☐ He was a good father. |
| ☐ She loves the water. | ☐ He liked to fish. |
| ☐ She is brave. | ☐ He died in an accident. |

**F. EXTEND** Work with a partner. Find a sentence in the blog post to support the statements you checked in Activity E. Discuss why you didn't check the other statements.

# WORK WITH THE VIDEO

**A. PREVIEW** Have you ever quit doing an activity? Why?

## VIDEO VOCABULARY

**instill (v.)** to make someone feel a particular way over time

**pick on (v.)** to treat unfairly by blaming, criticizing, or punishing

**self-esteem (n.)** a feeling of being happy with your own character and abilities

**rule of thumb (n.)** a practical method of measuring something, usually based on past experience

**stamina (n.)** physical or mental strength that enables you to do something for long periods

**iQ RESOURCES** Go online to watch the video about children who want to quit doing an activity. *Resources > Video > Unit 3 > Unit Video*

**B. COMPOSE** Watch the video two or three times. Take notes in the first part of the chart.

|  | Reasons children quit | Ways to help children commit |
|---|---|---|
| Notes from the video |  |  |
| My ideas |  |  |

**C. EXTEND** Why else do children quit? What are some other ways parents can help children commit to activities? Write your ideas in the chart above. Discuss your ideas with a partner.

# WRITE WHAT YOU THINK

**SYNTHESIZE** Think about Reading 1, Reading 2, and the unit video as you discuss these questions. Then choose one question and write a paragraph of 5–7 sentences in response.

1. Number 6 of Ms. Hurley's list of lessons talks about fitting in. How does the idea of counting your friends on two hands illustrate the idea of belonging?

2. Choose one of the tips from Reading 2 (besides number 6). Explain how this tip also is about belonging instead of fitting in.

3. Think about what you have read and watched about caring and coping. Who in your life helped you learn to connect, care, and cope? Give examples.

## VOCABULARY SKILL Prefixes and suffixes

A **prefix** is a group of letters that comes at the beginning of a word. When you add a prefix to a word, it usually changes the word's meaning.

| Prefix | Meaning | Example |
|---|---|---|
| **anti-** | against | antiwar |
| **co-** | together | cooperation |
| **extra-** | more | extracurricular |
| **in-** | not | independence |
| **inter-** | go between | interaction |
| **mid-** | middle | mid-fifties |
| **mis-** | incorrect, badly | misunderstanding |
| **re-** | again | reread |

**ACADEMIC LANGUAGE**
The corpus shows that
*the significance of* is
often used in academic
writing.
*. . . the significance of
Dr. Brown's research . . .
. . . the significance of
the parents' actions . . .*

_____ **OPAL**
Oxford Phrasal Academic Lexicon

A **suffix** is a group of letters that comes at the end of a word. When you add a suffix to a word, it usually changes the part of speech of that word. For example, adding the suffix *-tion* to the verb *inform* makes it the noun *information*.

| | | |
|---|---|---|
| Suffixes that form nouns | **-ence / -ance** | competence, significance |
| | **-tion** | foundation, connection |
| Suffixes that form adjectives | **-ent / -ant** | consistent, important |
| | **-ful** | resentful, meaningful |
| Suffixes that form verbs | **-ate** | investigate, motivate |
| | **-ize** | organize, realize |

**iQ** PRACTICE  Go online to watch the the Vocabulary Skill video.
*Resources ‣ Video ‣ Unit 3 ‣ Vocabulary Skill Video*

**A. APPLY** Complete the word in each sentence with the correct prefix from the Vocabulary Skill chart on page 79. Then check your answers in the dictionary.

1. He _____ pronounced the word, so she didn't understand what he had said.

2. They were both _____ ordinary students. They excelled at school and were talented in sports and poetry as well.

3. Many parts of the brain are _____ connected. They work together to enable the brain's many functions.

4. His job required that he _____ locate often, so he had lived in many places.

5. Fatimah knew she wasn't ready for _____ term exams, but she hoped she'd do better on the final.

6. People assumed Ali was _____ social because he rarely spoke with other children.

7. Some siblings have to learn to _____ exist peacefully with each other.

8. We're going to have a(n) _____ formal gathering tonight. Come by if you want.

**B. IDENTIFY** Read each word. Check (✓) the correct part of speech. Use information from the Vocabulary Skill box on page 79 to help you. Then check your answers in the dictionary.

|  | Noun | Adjective | Verb |
|---|---|---|---|
| 1. recognize | ☐ | ☐ | ☐ |
| 2. reliance | ☐ | ☐ | ☐ |
| 3. peaceful | ☐ | ☐ | ☐ |
| 4. demonstrate | ☐ | ☐ | ☐ |
| 5. resilient | ☐ | ☐ | ☐ |
| 6. contribution | ☐ | ☐ | ☐ |
| 7. confidence | ☐ | ☐ | ☐ |
| 8. significant | ☐ | ☐ | ☐ |
| 9. substance | ☐ | ☐ | ☐ |
| 10. negotiate | ☐ | ☐ | ☐ |
| 11. imagination | ☐ | ☐ | ☐ |
| 12. cheerful | ☐ | ☐ | ☐ |

**C. COMPOSE** Choose five words from Activity B. Write a sentence for each.

**iQ PRACTICE** Go online for more practice with prefixes and suffixes.
*Practice > Unit 3 > Activity 9*

# WRITING

**OBJECTIVE ▶**

At the end of this unit, you will write a narrative essay about someone or something that influenced you when you were younger. This essay will include specific information from the readings, the unit video, and your own ideas.

---

**WRITING SKILL** **Writing a narrative essay and varying sentence patterns**

A **narrative essay** tells a story about a personal experience, event, or memory.

## Organization

- The **introduction** sets the scene for the reader. It should give information about the people, place, and time, and should create interest in the story. The introduction may include a **thesis statement** that tells why the story is important or memorable.

- There can be one or more **body paragraphs**. These tell the main events or actions of the story. They are usually in the order in which the events happened. They may also include important or interesting details to support the ideas in the main event.

- The **conclusion** gives the outcome or result of the actions in the story. It often tells what the writer learned from the experience.

## Expressing the order of events

In a narrative essay, you use **time phrases** and **clauses** to explain when the events happened in the story and the order of events.

**Prepositional phrases: in** 1978, **on** June 5, **before/after** class, **for** five years

**Time expressions:** a week **ago**, **last** month, **earlier** this year, the week **before**, an hour **later**, the **next** day

**Time clauses: after** we spoke, **before** I ate, **as** they were leaving, **when** we met

## Varying sentence patterns

Varying sentence patterns in your writing will help the reader maintain interest and focus on important information. Here are some ways to add variety to your writing.

- Shorter sentences emphasize or stress one important point.

- Longer sentences combine closely related ideas. Longer sentences can be made by using conjunctions, subordinators, or relative clauses to combine shorter sentences.

| | |
|---|---|
| **Shorter:** | There was a sudden noise. |
| **Longer** (with conjunction): | Then a cat jumped out of the bushes **and** ran up the path. |
| **Longer** (with subordinator): | **Even though** it was only a cat, my heart started beating faster. |
| **Longer** (with relative clause): | The next noise **that I heard** was definitely not a cat. |

### A. CREATE Brainstorm ideas for a narrative essay.

1. Draw a timeline of four or five events that you remember from your childhood. Put on your timeline how old you were and a short phrase indicating what happened. Look at the example.

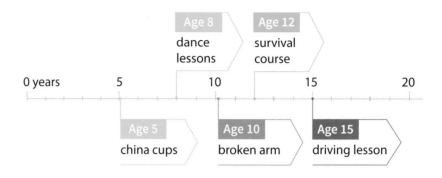

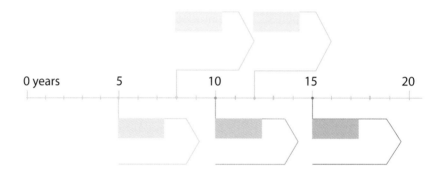

**WRITING TIP**

Using a **timeline** is a good way to plan a narrative essay. A timeline can help you map out important events in the order in which they occurred.

2. Choose one of the events on your timeline and answer these questions.

   a. What happened?

   _____

   b. Who was with you?

   _____

   c. Where were you?

   _____

   d. When did it happen?

   _____

   e. What did you learn?

   _____

**B. WRITING MODEL** Read the model narrative essay. Notice the organizational structure. Then answer the questions that follow.

## My Mother's China Cups

introduction

1    When I think about my mother, one thing I remember is her collection of china cups and saucers. She had collected them throughout her life, and they were very important to her. They were displayed on shelves in our kitchen. Some of them were quite old; some she had gotten from faraway places. And each one had a special memory for her.

body paragraph 1

2    From a very young age, I always wanted to take down those beautiful cups and wash them. It was my chance to see them up close. My mother never really wanted to let me do it. She knew the cups were fragile and I could easily break them. But sometimes I begged until she let me take them down and clean them.

body paragraph 2

3    My earliest memory of this was when I was five. I pulled a chair near the kitchen table and took down the small cups. I started with my favorites: the very old blue and white one that had belonged to my great-grandmother and the one from Japan with exotic buildings on it. I moved them all, one by one, to the kitchen counter. After I had put them on the counter, I moved my chair to the sink, filled the sink with soapy water, and began to wash the tiny cups.

body paragraph 3

4    I had only washed a few when the beautiful blue and white cup slipped from my small hands and fell back into the sink. The handle broke off. My mother's special cup was ruined, and I was sure she would be angry. I cried and waited for quite a while before I could find the courage to tell her. My mother, who was probably upset, only smiled and said we would glue it back together. I happily finished washing the precious cups. When I had cleaned and dried them all, we carefully placed them back on the shelves. Then my mother glued the handle back on the broken cup before we set it back in its place, too.

conclusion

5    I washed those cups many times as a child, and almost every time, I broke one. By the time I was grown, several showed the signs of my efforts. I am an adult now and my mother is gone, but I will always remember that she cared more about encouraging me than about her valuable cups. Now, as a mother myself, I understand the patience it took to allow me to handle her precious things. I try to demonstrate that same level of caring to my own children.

1. Who are the people in the narrative?

_____

2. Where does the action take place?

_____

3. When does the action take place?

_____

**C. RESTATE** Complete the outline of the essay. You do not have to use the writer's exact words.

I. Introductory ideas: _____

_____

**WRITING TIP**
When writing a narrative, use details and descriptive language to make the story come alive for the reader. See the Writing Skill on page 51 for more information.

II. Body paragraph 1: Main event in story

When I was a child, I always wanted to wash my mother's china cups.

   A. Important or interesting detail: _____

   _____

   B. Important or interesting detail: _____

   _____

III. Body paragraph 2: Main event in story

   _____

   A. Important or interesting detail: I started with my favorites—

   the old blue and white one and the one from Japan.

   B. Important or interesting detail: _____

   _____

IV. Body paragraph 3: Main event in story

   _____

   A. Important or interesting detail: _____

   _____

   B. Important or interesting detail: My mother glued the handle on

   the cup before we put it back on the shelf.

V. Conclusion (what I learned): _____

_____

**D. IDENTIFY** Look at body paragraph 3 of "My Mother's China Cups" on page 83. Circle the conjunctions. Underline the subordinators. Put a star (*) next to the relative clause. Then answer these questions.

1. Write the shortest sentence here. _____

2. How many conjunctions did you find? ____

3. How many subordinators? ____

4. The relative clause has commas around it. Who does the relative clause describe? _____

**TIP FOR SUCCESS**
You do not have to use all the techniques in everything you write. Just be sure to vary the patterns that you use.

**E. RESTATE** Work with a partner to rewrite the paragraph below. Vary the sentence patterns by keeping some shorter sentences and by using conjunctions, subordinators, and relative clauses to make longer sentences.

> The toughest weekend of my life was also one of the best. I was 12. My father and I attended a short survival course. I will never forget it. I woke up early on a Saturday morning. It was still dark. I wanted to go back to sleep. My father was wide awake. My father was excited about the day ahead. We ate a quick breakfast. We drove to the school at the edge of the desert. We arrived at 7 a.m. The desert was already hot. I felt nervous. I didn't want to show it. The other students arrived. One was a boy. He was about my age. He was with his father, too. The instructor came out to greet us.

**Example:** The toughest weekend of my life was also one of the best. When I was 12, my father and I attended a short survival course that I will never forget. . . .

**F. IDENTIFY** Go back to your paragraph from Activity E. Circle the conjunctions. Underline the subordinators. Put a star (*) next to the relative clauses. Then answer these questions.

1. How many short sentences do you have? ____

2. How many sentences have conjunctions? ____

3. How many sentences have subordinators? ____

4. How many sentences have relative clauses? ____

**G. IDENTIFY** Read the rest of the essay from Activity E. Choose one of the paragraphs in the essay. Circle the conjunctions. Underline the subordinators. Put a star (*) next to the relative clauses.

> The instructor—a tall, athletic man—looked at us seriously. "You are going to learn about survival," he said. "This may be the most challenging and rewarding weekend of your life." I looked at my father. I wasn't sure that I wanted to continue, but he was still very excited. "You will learn how to do such things as find food, find shelter, and keep warm. I won't tell you that it is going to be easy. In fact, it won't be. However, at the end of the weekend, I hope you'll think that it was worth the effort."

> continued on page 86

We set out with only our water bottles and knives. We hiked through the desert for miles in the hot sun. I was afraid that we would run out of water, but our guide said that we would be fine as long as we didn't waste any. Along the way, we looked for food. We found an edible plant that people call a barrel cactus. We also caught a lizard that people can boil and eat, but no one wanted to. We were hungry and tired when the instructor had us stop near some flowering cactus. We ate the flowers, which tasted OK, and we rested in the shade of some large rocks.

I don't remember much about the rest of the first day, but I do remember that the air got cold quickly when the sun set and I was happy to sit close to my father, near the fire that we had helped build. I looked up at the stars and smiled. They were so beautiful, out away from the city. I looked up at my father and saw his face more peaceful than I could remember ever seeing it before.

It was a tough weekend, but I am glad we went. I learned about the desert and how to survive in it, but more importantly, I learned about myself and my father. We had shared a difficult time in the desert, and we grew closer because of it. Long afterward, whenever we saw the stars, one or the other would say, "Remember that night in the desert?" and we would both smile.

**iQ PRACTICE** Go online for more practice with writing narrative essays and varying sentence patterns. *Practice > Unit 3 > Activity 10*

## GRAMMAR  Past perfect and past perfect continuous

### Order of events in the past

The **past perfect** shows that one event happened before another event in the past. The past perfect expresses the earlier event. The simple past is often used to express the later event. The past perfect often gives background information about events or situations. It has the same form for all subjects: subject + *had* (+ *not*) + past participle.

earlier event · later event

Every morning, no matter how late he **had gone** to bed, my father **rose** at 5:30.

past perfect · simple past

later event · earlier event

I **got** the job because I **had lived** in China for several years.

simple past · past perfect

## Past perfect with past time clauses

The past perfect is often used in sentences with **past time clauses**. A past time clause usually begins with a subordinator such as *when, until,* or *by the time*. Notice the use of a comma when the past time clause comes first.

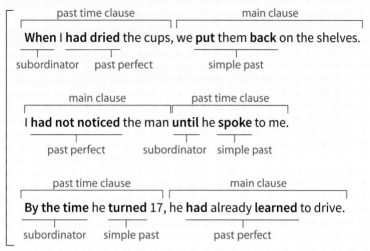

## Past perfect continuous

The **past perfect continuous** is used for actions that began in the past and continued up to another past event or state in the past. It is often used with *for* to indicate how long a situation lasted. Like the past perfect, it often gives background information. The past perfect continuous is subject + *had* + *been* + verb + *-ing*.

> I **had been living** there for six months when the Smiths moved next door.
>
> She **had been writing** stories for many years when her first story was published.
>
> When she finally arrived, he**'d been waiting** for her for two hours.

A. **IDENTIFY** Read the sentences. Underline the past perfect and past perfect continuous verbs and circle the simple past verbs in each example. Label the verbs *1* for the earlier event and *2* for the later event.

1. My mother (had) a collection of very small china cups and saucers.
   She had collected them throughout her life.

2. I had only washed a few when the beautiful blue and white cup slipped from my small hands.

3. I had forgotten to call my brother, so he was angry with me.

4. She had thought seriously about studying medicine, but in the end, she decided to study business.

5. Until he got an internship at a big ad agency, he hadn't been interested in working in advertising.

6. I didn't answer the man because I hadn't heard him clearly.

7. We had been working on the project for hours when we finally finished it.

**B. RESTATE** Combine the sentences using the time expression indicated. Change the simple past verb to the past perfect or past perfect continuous for the event that happened first. The sentences are in the order that they happened.

1. She was studying English. She moved to the United States. (when)

   _____

2. I did not leave my home country. I visited Canada. (until)

   _____

3. He already finished reading the book. He watched the movie. (when)

   _____

4. They recalled important events from their past. The students wrote stories about their memories of childhood. (after)

   _____

   _____

5. I had lunch. She arrived at the restaurant. (by the time)

   _____

6. I offered to pay for lunch. I realized that I didn't have any money. (when)

   _____

**iQ** PRACTICE  Go online for more practice with the past perfect and past perfect continuous. *Practice > Unit 3 > Activities 11–12*

**UNIT ASSIGNMENT**

**OBJECTIVE ▶**

## Write a narrative essay

In this assignment, you are going to write a three-paragraph narrative essay about someone or something that influenced you when you were younger. As you prepare your essay, think about the Unit Question, "What important lessons do we learn as young people?" Use information from Reading 1, Reading 2, the unit video, and your work in this unit to support your essay. Refer to the Self-Assessment checklist on page 90.

**iQ** PRACTICE  Go online to the Writing Tutor to read a model narrative essay. *Practice > Unit 3 > Activity 13*

# PLAN AND WRITE

**A. BRAINSTORM** Follow these steps to help you organize your ideas.

1. Create a chart. Write down the names of some people or things that influenced you when you were younger.

**TIP FOR SUCCESS**

To help you remember all the details of your memory, ask and answer the six *wh-* questions: *who, what, where, when, why,* and *how.*

2. Think about memories associated with those people or things. Write notes about the memories and specific details such as people, times, and places. Look at the example.

|  | Memories | Details |
|---|---|---|
| People: My older brother | The time I fell off my bike when we were kids | I was 6. We were in Greenway Park. I cut my head. We went to see Dr. Garcia. |
| Things: Greenwich Elementary School | My first day of school | I was lost on my first day. Mrs. Lu found me on the school playground. She took me back to class. |

**B. PLAN** Follow these steps to plan your essay.

1. Choose one of the people or things from Activity A to write about.

2. Circle the most interesting memories and the most important details.

**iQ** RESOURCES  Go online to download and complete the outline for your narrative essay. *Resources > Writing Tools > Unit 3 > Outline*

**C. WRITE** Use your planning notes to write your essay.

1. To clearly express the order of the events, use time words and time clauses, the past perfect and past perfect continuous, and other past verb forms.

2. Look at the Self-Assessment checklist below to guide your writing.

**iQ** PRACTICE  Go online to the Writing Tutor to write your assignment.
*Practice › Unit 3 › Activity 14*

# REVISE AND EDIT

**iQ** RESOURCES  Go online to download the peer review worksheet.
*Resources › Writing Tools › Unit 3 › Peer Review Worksheet*

**A. PEER REVIEW** Read your partner's essay. Then use the peer review worksheet. Discuss the review with your partner.

**B. REVISE** Based on your partner's review, revise and rewrite your essay.

**C. EDIT** Complete the Self-Assessment checklist as you prepare to write the final draft of your essay. Be prepared to hand in your work or discuss it in class.

| SELF-ASSESSMENT | Yes | No |
|---|---|---|
| Does the introduction tell why the story is important? | ☐ | ☐ |
| Are the events in the order in which they happened? | ☐ | ☐ |
| Does the conclusion tell why the memory is important today? | ☐ | ☐ |
| Are time phrases and time clauses used to clearly express the order of the events? | ☐ | ☐ |
| Are the past perfect and past perfect continuous used appropriately to give background for other past events or situations? | ☐ | ☐ |
| Does the essay include vocabulary from the unit? | ☐ | ☐ |
| Did you check the essay for punctuation, spelling, and grammar? | ☐ | ☐ |

**D. REFLECT** Discuss these questions with a partner or group.

1. What is something new you learned in this unit?

2. Look back at the Unit Question—What important lessons do we learn as young people? Is your answer different now than when you started the unit? If yes, how is it different? Why?

**iQ** PRACTICE  Go to the online discussion board to discuss the questions.
*Practice › Unit 3 › Activity 15*

# TRACK YOUR SUCCESS

**iQ** PRACTICE  Go online to check the words and phrases you have learned in this unit. *Practice > Unit 3 > Activity 16*

Check (✓) the skills and strategies you learned. If you need more work on a skill, refer to the page(s) in parentheses.

| | |
|---|---|
| CRITICAL THINKING | ☐ I can relate what the author writes to my own experience. (p. 70) |
| READING | ☐ I can make inferences about a text. (p. 71) |
| VOCABULARY | ☐ I can recognize and understand prefixes and suffixes. (p. 79) |
| WRITING | ☐ I can organize and write a narrative essay and vary sentence patterns. (p. 81) |
| GRAMMAR | ☐ I can understand and use the past perfect and past perfect continuous. (pp. 86–87) |

OBJECTIVE ▶  ☐ I can gather information and ideas to write a narrative essay about someone or something that influenced me when I was younger.

# Science and Technology

## 4

| | |
|---|---|
| CRITICAL THINKING | categorizing information |
| READING | understanding comparisons and contrasts |
| VOCABULARY | using the dictionary to distinguish between homonyms |
| WRITING | writing a compare and contrast essay |
| GRAMMAR | subordinators and transitions to compare and contrast |

## UNIT QUESTION

# How can science improve lives?

**A. Discuss these questions with your classmates.**

1. Have you experienced a time without electricity? How did it affect your activities?

2. Which electronic device (an object or piece of equipment) would you miss the most if you didn't have it?

3. Look at the photo. What might the device do? How could it improve people's lives?

**B. Listen to *The Q Classroom* online. Then answer these questions.**

1. Marcus focuses on technology as one way that science can improve lives. What does Sophy focus on in her answer?

2. Yuna thinks that science sometimes doesn't help us and gives examples of air and water pollution. What is Felix's response to Yuna?

**iQ** PRACTICE   Go to the online discussion board to discuss the Unit Question with your classmates. *Practice > Unit 4 > Activity 1*

**UNIT OBJECTIVE**

Read a product review and a news article. Gather information and ideas to write an essay comparing and contrasting two new technologies that can improve lives.

**READING 1**

# Five Innovative Technologies That Bring Energy to the Developing World

**OBJECTIVE ▶**

You are going to read a product review by Joseph Stromberg for Smithsonian.com. The review looks at innovative energy technologies. Use the review to gather information and ideas for your Unit Assignment.

## PREVIEW THE READING

**A. PREVIEW** Read the title. Read the headings and look at the pictures.

1. Try to guess what the five technologies are from their names and pictures.

2. Which of the five technologies seems most interesting? Why?

**B. QUICK WRITE** Imagine your life without electricity. How would it be different than your life with electricity? Compare the two. Write for 5–10 minutes in response. Remember to use this section for your Unit Assignment.

**C. VOCABULARY** Check (✓) the words you know. Use a dictionary to define any new or unknown words. Then discuss with a partner how the words will relate to the unit.

| | |
|---|---|
| alleviate *(v.)* | grid *(n.)* 🔑+ |
| dedicated *(adj.)* 🔑+ | innovative *(adj.)* 🔑+ |
| developing *(adj.)* | intuitively *(adv.)* |
| enterprise *(n.)* 🔑+ | motion *(n.)* 🔑+ |
| existence *(n.)* 🔑+ OPAL | replacement *(n.)* 🔑+ OPAL |
| generate *(v.)* 🔑+ OPAL | resemble *(v.)* 🔑+ |

🔑+ Oxford 5000™ words                    OPAL Oxford Phrasal Academic Lexicon

**iQ PRACTICE** Go online to listen and practice your pronunciation.
*Practice > Unit 4 > Activity 2*

# WORK WITH THE READING

 **A. INVESTIGATE** Read the review and gather information about innovative energy technologies.

# FIVE INNOVATIVE TECHNOLOGIES THAT BRING ENERGY TO THE DEVELOPING WORLD

*By Joseph Stromberg*

1    In the wealthy world, improving the energy system generally means increasing the central supply of reliable, inexpensive, and environmentally-friendly power. This power is then distributed through the power **grid**. Across most of the planet, though, millions of people are without electricity and depend on burning wood or kerosene[1] for heat and light. Simply providing new energy sources would open up new opportunities for these people and for engineers and designers.

2    With that in mind, engineers and designers have recently created a range of **innovative** devices that can increase the supply of safe, cheap energy on a user-by-user basis. The devices do not need the years it takes to extend the power grid to remote places. They also make it easier for countries to produce more energy without spending a lot more money. Here are a few of the most promising technologies.

## VOTO

👍 Like    💬 Comment

3    Millions of people around the world use charcoal[2] and wood-fueled stoves on a daily basis. VOTO, developed by the company Point Source Power, converts the energy these fires release as heat into electricity. That electricity can power a handheld light, charge a phone, or even charge a spare battery. The company initially designed VOTO for backpackers and campers in wealthy countries, so they can charge their devices during trips. Now it is also trying to find a way for residents of the **developing** world to use it every day.

VOTO

## The Window Socket

👍 Like    💬 Comment

4    This is perhaps the simplest solar charger in **existence**. Just stick it on a sunny window for 5–8 hours, with the built-in suction cup[3]. The solar panels on the back will store about ten hours' worth of electricity that can be used with any device. If there's no window available, a user can just leave it on any sunny surface, including the ground. Once it's fully charged, it can be removed and taken anywhere. It can be stored in a bag or carried around in a vehicle. The designers, Kyuho Song and Boa Oh of Yanko Design, created it to **resemble** a normal wall outlet[4] as closely as possible. In that way, it can be used **intuitively** without any special instructions.

The Window Socket

[1] **kerosene:** a type of fuel oil made of petroleum and that is used for heat and light
[2] **charcoal:** a black substance made by burning wood slowly in an oven with little air; used as a fuel
[3] **suction cup:** a cup-shaped device that produces a partial vacuum that makes it stick to a surface
[4] **wall outlet:** a device in a wall that you plug into to connect electrical equipment

## The Berkeley-Darfur Stove

👍 Like  💬 Comment

5    In the past few years, a number of health researchers have come to the same conclusion: Providing a safe, energy-efficient, wood-burning cookstove to millions of people in the developing world has three major benefits. This kind of cookstove can directly improve health by reducing smoke inhalation[5]. It can aid the environment by reducing the amount of wood needed for fuel. It can **alleviate** poverty by reducing the amount of time needed to devote to gathering wood every day.

The Berkeley-Darfur Stove

6    Many projects have pursued this goal. Potential Energy, a nonprofit **dedicated** to adapting technologies to help improve lives in the developing world, is the furthest along. Potential Energy has distributed more than 25,000 of their Berkeley-Darfur Stoves in Darfur and Ethiopia. Their stove's design achieves these aims with features such as a wind collar that keeps the fire from burning too fast and air vents that reduce the amount of wind allowed to affect the fire, which decreases the amount of fuel wasted. It also has ridges that let the cook pot be at the best distance from the fire in order to use the fuel in the most efficient manner.

## The GravityLight

👍 Like  💬 Comment

7    Kerosene-burning lamps provide light throughout the developing world. However, these lamps are targets for **replacement** because the fumes[6] **generated** by burning kerosene in close quarters are a major health problem. A seemingly simple solution is GravityLight, developed by deciwatt.org.

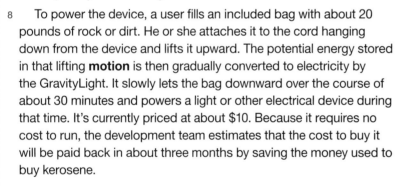

The GravityLight

8    To power the device, a user fills an included bag with about 20 pounds of rock or dirt. He or she attaches it to the cord hanging down from the device and lifts it upward. The potential energy stored in that lifting **motion** is then gradually converted to electricity by the GravityLight. It slowly lets the bag downward over the course of about 30 minutes and powers a light or other electrical device during that time. It's currently priced at about $10. Because it requires no cost to run, the development team estimates that the cost to buy it will be paid back in about three months by saving the money used to buy kerosene.

## SOCCKET

👍 Like  💬 Comment

9    Soccer is easily the most popular sport in the world. The newest product of Uncharted Power, a for-profit social **enterprise**, seeks to take advantage of the millions of people already playing the sport. Uncharted Power wants to replace kerosene lamps with electric light that is generated in a much different manner. Their ball uses an internal motion-powered device to generate and store electricity. After about 30 minutes of play, the ball stores enough energy to power an attachable LED lamp for 3 hours. A percentage of all retail sales will go to providing SOCCKETs to schools in the developing world.

SOCCKET

[5] **inhalation:** the taking in of air, smoke, gas, etc., into the lungs as you breathe
[6] **fumes:** smoke, gas, or something similar that smells or is dangerous to breathe in

**B. VOCABULARY** Here are some words and phrases from Reading 1. Read the sentences. Circle the answer that best matches the meaning of each bold word.

1. Being connected to the power **grid** is a luxury. But we seldom think about the ____ until something disrupts it.

   a. network　　　　b. plan　　　　c. power

2. In our rapidly changing world, we depend on **innovative** solutions to the problems we face. We need ____ ideas and ways of doing things.

   a. big　　　　b. new　　　　c. smart

3. Providing technology to help people is the goal of most **developing** nations. These ____ societies, like wealthy societies, are trying to improve lives.

   a. rich　　　　b. advanced　　　　c. poor

4. This is the best technology in **existence** today. The technology is ____.

   a. not available yet　　b. real and available　　c. no longer available

5. Both daughters **resemble** their mother. They ____ her.

   a. like　　　　b. look like　　　　c. differ from

6. They didn't read the instructions. Rather, they still succeeded in using the device **intuitively**. They understood how to do it ____.

   a. well　　　　b. quickly　　　　c. without help

7. The ceiling fans **alleviated** our discomfort. Our problems were ____.

   a. made less severe　　b. worsened　　　　c. unaffected

8. They are **dedicated** to helping as many people as possible. They are ____ to achieving their goal because the work is important.

   a. committed　　　　b. on their way　　　　c. unwilling

9. We need a **replacement** for this policy, which is having a negative impact on the environment. We must provide ____.

   a. a place with clean air　　b. a new reason　　c. something better

10. Electricity can be **generated** by using wind. It can also be ____ by using the sun and water, for example.

    a. produced　　　　b. consumed　　　　c. wasted

11. **Motion** is necessary for good health. The ____ keeps us fit.

    a. ability to move　　b. need for movement　　c. process of moving

12. Much of the innovation in technology is the result of the efforts of an individual or small **enterprise**. Innovation seems to happen less often in a large ____.

   a. industry           b. company           c. government organization

**iQ** PRACTICE   Go online for more practice with vocabulary. *Practice > Unit 4 > Activity 3*

**C. EXPLAIN** Discuss the questions with a partner.

1. What is the purpose of the review?

2. What are the advantages of all five of these technologies?

3. Who are the targeted users of these technologies?

4. Which technology uses solar power?

5. Which technology utilizes heat to provide electricity?

6. How does the GravityLight power a light?

 **CRITICAL THINKING STRATEGY**

### Categorizing information

When you **categorize information**, you put it into groups by type. This can help you see the relationships between ideas more clearly. For example:

What the device produces or conserves

| Electricity | | Heat |
| --- | --- | --- |
| VOTO | Window Socket | Berkeley-Darfur Stove |
| GravityLight | SOCCKET | |

**iQ** PRACTICE   Go online to watch the Critical Thinking Skill Video and check your comprehension. *Practice > Unit 4 > Activity 4*

**D. CATEGORIZE** Reread the descriptions of each technology in Reading 1. Then use the information to complete the charts.

| What the electricity is used for | |
| --- | --- |
| Recharging devices | Producing light |
| | |

| What the device replaces | | |
| --- | --- | --- |
| Non-portable chargers | Less efficient stoves | Kerosene lamps |
| | | |

**E. CATEGORIZE** Read the statements. Write *T* (true) or *F* (false) and the paragraph number where the answer is found. Then correct each false statement to make it true according to the review.

____ 1. Few people today live off the power grid. (paragraph ____)

____ 2. Providing energy sources can open up new opportunities in developing countries. (paragraph ____)

____ 3. The VOTO converts the energy of wood-fueled stoves into energy to power lights, etc. (paragraph ____)

____ 4. The Window Socket uses solar panels to store ten hours of electricity. (paragraph ____)

____ 5. The Berkeley-Darfur Stove reduces the amount of wood needed for fuel. (paragraph ____)

____ 6. The GravityLight, designed to replace kerosene-burning lights, is expensive to buy. (paragraph ____)

____ 7. It costs a lot to use the GravityLight. (paragraph ____)

____ 8. Uncharted Power's SOCCKET is a solar energy light designed to replace kerosene lamps. (paragraph ____)

**F. SYNTHESIZE** Look back at your Quick Write on page 94. How would your life be without electricity? Add any new ideas or information you learned from the reading.

**iQ** PRACTICE   Go online for additional reading and comprehension.
*Practice > Unit 4 > Activity 5*

# ? WRITE WHAT YOU THINK

**A. DISCUSS** Discuss the questions in a group. Think about the Unit Question, "How can science improve lives?"

1. Which of the five technologies seems most practical? Least practical?

2. Which of the five technologies seems easiest to provide to people in areas that don't have access to electricity?

3. How can access to energy open up opportunities to people in developing nations? Give specific examples.

**B. SYNTHESIZE** Choose one of the questions from Activity A and write a paragraph of 5–7 sentences in response. Look back at your Quick Write on page 94 as you think about what you learned.

---

**READING SKILL** Understanding comparisons and contrasts

Writers **compare and contrast** information in order to examine the similarities and differences between two or more things. Phrases that signal similarities include *all (of), both, each, similarly, like,* and *likewise.* Phrases such as *in comparison with, by comparison, in contrast,* and *differs from* show differences. Comparisons can also be made using comparative and superlative adjectives: *better/worse, more/less . . . than, the best/worst.* Look at this paragraph:

> Five innovative technologies seek to improve lives in developing countries with quick, efficient energy sources. There are similarities and differences in how each of the five technologies provides energy. **All of** the technologies seek to provide safe sources of energy on a user-by-user basis. **Likewise,** each technology is designed to provide energy as cheaply as possible. The technologies **differ** in how they provide energy. Two use wood-burning stoves. The VOTO converts heat from existing wood-burning stoves into electricity to power various devices. **By comparison,** the Berkeley-Darfur Stove is a **better** wood-burning stove that is **more** efficient. The other three technologies seek to provide electricity in **less** harmful ways by harnessing existing clean energy sources. The Window Socket uses solar energy to provide electricity. **In contrast,** the GravityLight and the SOCCKET are designed to generate power using motion.

When a reading doesn't explicitly make comparisons, as is the case with Reading 1, it is up to the reader to understand and infer the similarities and differences using the information provided. You can use a simple T-chart to quickly identify and separate the information.

| | Application of technology | |
|---|---|---|
| Utilizes charcoal-/wood-fueled stoves | Harnesses existing clean energy sources to create electricity | |
| The **VOTO** converts heat from wood-fueled stoves into electricity.<br><br>The **Berkeley-Darfur Stove** provides a better wood-fueled stove that creates energy more efficiently. | The **Window Socket** provides electricity using solar power.<br><br>The **GravityLight** replaces kerosene-burning lights with an electricity-generated light using gravity.<br><br>The **SOCCKET** replaces kerosene-burning lights with an electric one using an internal motion-powered device. | |

You can also divide the information further by adding categories or topic areas down the side of the chart. After you chart the information, you can easily examine the ideas for similarities and differences.

**A. CATEGORIZE** Reread paragraphs 3–9 of Reading 1. Underline the phrases that describe each technology. Then write the information in the chart.

| Device | Materials | Manner | Source of energy |
|---|---|---|---|
| VOTO | Charcoal-/wood-burning stove + VOTO device | | |
| Window Socket | | Solar panels store energy to use with any device (simple charger) | |
| Berkeley-Darfur Stove | | | Fire/Heat |
| GravityLight | | | |
| SOCCKET | | | |

**B. DISCUSS** Discuss your chart with a partner and add any points that you missed. What similarities and differences do you see in the points?

**iQ** PRACTICE   Go online for more practice with understanding comparisons and contrasts. *Practice > Unit 4 > Activity 6*

# READING 2
## This Device Pulls Water Out of Desert Air

**OBJECTIVE ▶**

You are going to read a news article by reporter Emily Matchar for Smithsonian.com. The article takes a look at a device that helps people live in arid places. Use the article to gather information and ideas for your Unit Assignment.

# PREVIEW THE READING

**A. PREVIEW** Look at the title and subtitle. Why would a device like this be useful? Read the last paragraph. What do you think "water-stressed regions" are? How much water "satisfies the basic needs of the individuals"?

**B. QUICK WRITE** The average person needs about 10 gallons (38 liters) of clean water a day for drinking and cleaning. Imagine you had only 2 gallons (7.5 liters). What would you have to give up or do differently? Write for 5–10 minutes in response. Remember to use this section for your Unit Assignment.

**C. VOCABULARY** Check (✓) the words you know. Use a dictionary to define any new or unknown words. Then discuss with a partner how the words will relate to the unit.

| | |
|---|---|
| absorb *(v.)* 🔊+ | organic *(adj.)* 🔊+ |
| caution *(v.)* 🔊+ | porous *(adj.)* |
| drought *(n.)* 🔊+ | potentially *(adv.)* 🔊+ OPAL |
| extract *(v.)* 🔊+ | premise *(n.)* 🔊+ |
| framework *(n.)* 🔊+ OPAL | shortage *(n.)* 🔊+ |
| implication *(n.)* 🔊+ | yield *(n.)* 🔊+ OPAL |

🔊+ Oxford 5000™ words                    OPAL Oxford Phrasal Academic Lexicon

**iQ PRACTICE**  Go online to listen and practice your pronunciation.
*Practice › Unit 4 › Activity 7*

# WORK WITH THE READING

🔊 **A. INVESTIGATE** Read the article and gather information about a device that helps people live in arid places.

# THIS DEVICE PULLS WATER OUT OF DESERT AIR

A water harvester based on MOF technology

A new water harvester[1] can extract water from extremely dry air using only solar energy.

By Emily Matchar

1    **Droughts** have been making headlines across the world in recent years, from the California water crisis to Cape Town's severe water **shortage**. Research suggests 25 percent of the globe could eventually be left in permanent drought due to climate change. But what if you could simply pull water from the air?

2    That's the **premise** of a new technology developed by University of California, Berkeley researchers. It's a water harvester that can **extract** water from the air, even in extremely dry climates. It uses no energy other than ambient[2] sunlight.

3    The key to the water harvester is a new class of materials called *metal-**organic frameworks*** (MOFs). These MOFs are solid but **porous** materials with enormous surface areas. An MOF the size of a sugar cube can have the internal surface area as big as many football fields. This means that they can **absorb** gases and liquids, and then release them quickly when heat is added.

4    "Certain MOFs have an extraordinary ability to suck in water vapor from the atmosphere, but then at the same time do not hold on to the water molecules inside their pores too tightly so that it is easy to get the water out," says Omar Yaghi. He is a professor of chemistry at Berkeley and led the research.

5    The researchers tested the harvester in Scottsdale, Arizona. It is a desert town with a high of 40 percent humidity at night

---

[1] **water harvester:** a machine that gathers water
[2] **ambient:** relating to the surrounding area; on all sides

and 8 percent humidity during the day. The researchers believe that the harvester could ultimately extract about 3 ounces of water per pound of MOF per day.

6    The harvester itself is a box inside a box. The inner box contains a bed of MOFs. The outer box is a two-foot transparent[3] plastic cube. At night, the researchers left the top off the outer box to let air flow past the MOFs. In the day, they put the top back on, so the box would be heated by the sun. The heat would pull the water out of the MOFs, where it would condense on the inner walls of the plastic cube before dripping to the bottom, where it could be collected.

7    "The most important aspect of this technology is that it is completely energy-passive," says Eugene Kapustin, a Berkeley graduate student who worked on the research. That is to say, it needs no energy besides the sun. This makes it environmentally friendly and accessible[4] to people in places with limited electricity. The results of the trials were published in the journal *Science Advances* (Fathieh, 2018).

8    The team needs to conduct more trials on the current models to figure out which factors most affect how much water can be harvested. They also hope to learn more about how specific climate conditions affect water **yield**. The next trial is planned for late summer in Death Valley, where the nighttime humidity can be as low as 25 percent.

9    Yaghi has also developed a new aluminum-based MOF. He says it is 150 times cheaper and can capture twice as much water as the current MOFs. He and his team are designing a new water harvester that actively pulls air into the MOFs at high speed. It thus delivers a much larger volume of water.

10   The team is now partnering with industry to test harvesters on an industrial scale. They also continue to search for newer, better, and cheaper MOFs. "I am very happy to see that more and more researchers around the world are joining our efforts in this regard," Yaghi says.

11   The idea of sucking water out of the atmosphere is not new, says Eric Hoek. He is an engineering professor at the University of California, Los Angeles and editor of the journal *npj Clean Water*. It's long been noted that when you run an air conditioner, water drips out. This is because the machine is cooling the air to the dew point, the temperature at which the air is saturated with water vapor and condensation occurs.

12   But creating water harvesters based on cooling technology is incredibly energy intense. In very dry climates, the dew point is below zero. Cooling the air to that temperature at any large scale is unfeasible.

13   "The real innovation [of Yaghi's research] is a materials innovation," Hoek says. "These materials [the MOFs] pull water out and more easily give it up." But the concept is challenging to scale[5], Hoek **cautions**, as the amount of water produced per square inch of harvester is relatively low. Thus a large harvester would **potentially** take up a huge amount of land. "But maybe for a household or village, it could be a very interesting way for someone to get fresh water," Hoek says.

14   Yaghi imagines exactly that: a future where everyone without easy access to fresh water has a harvester in their yard.

15   "My vision is to achieve 'personalized water,' where people in water-stressed regions have a device at home running on ambient solar, delivering the water that satisfies the basic needs of the individuals," he says. "More than one third of the population in the world lives in water-stressed regions or is suffering from a lack of clean water. The potential **implications** of this technology in transforming people's lives and improving the global public health conditions are tremendous."

**Reference** Fathieh, Farhad et al. (2018). Practical Water Production from Air. *Science Advances, 4* (6)

[3]**transparent:** something that can be seen through
[4]**accessible:** something that can be reached, entered, used, seen, etc.
[5]**scale:** to change the size of something

**B. VOCABULARY** Here are some words from Reading 2. Read the sentences. Then write each bold word next to the correct definition. You may need to change verbs to their base form and nouns to the singular form.

1. The **premise** that drives their research is the idea that many people need access to clean water.

2. The **implication** of the research is that, with this technology, it is possible to ensure an adequate supply of water.

3. The device uses a simple **framework** of two boxes, one inside the other.

4. **Organic** materials always contain some carbon since carbon is a basic element of living things.

5. Long **droughts** often lead to wildfires because plants dry up and burn easily.

6. If we have a **shortage** of water, we may need to give up taking long showers.

7. The purpose of a paper towel is to **absorb** water or other liquids.

8. We put sand in the soil to make the soil more **porous**, letting water move through it more easily.

9. The professor **cautioned** us to not spend too much time on our project.

10. We wanted to **extract** the salt from the sea water so that we could drink the water.

11. There are **potentially** many uses for this device; the possibilities are many.

12. Farmers need to estimate the **yield** for each field, so they can estimate how much money they will make.

a. _____ (n.) a possible effect or result of an action or a decision

b. _____ (n.) the parts of an object that support its weight and give it shape

c. _____ (n.) a statement or an idea that forms the basis of an argument

d. _____ (v.) to take in a liquid, gas, or other substance from the surface or space around

e. _____ (n.) a situation when there is not enough of the people or things that are needed

f. _____ (adj.) having many small holes that allow water or air to pass through slowly

g. _____ (v.) to remove or obtain a substance from something

h. _____ (n.) a long period of time when there is little or no rain

i. _____ (v.) to warn somebody about the possible dangers or problems of something

j. _____ (n.) the total amount of crops, profits, etc., that are produced

k. _____ (adv.) used to say that something may happen; possibly

l. _____ (adj) produced by or from living things

**iQ** PRACTICE  Go online for more practice with the vocabulary.
*Practice > Unit 4 > Activity 8*

**C. IDENTIFY** Circle the correct answer. Then write the paragraph number where the answer is found.

1. What are MOFs (metal-organic frameworks)? (paragraph ____)
   a. solid materials that are small but have a lot of surface area
   b. materials that take in liquids and gases
   c. materials that release liquids and gases when they are heated
   d. all of the above

2. A water harvester is a box inside a box. What is the purpose of the outside box? (paragraph ____)
   a. It protects the inside box from animals.
   b. It collects the water that evaporates.
   c. It makes the water harvester easier to see.
   d. It focuses the sunlight on the box.

3. Why is the lid taken off the water harvester at night? (paragraph ____)
   a. to make it easier to inspect
   b. to allow the MOFs to absorb water
   c. to dry the MOFs
   d. to let insects drink the water from the box

4. Why is the lid put on the water harvester during the day? (paragraph ___)

    a. so that the MOF can absorb sunlight

    b. so that it can reflect the heat away from the box

    c. so that the box will trap the water released by the MOF

    d. so that dirt and animals don't get into the box

5. What is the main problem with water harvesters? (paragraph ___)

    a. They don't yield much water for their size.

    b. They use a lot of energy.

    c. They are hard to maintain.

    d. They weigh too much.

## D. RESTATE Write the meaning of these phrases from the article.

1. energy-passive (paragraph 7) _____

2. conduct more trials (paragraph 8) _____

3. nighttime humidity (paragraph 8) _____

4. sucking water out of the atmosphere (paragraph 11)

    _____

5. dew point (paragraphs 11 and 12) _____

6. "personalized water" (paragraph 15) _____

## E. EXPLAIN Discuss the questions with a partner.

1. What is the major benefit of the water harvesters?

2. Why do the scientists test the water harvesters in deserts?

3. What are two benefits of the water harvesters being "energy-passive"?

4. Why would Omar Yaghi "test harvesters on an industrial scale" (paragraph 10)?

5. Why don't scientists cool the air to get the water out of it?

6. Reread the last sentence in the article. How could a water harvester transform someone's life?

# WORK WITH THE VIDEO

**A. PREVIEW** Can we do something about global warming? If so, what?

## VIDEO VOCABULARY

**reflective (adj.)** sending back heat or light

**enhance (v.)** to increase or further improve the good quality of something

**particle (n.)** a very small piece of something

**vapor (n.)** a mass of very small drops of liquid in the air

**replicating (n.)** producing exact copies of

**iQ RESOURCES** Go online to watch the video about geoengineering inventions used to save the planet by combatting global warming.
*Resources ⟩ Video ⟩ Unit 4 ⟩ Unit Video*

**B. COMPOSE** Watch the video two or three times. Take notes in the chart.

| | Putting tiny reflective lenses into space | Making clouds thicker and more reflective | Releasing sulfur into the stratosphere |
|---|---|---|---|
| Notes from the video | | | |
| My ideas | | | |

**C. EXTEND** What are the advantages and disadvantages of each invention? Which idea seems the most likely to work? Write your ideas in the chart above. Discuss your ideas with a partner.

# WRITE WHAT YOU THINK

**SYNTHESIZE** Think about Reading 1, Reading 2, and the unit video as you discuss these questions. Then choose one question and write a paragraph of 5–7 sentences in response.

1. Some inventions start out being for one group of people but end up being useful for other groups of people as well, such as the VOTO in Reading 1. Which of the technologies in the readings and the video could you use?

2. Many technologies have both positive and negative aspects. Choose a technology that you use (cell phone, automobile, etc.). What are the positive and negative points of that technology?

3. A popular expression in English is, "Necessity is the mother of invention." Think of a need you know of in any country, in any field. What technology, existing or imagined, would address that need?

---

## VOCABULARY SKILL  Using the dictionary to distinguish between homonyms

### Finding the correct meaning

There are many words that have the same spelling and pronunciation but different meanings. These words are called *homonyms*.

> **lift** *(v.)* to raise something to a higher position
>> I **lifted** the lid of the box and peered in.
>
> **lift** *(v.)* to copy ideas or words without asking permission
>> She **lifted** most of the ideas from a book she had been reading.
>
> **lift** *(v.)* to become or make more cheerful
>> His heart **lifted** at the sight of a house in the distance.
>
> **field** *(n.)* (usually in compounds) an area of land used for the purpose mentioned
>> Her excitement grew as she kicked the ball down the soccer **field**.
>
> **field** *(n.)* a particular subject or activity that somebody works in or is interested in
>> He is an expert in the **field** of chemistry.

Some homonyms may have different parts of speech, for example, a noun form and a verb form.

> **scale** *(n.)* the size of something
>> The team is now testing harvesters on an industrial **scale**.
>
> **scale** *(v.)* to change the size of something
>> The concept is challenging to **scale**.

Advanced dictionaries will list all the word forms and definitions for them. When using a dictionary to find the correct meaning of a word, it is important to read the entire sentence where you found the word and consider the use and context.

## A. IDENTIFY Look at the dictionary entry for *range*. Check (✓) the correct answers.

**range** ⓘ ● /reɪndʒ/ *noun, verb*
● *noun*
> VARIETY **1** [C, usually sing.] ~ **(of sth)** a variety of things of a particular type: *The hotel offers a **wide range** of facilities.* ◆ *There is **a full range of** activities for kids.*
> LIMITS **2** [C, usually sing.] the limits between which something varies: *Most of the students are in the 17–20 **age range**.* ◆ *There will be an increase **in the range** of 0 to 3 percent.* ◆ *It's difficult to find a house in our **price range** (= that we can afford).* ◆ *This was **outside the range of** his experience.*
> DISTANCE **3** [C, U] the distance over which something can be seen or heard: *The child was now out of her **range of vision** (= not near enough for her to see).* **4** [C, U] the distance over which a gun or other weapon can hit things: *These missiles have a range of 300 miles.* **5** [C] the distance that a vehicle will travel before it needs more fuel
> MUSIC **6** [C, usually sing.] all of the notes that a person's voice or a musical instrument can produce, from high to low: *She was gifted with an incredible vocal range.*
> ABILITY **7** [C, usually sing.] the full extent of a person's knowledge or abilities: *Those two movies give some indication of his range as an actor.*
> OF MOUNTAINS **8** [C] a line or group of mountains or hills: *the great mountain range of the Alps*
> FOR SHOOTING **9** [C] an area of land where people can practice shooting or where bombs, etc. can be tested: *a shooting range*
> OF PRODUCTS **10** [C] a set of products of a particular type SYN LINE: *our new range of hair products*
● *verb*
> VARY **1** [I] to vary between two particular amounts, sizes, etc., including others between them: ~ **from A to B** *to range in size/length/price from A to B* ◆ *Accommodations range from tourist class to luxury hotels.* ◆ ~ **between A and B** *Estimates of the damage range between $1 million and $5 million.* **2** [I] to include a variety of different things in addition to those mentioned: ~ **from A to B** *She has had a number of different jobs, ranging from chef to swimming instructor.* ◆ + **adv./prep.** *The conversation ranged widely (= covered a lot of different topics).*
> ARRANGE **3** [T, usually passive] ~ **sb/sth/yourself** + **adv./prep.** *(formal)* to arrange people or things in a particular position or order: *The delegates ranged themselves around the table.* ◆ *Spectators were ranged along the whole route of the procession.*
> MOVE AROUND **4** [I, T] to move around an area: + **adv./prep.** *He ranges far and wide in search of inspiration for his paintings.* ◆ ~ **sth** *Her eyes ranged the room.*

All dictionary entries adapted from the *Oxford American Dictionary for learners of English* © Oxford University Press 2011.

1. *Range* can be used as:

   ☐ a noun                    ☐ an adjective

   ☐ a verb                    ☐ an adverb

2. *Range* can mean:

   ☐ to vary                   ☐ light

   ☐ distance over which something    ☐ to move around
      can be heard or seen
                               ☐ music
   ☐ to lift

**B. IDENTIFY** Read the excerpts from Readings 1 and 2. Look up each bold word in your dictionary. Write the part of speech and the correct definition based on the context.

**Reading 1**

1. The devices do not need the years it takes to extend the **power** grid to remote places.

   _____

2. That electricity can power a handheld light, **charge** a phone, or even charge a spare battery.

   _____

3. Just **stick** it on a sunny window for 5–8 hours, with the built-in suction cup.

   _____

4. The solar panels on the back will **store** about ten hours' worth of electricity that can be used with any device.

   _____

5. With that in mind, engineers and designers have recently created a range of innovative devices that can increase the supply of **safe**, cheap energy on a user-by-user basis.

   _____

**Reading 2**

6. In the day, they put the top back on, so the box would be **heated** by the sun.

   _____

7. The heat would pull the water out of the MOFs, where it would **condense** on the inner walls of the plastic cube before dripping to the bottom, where it could be collected.

   _____

8. Cooling the air to that temperature at any large **scale** is unfeasible.

   _____

iQ PRACTICE Go online for more practice with using the dictionary to distinguish between homonyms. *Practice > Unit 4 > Activity 9*

# WRITING

OBJECTIVE ▶      At the end of this unit, you will write an essay comparing and contrasting two new technologies that can improve lives. This essay will include specific information from the readings, the unit video, and your own ideas.

## WRITING SKILL   Writing a compare and contrast essay

A **compare and contrast essay** describes the similarities and differences between two subjects. Comparisons show their similarities, while contrasts examine their differences.

### Introduction

The introduction describes the two subjects being compared and contrasted. It has a thesis statement that explains the relationship between the two subjects or gives reasons why the relationship is important.

### Body paragraphs

There are many different ways to organize the body paragraphs of a compare and contrast essay. Before you write a compare and contrast essay, it is important to decide which organization is best for your essay. Here are two ways to organize your ideas:

- In a **point by point essay**, you choose three or more key points to compare and contrast. Each body paragraph compares and contrasts one key point. This organization can be best when you want to balance your essay evenly between your two subjects.

- In a **similarities and differences essay**, the first body paragraph explains what is similar about the two subjects. The second body paragraph explains what is different about the two subjects. The third body paragraph discusses the most important similarities and differences. This organization can be best when you want to explain why one subject is better than the other subject, or what is significant about their similarities or differences.

### Conclusion

The conclusion summarizes the similarities and differences and gives the writer's opinion about the topic. It can explain why one of the subjects is better than the other or why they are of equal value.

**iQ** RESOURCES   Go online to watch the Writing Skill Video.
*Resources > Video > Unit 4 > Writing Skill Video*

**A. WRITING MODEL** Read the model compare and contrast essay. Then answer the questions that follow.

## The Dream of Flight

Otto Lilienthal

The Wright brothers

1    Flying has long been a dream of many people. Two sets of brothers are universally acknowledged to have contributed immensely to heavier-than-air flight. These brothers, the Lilienthals of Germany and the Wrights of the United States, share some similarities but also have some differences.

2    The Lilienthals, Otto and Gustav, worked together, as did the Wrights, Orville and Wilbur. Unlike the Wright brothers, who are usually spoken of together, the Lillienthal brothers weren't equally famous. Otto is usually spoken of individually. Otto opened a business that made boilers and steam engines, which made enough money for him to pursue his hobby of flight. When engaging with aircraft, Otto always worked with Gustav. The Wright brothers opened a printing business and then a bicycle shop. They developed their innovations to the airplane together as well. They shared credit for their inventions and depended on their businesses, including their work in aviation, to make a living.

3    While Otto Lilienthal was educated and employed as an engineer, the Wright brothers did not study at a university. The Wright brothers were mostly self-taught. In fact, one of the books that the Wrights were inspired by was authored by Otto Lilienthal.

4    Both Otto Lilienthal and the Wright brothers were inventors; many of their patents were related to aircraft. Otto and the Wright brothers were interested in gliders, specifically in how to control them. Both Otto Lilienthal and the Wrights studied birds in order to ascertain how birds were able to control themselves in flight. Otto, who made over 2,000 flights in gliders, was known as "the father of flight" because he was the first to sustain a controlled flight in a heavier-than-air aircraft, a glider. The Wrights are credited with the three-axis control (up and down, side to side, and forward and backward) for aircraft, which is still used in fixed-wing aircraft today. They are also credited with achieving the first sustained, controlled flight of an airplane. The Lilienthals and the Wrights were both influential in developing heavier-than-air aircraft, especially contributing to the control of the aircraft. Otto Lilienthal held patents on his inventions. Similarly, the Wright brothers held patents on their inventions and went on to build airplanes.

5    Despite their differences, the Lilienthals and the Wright brothers will always be remembered for their contributions to helping people achieve the dream of flight.

1. What is the thesis statement? Underline it.

2. How is the essay organized? _____

3. Why do you think the author organized it this way?

   _____

B. **CATEGORIZE** Reread the essay on page 113. Complete the chart with both the similarities and the differences for each key point. Then compare with a partner.

| Compare and contrast essay: Point by point | | |
|---|---|---|
| **Key points** | **The Lilienthal brothers** | **The Wright brothers** |
| 1. supporting businesses | | |
| 2. education | | |
| 3. inventions/interest in flight | | |

C. **CATEGORIZE** Work with a partner. Complete the chart below. Reorganize the information from the essay into a plan for a similarities and differences essay. Use the chart in Activity B to help you.

| Compare and contrast essay: Similarities and differences | | |
|---|---|---|
| **Similarities** | **Differences** | |
| | **The Lilienthal brothers** | **The Wright brothers** |
| | | |

D. **CATEGORIZE** Use the chart to help you think of examples of technology 100 years ago and technology now.

| Compare and contrast essay: Similarities and differences | | |
|---|---|---|
| **Similarities** | **Differences** | |
| | **Technology 100 years ago** | **Technology now** |
| | | |

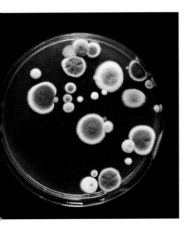

## Two Chemicals That Have Changed Lives

1    How has chemistry improved your life? When not one chemist made the top 50 scientists in *Science* magazine in 2014, the Royal Academy of Chemistry decided to try to understand why. It seems that when we think of innovations, chemistry is often overlooked. But, in fact, chemistry has led to many improvements in our lives. Two other important innovations in chemistry, penicillin and ammonia, have contributed to the world as we know it today, though each has done so in different ways.

2    Both penicillin and ammonia are naturally occurring on earth. Penicillin is a mold, and ammonia is a chemical compound. They were also both discovered around the same time. Penicillin was discovered in 1928, by Scottish bacteriologist Alexander Fleming. Just more than a decade later, Australian pharmacologist Howard Florey purified penicillin into useable amounts, and in 1944, chemical engineer Margaret Hutchinson Rousseau was able to put it into production. Similarly, in 1910, German chemists Fritz Haber and Carl Bosch were working on the formulation that would become ammonia. They did it by combining nitrogen and hydrogen. This process of making ammonia, called the *Haber-Bosch process*, allowed for the greater access to nitrogen of both plants and animals. Both penicillin and ammonia have been used to improve our lives.

3    While penicillin and ammonia share similarities, there are differences. The main difference is in how they are used. Penicillin is an important medical treatment used to cure many bacterial diseases. It has saved the lives of millions of people since it was first put into full-scale production in 1944. Ammonia, on the other hand, has been used mostly as a fertilizer, resulting in increased food production, cited as the most important factor in the population explosion over the last century.

4    However, the most significant similarity between these two innovations is how they are used and perceived today. With both, there is caution in their use. The reasons for that caution are very similar. Penicillin's use (or some would argue, overuse) has resulted in bacteria that are increasingly resistant to penicillin. Therefore, doctors are much more careful now in prescribing it to their patients. Similarly, ammonia is now understood to be a toxic chemical compound that is irritating and caustic. This has resulted in efforts to find alternatives to using it.

5    In conclusion, no one would dispute that these two chemistry inventions, penicillin and ammonia, have improved our lives since their discovery and development in the early twentieth century. But they have also shown us that even a good thing must be used carefully. Chemists must continue to conduct research on the chemicals that we use to improve lives.

1. What is the thesis statement? Underline it.

2. How is the essay organized?

_____

3. Why do you think the author organized it this way?

_____


**F. CATEGORIZE** Create a chart for the essay "Two Chemicals That Have Changed Lives" like the ones in Activities C and D.

**iQ** PRACTICE  Go online for more practice writing a compare and contrast essay. *Practice > Unit 4 > Activity 10*

You can use different words and phrases to **compare and contrast** ideas.

**Subordinators showing contrast**

You can use an adverb clause to show an idea that contrasts with the main clause. The subordinators *although* and *though* show contrasting ideas. *Whereas* and *while* often signal more direct opposition. Notice the comma when the adverb clause comes first.

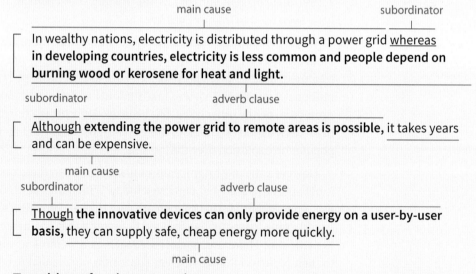

**Transitions showing comparison**

You can use some transition words to show comparison. Some common transition words to introduce comparison are *similarly, likewise,* and *in addition*. These are used to discuss similarities.

> The GravityLight is a replacement for kerosene lamps. **Similarly,** the SOCCKET replaces kerosene lamps with an electric light.
>
> All of the innovative devices provide energy on a user-by-user basis. **In addition,** they use sources that are readily available.
>
> Providing new energy sources would open up new opportunities for people in developing countries. **Likewise,** it opens up opportunities for engineers and designers.

### Transitions showing contrast

You can use other transition words to show contrast or differences.

| Contrast | More direct opposition | Concession |
|---|---|---|
| however<br>though | on the other hand<br>in contrast | nevertheless<br>in spite of this<br>nonetheless<br>despite this |

> Both the GravityLight and the SOCCKET replace kerosene lamps. **However,** they use different methods to generate electricity.
>
> The GravityLight uses the energy generated by a falling motion to create electricity for the light. **On the other hand,** the SOCCKET uses an internal motion-powered device to generate and store electricity.

**ACADEMIC LANGUAGE**

The corpus shows that *in contrast* and *in contrast to* are often used in academic writing.
. . . *In contrast, ammonia is . . .*
. . . *In contrast to penicillin, ammonia is . . .*

———————— **OPAL**
Oxford Phrasal Academic Lexicon

**A. IDENTIFY** Read each sentence. Underline the word or phrase that indicates a comparison or a contrast. Then write *CP* (comparison) or *CT* (contrast).

____ 1. The GravityLight and the SOCCKET each uses motion to generate energy, though they use different types of motion.

____ 2. The Berkeley-Darfur Stove helps users directly, improving health by reducing the amount of smoke inhaled. Similarly, it helps users by shortening the amount time spent gathering wood to fuel the stove.

____ 3. Each of the innovative technologies described in the review provides energy simply and safely. Nonetheless, some of them are more effective than others.

____ 4. While the Window Socket uses solar energy to generate power, VOTO uses the heat produced by a charcoal- or wood-burning stove.

____ 5. The electricity produced by VOTO can power a phone. Likewise, VOTO can even charge a spare battery.

**B. IDENTIFY** Circle the best phrase to complete each sentence.

1. The Wright brothers shared fame equally whereas *Otto Lilienthal was more famous than his brother, Gustav / the Lilienthal brothers were also equally famous.*

2. The Wright brothers had patents. Likewise, Otto Lilienthal *never had patents / had patents.*

3. Although the Wright brothers were self-educated, Otto Lilienthal *was also self-educated / was an engineer.*

4. The Wright brothers were self-educated. Despite this, they *built airplanes / didn't build airplanes.*

5. Otto Lilienthal is credited with the first heavier-than-air flight in a glider. In contrast, the Wright brothers *also are credited with heavier-than-air flight in a glider / are credited with heavier-than-air flight in an airplane.*

**C. APPLY** Complete the sentences using your own ideas. Make sure you use correct punctuation.

1. I think that science can improve lives. Nevertheless _____
   _____.

2. Although penicillin has saved many lives _____
   _____.

3. Water is essential to all living things. Similarly _____
   _____.

4. I think I could live without a television. On the other hand _____
   _____
   _____.

5. Technology has benefitted us in many ways. However _____
   _____
   _____.

6. Whereas many people in the world get electricity from a power grid _____
   _____
   _____.

**iQ** PRACTICE   Go online for more practice with subordinators and transitions to compare and contrast. *Practice > Unit 4 > Activities 11–12*

**UNIT ASSIGNMENT** Write a compare and contrast essay

**OBJECTIVE ▶**

In this assignment, you are going to write a five-paragraph essay comparing and contrasting two innovative technologies that can improve lives. As you prepare your essay, think about the Unit Question, "How can science improve lives?" Use information from Reading 1, Reading 2, the unit video, and your work in this unit to support your essay. Refer to the Self-Assessment checklist on page 120.

**iQ** PRACTICE  Go online to the Writing Tutor to read a model compare and contrast paragraph. *Practice > Unit 4 > Activity 13*

# PLAN AND WRITE

**WRITING TIP**
When you brainstorm ideas using both a point by point and a similarities and differences chart, it will help you discover which organization works best for your subject, and you may get more ideas.

**A. BRAINSTORM** Follow these steps to help you organize your ideas.

1.  Complete the chart. List new technologies that scientists have discovered, invented, or designed to improve lives in the fields indicated. Add another field and technologies you are familiar with. Compare charts with a partner.

| Field | Technologies |
|---|---|
| Chemistry | |
| Physics | |
| Engineering | |
| Education | |
| | |

2.  Choose the two technologies you would like to use as your subject to compare and contrast.

3.  Write points to compare and contrast and similarities and differences for your subject. (Refer to the charts on p. 114 to help you organize your ideas.)

**B. PLAN** Plan your essay.

Look at your ideas from question 3 in Activity A. Decide whether your essay would be best organized as a point by point essay or a similarities and differences essay.

**iQ** RESOURCES  Go online to download and complete the outline for your compare and contrast essay. *Resources > Writing Tools > Unit 4 > Outline*

**C. WRITE** Use your planning notes to write your essay.

1.  Write your essay comparing and contrasting two innovative technologies to improve lives. Be sure to include an introduction with a thesis statement, three body paragraphs, and a conclusion.

2.  Look at the Self-Assessment checklist on page 120 to guide your writing.

**iQ** PRACTICE   Go online to the Writing Tutor to write your assignment.
*Practice > Unit 4 > Activity 14*

# REVISE AND EDIT

**iQ** RESOURCES   Go online to download the peer review worksheet.
*Resources > Writing Tools > Unit 4 > Peer Review Worksheet*

**A. PEER REVIEW**  Read your partner's essay. Then use the peer review worksheet. Discuss the review with your partner.

**B. REWRITE**  Based on your partner's review, revise and rewrite your essay.

**C. EDIT**  Complete the Self-Assessment checklist as you prepare to write the final draft of your essay. Be prepared to hand in your work or discuss it in class.

| SELF-ASSESSMENT | Yes | No |
|---|---|---|
| Does the thesis statement explain the relationship between the two subjects or give reasons why the relationship is important? | ☐ | ☐ |
| Is the essay organized using one of the compare and contrast essay types? | ☐ | ☐ |
| Does the essay contain an introduction, three body paragraphs, and a conclusion? | ☐ | ☐ |
| Does the essay use subordinators and transitions to compare and contrast? | ☐ | ☐ |
| Does the essay include vocabulary from the unit? | ☐ | ☐ |
| Did you check the essay for punctuation, spelling, and grammar? | ☐ | ☐ |

**D. REFLECT**  Discuss these questions with a partner or group.

1. What is something new you learned in this unit?

2. Look back at the Unit Question—How can science improve lives? Is your answer different now than when you started the unit? If yes, how is it different? Why?

**iQ** PRACTICE   Go to the online discussion board to discuss the questions.
*Practice > Unit 4 > Activity 15*

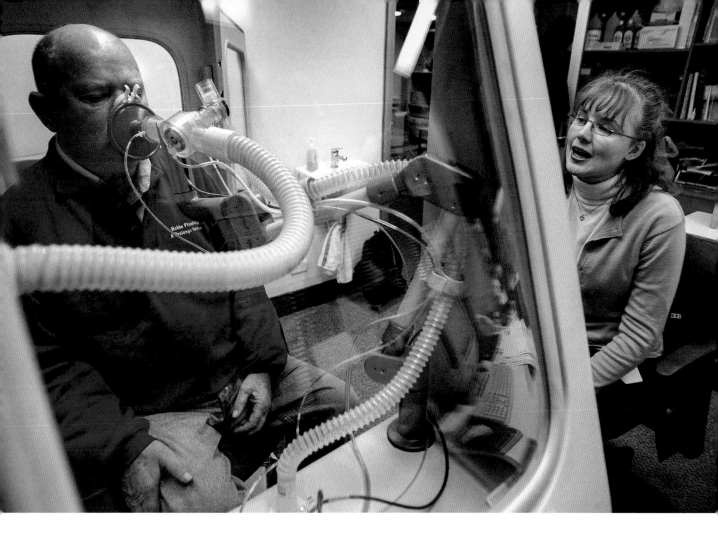

# TRACK YOUR SUCCESS

**iQ** PRACTICE  Go online to check the words and phrases you have learned in this unit. *Practice > Unit 4 > Activity 16*

Check (✓) the skills and strategies you learned. If you need more work on a skill, refer to the page(s) in parentheses.

CRITICAL THINKING  ☐ I can categorize information. (p. 98)

READING  ☐ I can understand comparisons and contrasts. (p. 100)

VOCABULARY  ☐ I can use the dictionary to distinguish between homonyms. (p. 109)

WRITING  ☐ I can write a compare and contrast essay. (p. 112)

GRAMMAR  ☐ I can use subordinators and transitions to compare and contrast. (p. 116)

OBJECTIVE ▶  ☐ I can gather information and ideas to write an essay comparing and contrasting two new technologies that can improve lives.

# 5 Nutritional Science

| | |
|---|---|
| READING | recognizing bias |
| CRITICAL THINKING | analyzing texts for cause and effect relationships |
| VOCABULARY | cause and effect collocations |
| WRITING | writing a cause and effect essay |
| GRAMMAR | agents with the passive voice |

# Should science influence what we eat?

**A.** Discuss these questions with your classmates.

1. Do you think you have a generally healthy diet? What have you eaten so far today?

2. Which is more important to you: eating for pleasure or eating for health? Why?

3. Look at the photo. Would you eat food that was grown in a lab? Why or why not?

**B.** Listen to *The Q Classroom* online. Then answer these questions.

1. Who agrees that science should influence what we eat? What reasons do they give?

2. Who thinks science shouldn't influence what we eat? What reasons do they give? Do you think science should influence what we eat? Why or why not?

**iQ PRACTICE** Go to the online discussion board to discuss the Unit Question with your classmates. *Practice > Unit 5 > Activity 1*

**UNIT OBJECTIVE**

Read an article from a health magazine and an article from a science magazine. Gather information and ideas to write a cause and effect essay about the effects of science on the food we eat.

# READING

READING 1

## Eating Well: Less Science, More Common Sense

You are going to read an article from a health magazine about ways that we can eat well. Use the article to gather information and ideas for your Unit Assignment.

## PREVIEW THE READING

**A. PREVIEW** Read the title and look at the pictures. Answer these questions.

1. Does the author think science should help us choose the foods we eat? Explain.

2. What suggestions for eating well do you think the author will talk about?

**B. QUICK WRITE** How do you know what to eat? Do you pay attention to scientific studies about food? Write for 5–10 minutes in response. Be sure to use this section for your Unit Assignment.

**C. VOCABULARY** Check (✓) the words you know. Use a dictionary to define any new or unknown words. Then discuss how the words will relate to the unit with a partner.

| | |
|---|---|
| access *(n.)* 𝕝+ OPAL | expert *(n.)* 𝕝+ OPAL |
| approach *(n.)* 𝕝+ OPAL | finding *(n.)* 𝕝+ OPAL |
| benefit *(n.)* 𝕝+ OPAL | link *(n.)* 𝕝+ OPAL |
| challenge *(v.)* 𝕝+ OPAL | participate *(v.)* 𝕝+ OPAL |
| eliminate *(v.)* 𝕝+ OPAL | physical *(adj.)* 𝕝+ OPAL |
| encourage *(v.)* 𝕝+ OPAL | practical *(adj.)* 𝕝+ OPAL |

𝕝+ Oxford 5000™ words      OPAL Oxford Phrasal Academic Lexicon

**iQ** PRACTICE Go online to listen and practice your pronunciation.
*Practice > Unit 5 > Activity 2*

**124** UNIT 5 Should science influence what we eat?

**A. INVESTIGATE** Read the article and gather information about how science influences what we eat.

# EATING WELL:
## LESS SCIENCE, MORE COMMON SENSE

Product labels can be misleading.

1    Food is life. We eat it to grow, stay healthy, and have the energy to do everyday activities. The food we consume makes all of these things possible, but not all food is created equal. Studies have shown, for example, that children who eat a nutritious breakfast do better in school than those with a poor diet. The well-fed child is able to pay attention longer, remember more, and **participate** more actively in class. Research has also shown that adults who have a healthy diet perform better on the job and miss fewer days of work. The **findings**, then, are clear. Because our food choices affect our health and behavior, we must do more than just eat; we must eat *well*. For many people today, though, making healthy food choices is not easy.

2    We are surrounded by information telling us what's good for us and what isn't, but usually this information is more confusing than helpful. In fact, different research about the same food often produces contradictory[1] results. Take one example: food studies done on eggs. For years, research showed a **link** between eating eggs and high cholesterol[2]. To prevent dangerous diseases like cancer or heart disease, people were **encouraged** to limit or completely **eliminate** eggs from their diets. However, recent studies now say that eggs are actually good for you and that most people can—and even *should*—eat one a day. It's hard to know who to believe.

3    Shopping for food can also be challenging. During a visit to a supermarket, we often need to make many different choices. Should you buy this cereal or that one? Regular or fat-free milk? Tofu or chicken? It's hard to know which to choose, especially when two items are very similar. Many shoppers read product labels to help them decide. Not surprisingly, people are more likely to buy items with the words *doctor recommended*, *low fat*, or *all natural* on them. But are these foods *really* better for you? Probably not. Indeed, many food labels are often misleading. For instance, because doctors sometimes recommend that people eat yogurt for their digestion, a yogurt maker might then use the label "doctor-recommended" so that you buy their product. In reality, though, their specific yogurt isn't preferred by doctors, but shoppers may think it is because of the food label.

---

[1] **contradictory:** differing; opposite
[2] **cholesterol:** a substance found in foods like meat, milk, and cheese that can cause health problems

4    So how *do* we make healthy choices? Michael Pollan is a professor at the University of California, Berkeley who has written many books about eating well (including the bestseller *In Defense of Food*). In his opinion, our food needs to be defended against "needless complications" from "nutrition science and from the food industry." According to Pollan, we need to stop reading labels and listening to the so-called[3] scientific **experts**. Instead, he offers some simple, yet **practical** tips for eating well and staying healthy.

5    Tip 1: **"Eat food. Not too much. Mostly plants."** In other words, says Pollan, only eat "real food" or things your great-grandparents would recognize as food. Make fruit and vegetables your main source of food, and limit your meat intake. And when you eat, says Pollan, do so in moderation. He quotes the Okinawan people of Japan who have an expression: "*Hara Hachi Bu*: eat until you are 80 percent full."

6    Tip 2: **"Get out of the supermarket whenever possible."** Shopping for meat or dairy products at the market is probably OK, but a supermarket is also full of items like instant noodles, diet sodas, and similar products—the ones that aren't good for us. Instead, try to shop at a farmers' market or a local store when you can. The food there is fresher and healthier.

7    Tip 3: Pollan says that eating is not only about **physical** health and nutrition. "Food is also about pleasure, about community and family." In other words, choosing the right food to eat is only the first step. Learning how to cook and sharing a meal with others are also important parts of eating well and being healthy.

8    Thinking like Michael Pollan's is **challenging** the "scientific **approach** to eating." It is also helping people to reconnect[4] with food traditions. In cities around the world, for example, urban gardens—common since ancient times—are becoming popular again. On small pieces of land, neighbors are working together to grow fruit and vegetables. What are the **benefits** of these gardens? Better nutrition for one thing; people have **access** to more fresh fruit and vegetables, especially poorer people who are less likely to spend money on these items. The food also costs less than it would in a supermarket (where it was probably driven in from farms or shipped in from another country). There are other benefits, too. Working together in the garden helps people to exercise; it also promotes community and sharing.

9    Urban gardens have also been used to teach children about food production and healthy eating. At the Edible Schoolyard—a program at a public school in the U.S.—children learn how to plant and harvest[5] fruit and vegetables. They also learn how to clean and prepare them for meals—a skill that they will be able to use all their lives. And best of all, because the children want to eat the things they have grown, they learn to develop healthy eating habits.

The Edible Schoolyard program

10   Ultimately, making healthy food choices and eating well do not have to be difficult. Doing simple things—changing your shopping habits, learning to cook, planting a garden, and limiting your intake of certain foods—can result in a better diet and a healthier you. *Bon appétit*[6]!

---

[3] **so-called:** sometimes used to show that the word being introduced is not accurate or true
[4] **reconnect:** to discover a relationship with something again
[5] **harvest:** to pick and collect fruit, vegetables, and other plants
[6] **bon appétit:** a French expression used in English, said at the start of a meal to mean "Enjoy the food."

In Unit 4, you used the dictionary to find homonyms that have different meanings or are different parts of speech. Nine of the 12 vocabulary words in Activity B are homonyms—words that have the same spelling and pronunciation but different meanings. Use your dictionary to identify the nine homonyms.

**B. VOCABULARY** Complete the sentences with the vocabulary from Reading 1.

| | | | |
|---|---|---|---|
| access *(n.)* | challenge *(v.)* | expert *(n.)* | participate *(v.)* |
| approach *(n.)* | eliminate *(v.)* | finding *(n.)* | physical *(adj.)* |
| benefit *(n.)* | encourage *(v.)* | link *(n.)* | practical *(adj.)* |

1. If you want to lose weight, you should _____ junk food from your diet.

2. Dr. Carlson is a medical _____ who specializes in women's health and nutrition.

3. One _____ of a vegetarian diet is that you'll probably live longer.

4. Is there a(n) _____ between taking vitamins and better health?

5. Millions of people don't have _____ to clean drinking water. What can we do about this problem?

6. Do you want to _____ in our school's health study? You only have to answer a few questions.

7. One _____ from the study is that organic food is not always better for you.

8. You can _____ children to eat vegetables by eating more of them yourself.

9. Eating a large meal before bed isn't very _____. You won't be able to sleep.

10. To quit smoking, Leo tried chewing gum and exercising, but neither _____ has worked.

11. My dad had a(n) _____ exam today, and the doctor says he's in great health.

12. For years, people thought eating chocolate was bad for your skin, but recent studies _____ that belief. Research now says chocolate is good for you!

**iQ PRACTICE** Go online for more practice with the vocabulary.
*Practice > Unit 5 > Activity 3*

**C. EVALUATE** Read the statements. Would the author of the magazine article agree with them? Write *Y* (yes) or *N* (no) and the paragraph number where the answer is found. Discuss your answers with a partner.

_____ 1. Scientific research about diet gives us helpful information. (paragraph _____)

_____ 2. Food labels have made us better-informed consumers. (paragraph _____)

_____ 3. We don't need experts to tell us what to eat. (paragraph _____)

_____ 4. A lot of food found in a supermarket is not "real food." (paragraph _____)

_____ 5. The purpose of eating is mainly for health and nutrition. (paragraph _____)

_____ 6. An urban garden works well in modern cities. (paragraph _____)

_____ 7. Making healthy food choices is hard. (paragraph _____)

**D. IDENTIFY** Circle the correct answer.

1. According to the reading, which question is difficult for many people to answer?

   a. Why do some people have a healthier diet than others?

   b. How does our diet affect our health and behavior?

   c. Which are the healthiest foods to eat?

2. In paragraph 2, the studies on eggs are an example of _____.

   a. confusing results

   b. helpful advice

   c. similar findings

3. Food labels that read "low-fat" or "all-natural" _____.

   a. are usually on products recommended by doctors

   b. are mainly used to sell a product

   c. often help shoppers make healthy food choices

4. Which piece of advice would Michael Pollan probably agree with?

   a. Try to eat only one meal per day; you'll feel better and be healthier.

   b. Selecting healthy food and learning how to cook it are both important.

   c. Never shop at a supermarket; the food there is unhealthy.

5. At the Edible Schoolyard in the U.S., what are children *not* learning to do?

   a. plant fruit and vegetables

   b. cook and eat healthy meals

   c. read and understand nutrition labels

**E. IDENTIFY** Paragraph 8 of the article lists four benefits of having an urban garden. Write them below.

1. _____
2. _____
3. _____
4. _____

**F. CATEGORIZE** Complete the cause and effect chart with the benefits of an urban garden.

| Causes | Effects (Benefits) |
|---|---|
| 1. access to more fresh fruits and vegetables | |
| 2. food doesn't have to be brought to supermarkets | |
| 3. working in a garden | |
| 4. working together | |
| 5. participating in the Edible Schoolyard program | |

**G. SYNTHESIZE** Look back at your Quick Write on page 124. How do you know what to eat? Add any new ideas or information you learned from the reading.

**iQ** PRACTICE  Go online for additional reading and comprehension.
*Practice > Unit 5 > Activity 4*

# WRITE WHAT YOU THINK

**A. DISCUSS** Discuss the questions in a group. Think about the Unit Question, "Should science influence what we eat?"

1. Do you pay attention to the results of scientific food studies? What advice have you taken seriously?

2. Look again at Michael Pollan's tips for eating well in paragraphs 5–7 of Reading 1. Then describe the last three meals you have eaten and explain: Do you think you eat well? If yes, which of Pollan's tips are you following? If no, what do you need to do differently?

3. Look again at the benefits of an urban garden you listed in Activity E. Think of at least one more advantage and explain how it helps people.

B. **SYNTHESIZE** Choose one of the questions from Activity A and write a paragraph of 5–7 sentences in response. Look back at your Quick Write on page 124 as you think about what you learned.

## READING SKILL Recognizing bias

*Bias* means a strong feeling for or against something. Writers may present information in ways that support their biases in order to influence a reader's opinion. It is important to recognize a writer's bias in order to better evaluate his or her arguments and ideas. Look at these examples from Reading 1. They show some techniques that writers use to influence readers.

1. Choosing descriptive language and vocabulary that states or implies the author's bias (It is not necessarily supported with facts, examples, etc.)

   The food we consume makes all of these things possible, but **not all food is created equal**. (paragraph 1)

   [Pollan] offers some **simple, yet practical** tips for eating well and staying healthy. (paragraph 4)

2. Expressing direct criticism of the opposing point of view

   Our food needs to be **defended against "needless complications"** from "nutrition science and from the food industry." (paragraph 4)

3. Using adverbs like *in fact*, *in reality*, and *indeed* to emphasize particular points

   **In fact**, different research about the same food often produces contradictory results. (paragraph 2)

4. Claiming that the reader shares the author's bias by using pronouns like *we* and *our*.

   Because **our** food choices affect **our** health and behavior, **we** must do more than just eat; **we** must eat *well*. (paragraph 1)

A. **IDENTIFY** Read these sentences from Reading 1. Look at the words in bold. Write the number of the technique used from the Reading Skill box for each sentence. Some items have two answers.

<u>2, 4</u>     a. **We are surrounded** by information **telling us what's good for us** and what isn't, but usually **this information is more confusing than helpful**. (paragraph 2)

_____ b. Shopping for food can also be **challenging**. (paragraph 3)

_____ c. **Indeed**, many **food labels are often misleading**. (paragraph 3)

_____ d. **In reality**, though, their specific yogurt isn't preferred by doctors, but shoppers may think it is because of the food label. (paragraph 3)

_____ e. So how *do* **we make** healthy choices? (paragraph 4)

_____ f. According to Pollan, **we** need to **stop reading labels and listening to the so-called scientific experts.** (paragraph 4)

_____ g. A supermarket is also full of items like instant noodles, diet sodas, and similar products—**the ones that aren't good for us**. (paragraph 6)

_____ h. The food [at a farmers' market or a local store] is **fresher and healthier**. (paragraph 6)

**TIP FOR SUCCESS**

Pay attention to a writer's tone and choice of words to decide if he or she is biased. Writers may express strong opinions. However, those opinions need to be supported with facts, reasons, and examples.

**B. IDENTIFY** These statements each contain an example of bias. Underline language that shows bias. For each sentence, write the number of the technique used from the Reading Skill box on page 130.

__2__ a. You may have read that my colleagues do not agree with me on this topic. But let me make this clear: <u>my colleagues have ignored</u> the latest research data.

_____ b. Not all fats are bad for you. In reality, some are very good for you.

_____ c. Nutrition advice can sometimes be difficult to understand.

_____ d. We are all concerned about our weight getting out of control, so let's do something about it.

_____ e. Research into nutrition has been going on for decades, but, in fact, much is still unknown about foods as simple as the carrot.

_____ f. You and I both know that candy isn't good for our teeth, so why do we continue to eat it?

_____ g. Everyone wants to eat healthily. Many food manufacturers, however, are more interested in keeping costs down than in using healthy ingredients.

_____ h. You won't believe how delicious the cheesecake is: it's an absolute dream.

**iQ** PRACTICE  Go online for more practice recognizing bias.
*Practice > Unit 5 > Activity 5*

## CRITICAL THINKING STRATEGY

### Analyzing texts for cause and effect relationships

Some texts clearly describe cause and effect relationships. In other texts, the reader must analyze the information in the text to understand potential cause and effect between the events or elements presented.

An example of this can be found in Reading 1, Exercise F (p. 129). There you completed a chart on the benefits of an urban garden. To do this, you had to analyze the connection between causes and effects to determine whether they are related.

> **Cause**: Food doesn't have to be brought to supermarkets.
>
> **Effect**: Food is fresher. (Because it doesn't have to go to the supermarket, it can be eaten sooner after it is picked.)
>
> **Not an effect**: Children learn how to plant and grow vegetables. (This is true for programs aimed toward children, but it is not an effect of food not going to supermarkets. The two are not directly related.)

**iQ** PRACTICE Go online to watch the Critical Thinking Skill Video and check your comprehension. *Practice > Unit 5 > Activity 6*

C. **ANALYZE** Reread paragraphs 6, 7, and 8 of Reading 1. Consider the causes and the possible effects. Check *yes* (✓) if they are related and *no* (✓) if they are not. Use the information in the article and your own experience. Then compare answers with a partner and give reasons.

1. **Paragraph 6** Cause: shopping at a small local farmers' market instead of a large supermarket

   a. ☐ yes  ☐ no  Effect: eating fresher food

   b. ☐ yes  ☐ no  Effect: saving money

   c. ☐ yes  ☐ no  Effect: sharing a meal with others

2. **Paragraph 7** Cause: learning to cook

   a. ☐ yes  ☐ no  Effect: improving physical fitness

   b. ☐ yes  ☐ no  Effect: eating well

   c. ☐ yes  ☐ no  Effect: spending more money on food

3. **Paragraph 8** Cause: planting and growing a garden

   a. ☐ yes  ☐ no  Effect: learning how to read labels on food packages

   b. ☐ yes  ☐ no  Effect: getting exercise

   c. ☐ yes  ☐ no  Effect: learning how to grow plants

# A Personalized Nutrition Company Will Use Your DNA to Tell You What to Eat

**OBJECTIVE ▶**

You are going to read an article by Claire Maldarelli for the science magazine *Popular Science*. The article looks at about how science may influence your diet by using your own DNA. Use the article to gather information and ideas for your Unit Assignment.

## PREVIEW THE READING

**A. PREVIEW** Read the first paragraph. Answer these questions.

1. What is the name of the personalized nutrition company?

   _____

2. What does it offer? _____

   _____

3. Who is it targeting? _____

   _____

4. Why do the targeted people need help? _____

   _____

**B. QUICK WRITE** What could be an advantage to using people's DNA to determine what they should eat? What could be a disadvantage? Would you use such a service? Why or why not? Write for 5–10 minutes in response. Remember to use this section for your Unit Assignment.

**C. VOCABULARY** Check (✓) the words you know. Use a dictionary to define any new or unknown words. Then discuss with a partner how the words will relate to the unit.

| | |
|---|---|
| beverage *(n.)* | metabolize *(v.)* |
| complexity *(n.)* ₤+ OPAL | physician *(n.)* ₤+ |
| follow through with *(v. phr.)* | promising *(adj.)* ₤+ |
| genetic *(adj.)* ₤+ | series *(n.)* ₤+ OPAL |
| ingest *(v.)* | thus *(adv.)* ₤+ OPAL |
| initial *(adj.)* ₤+ OPAL | variation *(n.)* ₤+ OPAL |

₤+ Oxford 5000™ words                    OPAL Oxford Phrasal Academic Lexicon

**iQ PRACTICE** Go online to listen and practice your pronunciation.
*Practice > Unit 5 > Activity 7*

# WORK WITH THE READING

 **A.** **INVESTIGATE** Read the article and gather information about how science influences what we eat.

## A Personalized Nutrition[1] Company Will Use Your DNA[2] to Tell You What to Eat

### IS A DIET BASED ON YOUR GENOME[3] THE FUTURE OF NUTRITION?

By Claire Maldarelli *October 25, 2016*

1    Dieting in the United States is a multi-million-dollar industry. Over the past few decades, there have been diets that focus on increasing protein, eliminating fats, lowering calories—you name the food group, a diet fad has been centered around it. It's clear that Americans want to lose weight, but we are far from mastering the art. A California-based company is working to get at the root cause of why it believes diets fail: none of them focus on the dieter's unique **genetic** makeup. Habit's "personalized nutrition" program would analyze a person's DNA to create an individualized food plan and deliver those ingredients to the user's home.

2    A main focus behind any diet plan that focuses on weight loss is to decrease the number of calories a person **ingests**. But a growing body of research suggests that one of the reasons diets often fail is that the same foods can affect people in incredibly different ways. The same meal provides more calories for some and fewer

for others. It can spike[4] glucose[5] levels at varying degrees depending on the individual. For these reasons, it's hard to create a diet that will work for everyone. That's why many scientists are turning to the idea of personalized nutrition or nutrigenomics: analyzing our DNA to figure out what foods will make us healthiest.

3    "We have always taken a one-size-fits-all approach to dieting, and most [dieters] try and fail," says Alan Greene, a pediatrician and **physician**-advisor to Habit. He says we need to understand the **complexities** of our biologies first and figure out what fits these best. This will lead to success in an industry that has most often failed.

4    It's hard to create a diet that will work for everyone. Habit plans to use genetic markers to identify your ideal meal and send that meal directly to your door. Customers receive a blood sample kit. After a DIY[6] finger prick[7], you send your blood samples to a lab. They are used to

---

[1] **nutrition:** the process by which living things receive the food necessary for them to grow and be healthy

[2] **DNA:** the abbreviation for deoxyribonucleic acid (the chemical in the cells of animals and plants that carries genetic information)

[3] **genome:** the complete set of genes in a cell or living thing

[4] **spike:** to make something rise quickly and reach a high level

[5] **glucose:** a simple type of sugar that is an important energy source in living things

[6] **DIY:** Do It Yourself

[7] **prick:** to make a small hole in the skin so that blood comes out

identify a **series** of biomarkers that look for genetic **variations** in your DNA that affect how you break down and **metabolize** foods.

5   Customers are also sent a drink called a *metabolic challenge* meant to represent a typical American diet. The drink is a cocktail of fats, sugars, and carbohydrates that "challenges the system." After consumers drink the **beverage**, they take another series of blood samples. These test their blood sugar and lipid levels to see how well their bodies withstand the fat and sugar. Finally, consumers provide a series of body metrics like height, weight, and waist circumference. They also provide lifestyle habits, like how often they walk, run, or exercise. All of this analysis leads to a personalized meal plan that works best for the user's body.

6   Habit will likely be the first personalized direct-to-consumer complete nutrition program. It will suggest foods not based on calories, nutrient-type, or quantity, but on how customers' own personal genetic makeup responds to food. It will provide them with food deliveries, follow-up testing, and nutrition coaches. For example, some consumers (those lucky few) could be advised that their bodies process carbohydrates best. Others could be told that they are something called a *protein seeker*. They would **thus** benefit from a diet high in protein and low in carbohydrates and fat, as their bodies have a harder time processing those sugars and refined carbohydrates. Others may find they are particularly fast metabolizers and need to eat more calories than most people.

7   Scientists are still attempting to uncover all the factors that influence how we digest and metabolize food. In a 2015 study in the journal *Cell*, researchers gave 800 people the exact same meal and then tested their glucose levels soon after. They found that despite the meals being identical, the glucose levels among the group varied drastically. This was true not only for foods high in sugar like ice cream but also in foods with lower glycemic indexes[8], like whole-grain bread. This study also found that a genetics-based personal meal plan helped to decrease post-meal glucose levels overall.

8   Other studies have found similar results, and the idea of personalized nutrition is currently a large area of research. However, doing this kind of testing is quite expensive. Habit's CEO, Neil Grimmer, wanted to change this. His goal for Habit was to make this kind of service affordable for everyone. Habit currently costs $299 for the **initial** testing, diet recommendations, and a coaching session with a nutritionist. Food and follow up testing is not included in the initial cost.

9   Still, Habit is in its early stages, and in a similar light, researchers are still attempting to uncover all the factors that influence how we digest and metabolize food. Because of this, the Academy of Nutrition and Dietetics does not recommend nutrigenetic testing as a means of providing dietary advice. The Academy argues that it does not have enough evidence-based studies to prove effectiveness.

10   Studies also show that the gut microbiome[9] could have a significant effect on how we break down foods, as well as what nutrients and calories we extract from them. Further, depending on what a person eats, the gut microbiome can change. This potentially alters what might be suggested as the best food for that person's body. Habit doesn't currently analyze a consumer's microbiome or take that into account.

11   For now, the research alone on personalized nutrition and nutrigenomics makes Habit seem **promising** as an idea if the science follows through. It remains to be seen whether consumers will enjoy, and **follow through with**, the foods that they are *meant* to eat. Perhaps Habit, with its consumer-focused approach, will achieve what Hippocrates lectured long ago: "Let food be thy[10] medicine and medicine be thy food."

[8] **glycemic index:** a system for measuring the effect of foods containing carbohydrates on the level of sugar in the blood. Food with a low glycemic index has less effect on the sugar in the blood.

[9] **gut microbiome:** the collection of microbes that live in the human intestine. Gut microbiomes are unique to individuals.

[10] **thy:** an old form of *your*

**B. VOCABULARY** Here are some words from Reading 2. Read the sentences. Circle the answer that best matches the meaning of each bold word.

1. Scientists may use your body's **genetic** information to develop a diet for you.

    a. common, everyday          b. related to physical characteristics

2. To have enough energy, an athlete typically **ingests** a lot of calories in a day.

    a. eats, takes in          b. uses, burns

3. The company uses a **physician** to give health advice to workers.

    a. a medical doctor          b. someone who studies physics

4. We have a basic understanding of the **complexities** of the human body.

    a. aspects of someone's appearance          b. many parts working together

5. There is a **series** of steps that make up the process.

    a. events that are very important          b. events that happen one after another

6. You can observe many physical **variations** across a group of people; no two people are exactly the same.

    a. differences          b. disagreements

7. The gastroenterologists want to know how fast the study participants **metabolize** their food.

    a. turn into energy, cells, etc.          b. prepare and eat

8. The diets are based on a person's genetics and **thus** have been successful.

    a. also          b. because of this

9. The dieters take some **initial** tests before they start the program.

    a. happening at the beginning          b. not very difficult

10. At the restaurant, before we ordered our food, we each ordered a **beverage**.

    a. menu          b. type of drink

11. The research seems **promising**; we hope the diet will work.

    a. showing signs of being successful    b. showing signs of existing together

12. After dieters receive their results, they must **follow through with** the rest of the program to be successful.

    a. come after something          b. finish something that has been started

**iQ** PRACTICE   Go online for more practice with the vocabulary.
*Practice > Unit 5 > Activity 8*

**C. EXPLAIN** Answer the questions. Then discuss your answers with a partner.

1. Why is it hard to create a diet that works for everyone?

2. How does Habit's diet plan differ from most other plans?

3. What is *nutrigenomics*?

4. The dieters submit blood samples. What information is contained in the blood samples?

5. What are two problems with personalized nutrition right now?

6. What is the purpose of this article?

**D. IDENTIFY** Check (✓) all the services that Habit offers.

☐ 1. DNA analysis

☐ 2. a personalized diet plan

☐ 3. supplies for taking blood samples

☐ 4. cookbooks that fit the recommended diet

☐ 5. food that fits the recommended diet

☐ 6. counseling on dieting

☐ 7. microbiome analysis

**E. EXPLAIN** Answer the questions. Use information from Reading 2 and your own experience.

1. In paragraph 2, the article says, "A main focus behind any diet plan that focuses on weight loss is to decrease the number of calories a person ingests." Why do diet plans usually focus on calories?

_____

_____

2. In paragraph 3, the article says that understanding our biologies will lead to "... success in an industry that has most often failed." If dieters do not lose weight, is that the fault of the dieter, the diet industry, both, or neither? Why?

_____

_____

3. In paragraph 5, the article says, "Customers are also sent a drink called a *metabolic challenge* meant to represent a typical American diet." Why is this drink part of the analysis to determine an appropriate diet?

_____

_____

4. In paragraph 5, the article says, consumers "provide lifestyle habits, like how often they walk, run, or exercise." If the analysis is based on genetics, why do dieters provide this information?

_____

_____

5. In paragraph 10, the article says, "... depending on what a person eats, the gut microbiome can change. This potentially alters what might be suggested as the best food for that person's body." What does that imply about the product Habit has created?

_____

_____

# WORK WITH THE VIDEO

**A. PREVIEW** Do you take vitamins? Why? Why not?

**iQ** RESOURCES  Go online to watch the video about vitamin deficiencies and how in 1921, Dr. Joseph Goldberger, a physician and epidemiologist, proved a direct link between vitamins and health. *Resources › Video › Unit 5 › Unit Video*

## VIDEO VOCABULARY

**vitamin (n.)** a natural substance found in food that is essential for growing and staying healthy

**deficiency (n.)** a state of not having enough of something essential

**devastating (adj.)** causing a lot of damage and destruction

**rash (n.)** area of red spots on a person's skin, caused by an illness or a reaction to something

**infectious (adj.)** having the possibility of being passed easily from one person to another

**eradicate (v.)** to destroy or get rid of something completely, especially something bad

**B. COMPOSE** Watch the video two or three times. Take notes in the chart.

|  | Vitamin deficiency / disease | Symptoms | Additional information |
|---|---|---|---|
| Notes from the video |  |  |  |

**C. EXTEND** Why did Dr. Goldberger think pellagra wasn't an infectious disease? What are other benefits of having vitamins C, D, and B3 in our diet? Can you give an example of another vitamin that helps us stay healthy? Discuss your ideas with a partner.

# ? WRITE WHAT YOU THINK

**SYNTHESIZE** Think about Reading 1, Reading 2, and the unit video as you discuss these questions. Then choose one question and write a paragraph of 5–7 sentences in response.

1. What do you think Michael Pollan (Reading 1, p. 125–126) would say about genetic-based diets? What do you think he would say about adding vitamins to foods? Why?

2. Based on what you have read and heard about science and food, has science gone too far? Or are the changes for the best?

3. Which of the three—Reading 1, Reading 2, or the unit video—do you think is the most objective? Explain your answer.

## VOCABULARY SKILL  Cause and effect collocations

Many different collocations with prepositions are used to express cause and effect. Recognizing these phrases will help you understand how these ideas are related.

Some collocations are used when the cause is the subject of the sentence.

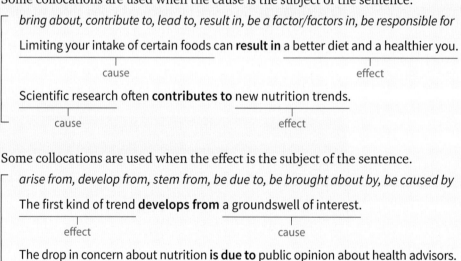

*bring about, contribute to, lead to, result in, be a factor/factors in, be responsible for*

Limiting your intake of certain foods can **result in** a better diet and a healthier you.
cause — effect

Scientific research often **contributes to** new nutrition trends.
cause — effect

Some collocations are used when the effect is the subject of the sentence.

*arise from, develop from, stem from, be due to, be brought about by, be caused by*

The first kind of trend **develops from** a groundswell of interest.
effect — cause

The drop in concern about nutrition **is due to** public opinion about health advisors.
effect — cause

**A. APPLY** In these sentences, the cause is the subject. Use a different collocation from the Vocabulary Skill box to complete each sentence. Use the correct form.

1. Tiredness and stress _are responsible for_____ many traffic accidents.

2. Greenhouse gases _____ global warming.

3. A good diet _____ excellent health.

4. Poverty _____ much of the crime in our society.

5. Eric's carelessness _____ his injury.

6. The poor economy _____ the failure of the company last year.

**B. APPLY** In these sentences, the effect is the subject. Use a different collocation from the Vocabulary Skill box to complete each sentence. Use the correct form.

1. Sylvie's good health _is due to_____ her excellent eating habits.

2. The hotel fire _____ an electrical problem.

3. My fight with my brother _____ a misunderstanding.

4. The high price of gas _____ a petroleum shortage.

5. The success of the book _____ the action-packed plot.

6. Harry's love of history _____ a childhood trip to the museum.

**C. COMPOSE** Work with a partner. Write six cause and effect sentences of your own: three with the cause as subject and three with the effect as subject. Use a different collocation in each sentence.

**Cause as subject**

1. _A sedentary lifestyle can lead to weight gain._

2. _____

3. _____

**Effect as subject**

1. _____

2. _____

3. _____

**iQ** PRACTICE Go online for more practice with cause and effect collocations.
*Practice > Unit 5 > Activity 9*

# WRITING

At the end of this unit, you will write a cause and effect essay about the positive or negative effects of science on the food we eat. This essay will include specific information from the readings, the unit video, and your own ideas.

## WRITING SKILL   Writing a cause and effect essay

A **cause and effect essay** examines the **reasons (causes)** an event, situation, or action occurs or the **results (effects)** of an event, situation, or action. There are many ways to structure a cause and effect essay.

**One effect with several causes**

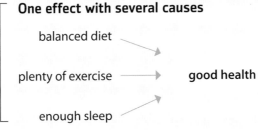

**One cause with several effects**

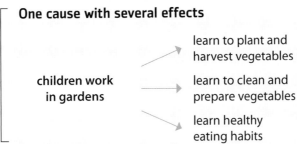

### Organization

- The introduction describes the event, situation, or action that you are examining. It includes the thesis statement. The thesis states the cause(s) and effect(s) you will examine or gives your opinion.

- Each body paragraph examines a cause or effect that you have chosen and provides supporting information, such as facts, examples, and descriptions. A strong body paragraph contains one main point and at least two pieces of information to support it.

- The conclusion summarizes the cause(s) and effect(s) discussed. It may also predict what will happen in the future or give advice.

**A. WRITING MODEL** Read the model cause and effect essay. Then answer the questions that follow.

## Why Do Weight-Loss Diets Fail?

1    The popularity of diet crazes over the last 30 years shows that many of us think we are overweight. It also suggests that we want to do something about it. Diet books with the latest scientific advice become bestsellers, and yet we continue to gain weight. Who's responsible? It's easy to blame scientific experts, but in my view, the problem is often with us, the dieters. We can't lose weight because of the way we think about food.

2    If we cannot follow a plan every day, no diet book can help. Many dieters change from one type of diet to another, so they never allow their bodies to get into a healthy rhythm. Others start out strongly on a program and lose a few pounds. Then when their weight stays the same for a few weeks, they become discouraged and lose their self-control. If the weight doesn't go away quickly, they give up.

3    But the number on the scale is not our only challenge. Modern life is so fast and stressful that many diets are ruined by "comfort eating." When we feel down, we want a slice of cheesecake or a chocolate brownie with ice cream to make us feel better. We use food as an escape. On the other hand, some of us use food as a reward. If we've done something well, we think we "deserve it."

4    We also need to pay attention to the food we eat. We should read food labels carefully and remember that we are often misled by them. Although a food package may say "low-fat," manufacturers sometimes replace the fat with carbohydrates, sugar, and other fattening substances. In addition, they may not take out much of the fat. Low-fat ice cream can have 70 percent of the fat of regular ice cream, so a scoop and a half of low-fat ice cream is more fattening than one scoop of regular.

5    These are just a few of the reasons why our diets fail, but they all arise from our state of mind and our ability to pay attention. The next time you reach for the cookie jar, remember: control your mind and you can control your body! The most important factor in losing weight is in our heads.

**ACADEMIC LANGUAGE**

The phrase *on the other hand* is often used in academic writing to introduce a contrasting point.

**OPAL**
Oxford Phrasal Academic Lexicon

1. Does the essay focus on the causes or the effects of diet failure?

   _____

2. What kind of information is used to support the thesis statement?

   _____

3. Why does the author think weight-loss diets fail?

   _____

   _____

**B. CATEGORIZE** Complete the outline of the essay on page 144. You do not have to use the writer's exact words.

   I.  Thesis statement: _____

     _____

  II.  Cause 1: _People don't follow the plan._____

      A.   Support 1: _____

      B.   Support 2: _____

 III.  Cause 2: _____

      A.   Support 1: _____

      B.   Support 2: _We use food as a reward._____

 IV.  Cause 3: _____

      A.   Support 1: _Low-fat foods may contain other fattening substances._

      B.   Support 2: _____

   V.  Concluding advice: _____

     _____

**C. CREATE** Write three causes and three effects for each topic below. Use your own ideas. Then determine whether the causes or the effects would make a better essay for each topic.

1.

   _____   ⟩ **good nutrition** ⟨   _____

2.

   _____   ⟩ **safe food** ⟨   _____

3.

   _____   ⟩ **enough food for all** ⟨   _____

## From Science to Common Sense

Citrus fruit prevents scurvy.

1    It is easy to say "less science, more common sense," but it is good to remember that our common sense is based on science. "What everyone knows" at one time was not common knowledge, and it was science that brought these ideas to light. Specifically, science has had huge effects on nutrition as well as on the safety and quantity of available food.

2    For one, common sense says that we need a variety of foods for a healthy diet, but it was science that found the link between our diet and nutritional deficit diseases. We can eat citrus fruit for the vitamin C that our bodies need to fight the disease called *scurvy*. We know, too, because of the efforts of science, that too much sugar or salt can cause health problems, and we are constantly looking at our food for ways that diet can improve our health.

3    Also, food safety has been greatly increased by science. We know that bacteria and other microbes can get into our food and make us sick, but it took Louis Pasteur in 1859 to prove that microbes could come from the air, not arise spontaneously from food. The process that he developed, known as pasteurization, has prevented many cases of food-caused illness, and because of science, we know more techniques to protect ourselves: refrigeration, washing our hands, and covering food to keep flies off it. These techniques might not seem like science, but it is science that showed the link between these practices and prevention of food-related illness.

4    Finally, having enough to eat has long been affected by science in many ways. Domesticating animals and plants, the beginning of agricultural science, started thousands of years ago and laid the foundations of having readily available food. Through the understanding of how to increase yields, discourage pests, and store food—all aspects of science—we have been able to provide enough food to feed our ever-growing population. In addition, science has increased our knowledge of mechanical forces so that we can transport food faster and for longer distances than ever before, thus increasing the variety and amount of available food.

5    Science has had an enormous effect on the food that we eat and in educating us about nutrition, keeping our food safe, and making it possible to have enough so that many people don't ever go hungry. We have not yet solved all of our food issues, but with science, we have a good chance of doing so.

1. Does the essay focus on causes or effects? _____

2. What kind of information is used to support the thesis statement?

   _____

   _____

3. What is a specific example that supports the thesis?

   _____

**iQ** PRACTICE   Go online for more practice writing a cause and effect essay.
*Practice ▸ Unit 5 ▸ Activity 10*

**iQ** PRACTICE   Go online for more practice writing a cause and effect essay.
*Practice ▸ Unit 5 ▸ Activity 10*

## GRAMMAR  Agents with the passive voice

In an active sentence, the subject is the **agent**—the person or thing that performs the action of the verb. In a passive sentence, the subject is the **receiver**—the person or thing that is affected by the action of the verb. The passive is formed with **be + past participle**. In a passive sentence, the agent is optional. If it is included, it follows the preposition *by*.

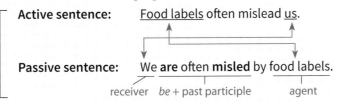

**Active sentence:**   Food labels often mislead us.

**Passive sentence:**   We **are** often **misled** by food labels.

receiver   *be* + past participle   agent

Most passive sentences do not include the agent because it is obvious or unnecessary.

Fruits and vegetables **are** usually **picked** ~~by people~~ when they are freshest.

People **were encouraged** ~~by experts~~ to eliminate eggs from their diets.

The passive is used with *by* + an agent to:

- complete the meaning of a sentence

  Many new trends **are promoted** <u>by the media</u>.

  Many diets **are ruined** <u>by "comfort eating."</u>

- give new, important, or surprising information

  The diet plan **was recommended** to me <u>by my doctor</u>.

  The apples **are picked** early in July <u>by machines</u>.

**iQ** RESOURCES   Go online to watch the Grammar Skill Video.
*Resources ▸ Video ▸ Unit 5 ▸ Grammar Skill Video*

**iQ** RESOURCES   Go online to watch the Grammar Skill Video.
*Resources ▸ Video ▸ Unit 5 ▸ Grammar Skill Video*

**A. IDENTIFY** Read these passive sentences. Check (✓) the sentence if the agent is necessary. If the agent is not necessary, cross it out.

☐ 1. I'm sorry, sir. All the cookies have been sold ~~by a salesclerk~~.

☐ 2. At the charity dinner, everything will be cooked by a famous chef.

☐ 3. We don't order pizza from that place anymore: it's always delivered cold by the delivery person.

☐ 4. That restaurant is far away. The food is delivered by a man on a motorcycle.

☐ 5. Karen got sick at the restaurant and was examined by a medical student.

☐ 6. My friend is going to the doctor's office and will be examined by the doctor at 10:30 a.m.

☐ 7. The professor was honored by the university for her achievements.

☐ 8. The documentary was watched by a TV audience of millions.

☐ 9. Our ideas about nutrition can be influenced by marketing.

☐10. Because my brother can never make up his mind, he is easily influenced by people.

**B. APPLY** Read these passive sentences. If the sentence is complete without an agent, add a period. If an agent is necessary to complete the meaning, add an appropriate agent.

**TIP FOR SUCCESS**

Only include the agent when it is specific. You do not usually write *by someone*, *by people*, etc.

1. That picnic table is going to be repainted _____

2. At my favorite restaurant, all the food is prepared _____

3. My treadmill is being repaired _____

4. The marathon runner was taken to the hospital _____

5. Many famous authors are influenced _____

6. I was trying to get to sleep, but I was disturbed _____

7. Everyone was shocked when the clinic was broken into _____

8. After the author's death, his last cookbook was finished _____

**iQ RESOURCES** Go online for more practice with agents with the passive voice. *Practice > Unit 5 > Activities 11–12*

## UNIT ASSIGNMENT
## OBJECTIVE ▶

### Write a cause and effect essay

In this assignment, you are going to write a five-paragraph cause and effect essay about the positive or negative effects of science on the food we eat. As you prepare your essay, think about the Unit Question, "Should science influence what we eat?" Use information from Reading 1, Reading 2, the unit video, and your work in this unit to support your essay. Refer to the Self-Assessment checklist on page 150.

**iQ** PRACTICE  Go online to the Writing Tutor to read a model cause and effect essay. *Practice ▸ Unit 5 ▸ Activity 13*

## PLAN AND WRITE

**A. BRAINSTORM** Follow these steps to help you organize your ideas.

1. Work with a partner. Brainstorm the positive and negative effects that science has had on food. Write them in the chart. Include ideas from the readings, the unit video, and your own ideas.

| Effects of science on food | |
| --- | --- |
| **Positive effects** | **Negative effects** |
| Food is safer. | Too many choices in supermarkets can be confusing. |

2. Compare the positive and negative effects. Decide whether you think science has had a positive or negative effect on the food we eat.

**WRITING TIP**
Your essay must have unity, so choose only the effects that support your thesis statement.

**B. PLAN** Follow these steps to plan your essay.

1. Look at your ideas from Activity A. Decide whether the subject of your cause and effect essay is positive or negative effects.

2. Choose three main effects to write about from the chart in question 1 in Activity A.

**iQ** RESOURCES  Go online to download and complete the outline for your cause and effect essay. *Resources ▸ Writing Tools ▸ Unit 5 ▸ Outline*

**C. WRITE** Use your planning notes to write your essay.

1. Write your essay on the positive or negative effects of science on the food we eat. Be sure to include an introduction with a thesis statement, three body paragraphs, and a conclusion.

2. Look at the Self-Assessment checklist below to guide your writing.

**iQ** PRACTICE Go online to the Writing Tutor to write your assignment.
*Practice > Unit 5 > Activity 14*

# REVISE AND EDIT

**iQ** RESOURCES Go online to download the peer review worksheet.
*Resources > Writing Tools > Unit 5 > Peer Review Worksheet*

**A. PEER REVIEW** Read your partner's essay. Then use the peer review worksheet. Discuss the review with your partner.

**B. REWRITE** Based on your partner's review, revise and rewrite your essay.

**C. EDIT** Complete the Self-Assessment checklist as you prepare to write the final draft of your essay. Be prepared to hand in your work or discuss it in class.

| SELF-ASSESSMENT | Yes | No |
|---|---|---|
| Does the essay clearly describe three effects of science on the food we eat? | ☐ | ☐ |
| Does the essay contain an introduction, three body paragraphs, and a conclusion? | ☐ | ☐ |
| Are passive verbs used correctly? Are agents included and omitted appropriately? | ☐ | ☐ |
| Does the essay use cause and effect collocations appropriately? | ☐ | ☐ |
| Does the essay include vocabulary from the unit? | ☐ | ☐ |
| Did you check the essay for punctuation, spelling, and grammar? | ☐ | ☐ |

**D. REFLECT** Discuss these questions with a partner or group.

1. What is something new you learned in this unit?

2. Look back at the Unit Question—Should science influence what we eat? Is your answer different now than when you started the unit? If yes, how is it different? Why?

**iQ** PRACTICE Go to the online discussion board to discuss the questions.
*Practice > Unit 5 > Activity 15*

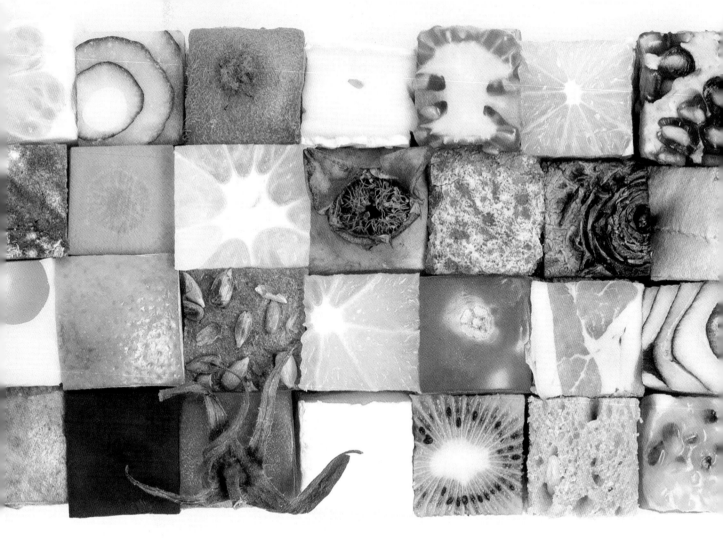

# TRACK YOUR SUCCESS

**iQ** PRACTICE  Go online to check the words and phrases you have learned in this unit. *Practice > Unit 5 > Activity 16*

Check (✓) the skills and strategies you learned. If you need more work on a skill, refer to the page(s) in parentheses.

| | |
|---|---|
| READING | ☐ I can recognize a writer's bias. (p. 130) |
| CRITICAL THINKING | ☐ I can analyze a text for cause and effect relationships. (p. 132) |
| VOCABULARY | ☐ I can identify and use cause and effect collocations. (p. 140) |
| WRITING | ☐ I can write a cause and effect essay. (p. 143) |
| GRAMMAR | ☐ I can use agents appropriately with the passive voice. (p. 147) |
| OBJECTIVE ▶ | ☐ I can gather information and ideas to write a cause and effect essay about the effects of science on the food we eat. |

# Education

| | |
|---|---|
| CRITICAL THINKING | justifying your opinions |
| READING | using an outline |
| VOCABULARY | word forms |
| GRAMMAR | reported speech with the present tense and shifting tenses |
| WRITING | writing a summary |

# Does school prepare you for work?

**A.** Discuss these questions with your classmates.

1. What skills and abilities do students learn in school that can help them in their careers?

2. What or who helps students prepare for adult life the most? School? Culture? Parents?

3. Look at the photo. What type of work are the people preparing to do? What skills are they learning?

**B.** Listen to *The Q Classroom* online. Then answer these questions.

1. In Sophy's opinion, how does writing essays and studying algebra prepare you for work?

2. In what ways does Yuna say work is different from school? Do you think school is preparing you for work? Why or why not?

**iQ PRACTICE** Go to the online discussion board to discuss the Unit Question with your classmates. *Practice > Unit 6 > Activity 1*

**UNIT OBJECTIVE** ▶ Read a magazine article and a blog post. Gather information and ideas to summarize a text.

## READING 1

# From Student to Employee: A Difficult Transition

**OBJECTIVE ▶**

You are going to read a magazine article that examines the transition from student to employee. Use the article to gather information and ideas for your Unit Assignment.

## PREVIEW THE READING

**A. PREVIEW** For many people, getting their first full-time job after graduating from school is an important turning point: it is the beginning of one's adult life. Read the title of the article and look at the picture. What is the author's opinion about students getting their first job after graduation?

_____

_____

**B. QUICK WRITE** Can you think of reasons for the author's opinion about students getting their first job after graduation? Write for 5–10 minutes in response. Be sure to use this section for your Unit Assignment.

**C. VOCABULARY** Check (✓) the words you know. Then work with a partner to locate each word in the reading. Use clues to help define the words you don't know. Check your definitions in the dictionary.

| | |
|---|---|
| adjust *(v.)* 🔑+ OPAL | expertise *(n.)* 🔑+ OPAL |
| ambiguous *(adj.)* | fixed *(adj.)* 🔑+ |
| analyze *(v.)* 🔑+ | interpret *(v.)* 🔑+ OPAL |
| anticipate *(v.)* 🔑+ | pattern *(n.)* 🔑+ OPAL |
| collaborative *(adj.)* | predictable *(adj.)* 🔑+ |
| constant *(adj.)* 🔑+ OPAL | transition *(n.)* 🔑+ OPAL |

🔑+ Oxford 5000™ words          OPAL Oxford Phrasal Academic Lexicon

**iQ PRACTICE** Go online to listen and practice your pronunciation.
*Practice › Unit 6 › Activity 2*

# WORK WITH THE READING

 **A. INVESTIGATE** Read the article and gather information about whether or not school prepares you for work.

# From Student to Employee:
## A Difficult Transition

by Mina Alonso

Many recent graduates struggle in the workplace.

1   It is a chilly January morning on the campus of San Jose State University, and the start of a new term. Twenty-two-year-old Ryan Adams is walking with some friends to their first class. Ryan is beginning his final semester as a college student; at the end of May, he will graduate with a degree in finance[1]. Even though graduation is a few months away, Ryan is already working on a résumé and plans to start applying for jobs in April. He is both excited and a little nervous about making the **transition** from student to full-time employee. "I'm hoping to have a job by the summer," he explains. "You know, it'll be good to finally get out into the working world. On the other hand, it'll be the first real job I've ever had, and that's a little scary."

2   By the time Ryan graduates, he will have spent four years in college and a total of 16 years of his life in school. Like many students, Ryan believes that the time and money spent on his education will pay off[2]: he will eventually be able to get a good job and do well in the field he has chosen. And yet, in spite of all of the years spent in school preparing to enter the workplace, many recent graduates say that they struggle with the transition from classroom to career world and have difficulty **adjusting** to life on the job.

3   Writer and editor Joseph Lewis, who blogs for the website WorkAwesome.com, suggests one reason why this is the case. Lewis believes that most of our school experiences—from childhood through university—are fairly **predictable**, while life in the working world is far more **ambiguous**. In school, for example, the **pattern** stays more or less the same from year to year. All students have to take a **fixed** number of classes each year, and in those classes, they have to do certain things to succeed: study assigned material, do homework, and take and pass tests. In the workplace, however, **constant** change is the norm, and one has to adapt quickly. A project you are working on this month might suddenly change next month—or next week—and it's often hard to **anticipate** what you'll be doing 6–12 months from now. Life in the workplace can be uncertain in other ways

[1] **finance:** the management and investing of money
[2] **pay off:** to bring good results

as well. Lewis notes that in school, for example, you advance each year to the next grade, "and that change carries with it a sense[3] of progress, a sense of . . . growth and importance." In the workplace, however, "you have no idea when you might be promoted; it depends on the economy[4], on your coworkers, on your boss or clients, or a hundred other things you can't control."

4    Another problem that graduates entering the workforce encounter is that they are unprepared to think analytically. In school, many students—including those in college—spend a lot of time memorizing facts and repeating what they "learned" on tests. But in the workplace, notes the Career Services Network at Michigan State University, employees "are often expected to think critically and make decisions about their work, not just follow a supervisor's[5] instructions." An employee who is facing a problem at work, for example, needs to be able to identify different solutions, select the best course of action[6], and explain his choice to others. Less time needs to be spent in school on testing, says one recent report, and more on helping students to **analyze** and **interpret** information, solve problems, and communicate their ideas effectively—skills that will prepare them to succeed in today's workplace.

5    Finally, many recent graduates say that one of the biggest difficulties they face is adjusting to teamwork on the job. In some ways, school does prepare one for the **collaborative** nature of the workplace. Learners sit in classes every day with many other students. They must listen to others' opinions, participate at times in group discussions, and learn how to get along outside the classroom. Nevertheless, in school, a student normally works independently to complete most tasks (tests, homework, and projects) and receives a grade according to how well he or she has done. In the workplace, however, employees must regularly interact with others and are often dependent on their coworkers for their success. In other words, if an employee has to work with others to complete a given project, that employee's success not only depends on his hard work and **expertise**, but also on how well his colleagues perform. Knowing how to participate effectively in teamwork—and deal with problems when they arise—is extremely important, and yet, it is also something many students don't get enough practice with in a school setting.

6    How can we better prepare young adults for the workplace? Recent graduates, looking back on their educational experience, have some advice. Many think that all students should be required to do an internship[7] while they are in school. Volunteering part time at a company, hospital, or government organization, for example, can help one gain experience and learn skills needed to succeed in the real world. Other graduates believe that teachers should include more teamwork as part of class activities; such tasks would familiarize students with the demands of collaborating with colleagues in the workplace. Still others feel there should be more focus on developing writing and public speaking skills—abilities many employees must regularly use on the job. Pairing this kind of practical work experience with classroom instruction, say the graduates, will help prepare students for the realities of the workplace and make the transition from school to career world less stressful.

---

**ACADEMIC LANGUAGE**

The phrases *dependent on* and *depends on* are often used in academic writing.

⌐ OPAL

Oxford Phrasal Academic Lexicon

---

[3] **sense:** a feeling

[4] **economy:** the financial system of a given country or region

[5] **supervisor:** a boss or manager

[6] **course of action:** a plan

[7] **internship:** a job or training program, often done without pay, to gain practical work experience

**B. VOCABULARY** Here are some words from Reading 1. Read the sentences. Circle the answer that best matches the meaning of each bold word.

1. Making the **transition** from student to full-time employee won't be easy, but you'll do fine.

   a. effort       b. goal       c. change

2. After the long summer vacation, it's hard to **adjust** to working in an office again.

   a. apply       b. leave       c. adapt

3. His job responsibilities have always been **ambiguous**. No one is really sure what he does.

   a. certain       b. unclear       c. helpful

4. Most people's lives follow a typical **pattern**: they graduate from school, get a job, and eventually get their own apartment.

   a. belief       b. order       c. behavior

5. In this job, you'll work a **fixed** number of hours: 8:00 to 5:30, Monday to Friday.

   a. flexible       b. short       c. certain

6. It's hard to study with **constant** interruptions every five minutes.

   a. occasional       b. frequent       c. brief

7. I knew getting a job would be hard, but I didn't **anticipate** that it would take six months.

   a. wish       b. hope       c. expect

8. The result of the election was **predictable**—polls had shown the voters supported him.

   a. expected       b. likeable       c. biased

9. Please **analyze** the information in the report carefully.

   a. skim       b. question       c. examine

10. How do you **interpret** the ending of that story? I didn't really understand it.

    a. explain       b. like       c. tell

11. The project was a **collaborative** effort; we all worked on it together.

    a. shared       b. difficult       c. unlikely

12. His **expertise** is in international banking. He's been in the field for almost 25 years.

    a. unusual habit       b. special skill       c. favorite hobby

**iQ** PRACTICE Go online for more practice with the vocabulary.
*Practice > Unit 6 > Activity 3*

**C. IDENTIFY** Circle the correct answer.

1. Which statement best describes the problem discussed in the article?

   a. Many recent graduates are bored by the jobs available to them.

   b. It's difficult for many recent graduates to find good jobs.

   c. Many graduates aren't ready for today's workplace challenges.

2. What is mainly responsible for this problem?

   a. students' performance in school

   b. employers' hiring practices

   c. schools' methods of instruction

3. Look at paragraphs 3–5. A good heading for this section would be ____.

   a. Three Ways Educators and Employers Can Work Together

   b. Difficulties Graduates Experience in the Workplace

   c. The Workplace: Yesterday, Today, and Tomorrow

4. Paragraphs 3–5 describe how school experiences ____ life in the workplace.

   a. are different from

   b. help us with

   c. are similar to

5. According to the article, which skills are essential in today's workplace?

   a. being able to solve problems and contribute to a team

   b. remembering facts quickly and working well independently

   c. speaking a second language and being able to work long hours

6. The purpose of paragraph 6 is to ____ the problem discussed in the article.

   a. describe how graduates have overcome

   b. suggest ways of solving

   c. criticize society for contributing to

**D. EXPLAIN** Answer these questions.

1. In paragraph 1, how does the writer introduce the topic? What do you think is the purpose of using a quote from a student?

   _____

   _____

2. Who is cited in paragraph 3? What problem does he discuss?

   _____

   _____

3. What network is cited in paragraph 4? What problem does the network raise?

_____

_____

4. Who is cited in paragraph 6? Why are they cited?

_____

**E. SYNTHESIZE** Look back at your Quick Write on page 154. Can you think of other reasons for the author's opinion about students getting their first job after graduation? Add any new ideas you learned from the reading.

## CRITICAL THINKING STRATEGY

### Justifying your opinions

Before you express an opinion, be sure to examine your reasoning to see if it is logical and reasonable. Then **justify your opinion** by explaining your reasoning. Be as specific as possible, and use facts and other evidence to support your reason. Look at the chart.

| Opinion | Reason (Why?) |
|---|---|
| Students should participate in teamwork while in school. | It will teach them how to collaborate with colleagues in a future job. |
| Schools should prepare students to use technology. | Many companies require technical skills. |

**iQ** PRACTICE  Go online to watch the Critical Thinking Skill Video and check your comprehension. *Practice > Unit 6 > Activity 4*

**F. IDENTIFY** Read the opinion. Check (✓) the reasons that support it.

**Opinion: While in school, students should intern with companies.**

☐ 1. Schools can teach students what they need to know.

☐ 2. Employers like applicants with experience.

☐ 3. Internships are hard to arrange.

☐ 4. Experience builds confidence.

☐ 5. Companies can help students learn what is necessary to succeed at a job.

☐ 6. Students can learn firsthand what fields interest them and adjust their coursework accordingly.

☐ 7. Schools can focus more on knowledge and not specific skill sets.

**G. CREATE** Give two reasons to justify the opinion in item 1. For item 2, express an opinion based on your own school experience and justify it with two reasons.

1. Schools should do more to prepare students for the workplace.

   a. _____

   b. _____

2. Students should _____.

   a. _____

   b. _____

**iQ** PRACTICE  Go online for additional reading and comprehension.
*Practice > Unit 6 > Activity 5*

# WRITE WHAT YOU THINK

**A. DISCUSS** Discuss the questions in a group. Think about the Unit Question, "Does school prepare you for work?"

1. In paragraph 6 of Reading 1, there are several suggestions to help young adults adjust to life in the workplace. In your opinion, are the solutions useful? Which one do you think would help the most? Why?

2. What other skill(s) should schools focus on to prepare students for the workplace? Think of at least one idea and explain why you think this skill is important.

3. Rate your own school experience on a scale from 1 (poor) to 5 (excellent) in terms of how it prepared (or is preparing) you for the workplace.
   Give at least two reasons that explain your rating.

**B. SYNTHESIZE** Choose one of the questions from Activity A and write a paragraph of 5–7 sentences in response. Look back at your Quick Write on page 154 as you think about what you learned.

---

**READING SKILL** Using an outline

An **outline** can help you understand how a text is organized. It shows the relationship between the main ideas and the specific information that supports them. There are many ways to organize an outline. One common way is to use Roman numerals (I, II, III) for the main ideas and letters (A, B, C) for the supporting points.

When you outline a text, you briefly summarize the ideas using some words from the text and some of your own words. You do not always need to write complete sentences.

**A. IDENTIFY** Look back at Reading 1 and follow these steps.

1. Underline the thesis statement in the introduction (paragraphs 1–2).

2. In paragraph 3, underline the main idea and circle two supporting points.

3. Compare the sentences in the article with those in the outline below. Notice that the sentences in the outline are shorter but still focus on the key information.

**TIP FOR SUCCESS**

An outline of a reading can help you study for a test. You can look over the outline to find the main ideas and supporting points instead of rereading the whole text.

> I. Introduction (paragraphs 1–2)
>
> Thesis statement: Many recent graduates have difficulty adjusting to life on the job.
>
> II. School experiences are fairly predictable; the working world is more ambiguous. (paragraph 3)
>
> A. In school, the pattern stays mostly the same; in the workplace, constant change is the norm.
>
> B. In school, you advance each year; in the workplace, you don't know when you might be promoted.

**B. CATEGORIZE** Reread paragraphs 4–6 in Reading 1 and complete the outline for sections III, IV, and V below.

III. Recent graduates are not prepared to think analytically.

  A. In school, _____.

  B. In the workplace, _____.

  C. Schools should spend less time on _____.

  D. Schools should spend more time on _____

  _____.

IV. Many recent graduates have difficulty _____.

  A. _____

  _____

  B. _____

  _____

V. _____

  _____

  A. _____

  B. _____

  C. There should be more focus on developing writing and public speaking skills.

**C. CATEGORIZE** Use your outline from Activity B and the reading to complete the chart comparing school and the workplace.

| School | Workplace |
|---|---|
| predictable | |
| | constant change |
| | don't know when you'll be promoted |
| memorize facts and take tests | |
| | interact with others and depend on coworkers |
| receive grades on individual work | |

**iQ** PRACTICE   Go online for more practice using an outline.
*Practice › Unit 6 › Activity 6*

## READING 2    Making My First Post-College Career Decision

**OBJECTIVE ▶**

You are going to read a blog post by Devin Reams, a graduating student who is considering his work options. Use the blog post to gather information and ideas for your Unit Assignment.

## PREVIEW THE READING

**A. PREVIEW** Choosing a job is one of the most important decisions a student makes after graduation. Read the title and paragraph headings of the blog post and skim the first paragraph. Answer these questions.

1. What two career options is Devin Reams trying to decide between?

_____

2. Which one do you think he's going to choose?

_____

**B. QUICK WRITE** Consider your answer to question 2 in Activity A. Why do you think the student will make that career choice? Write for 5–10 minutes in response. Be sure to use this section for your Unit Assignment.

**C. VOCABULARY** Check (✓) the words you know. Use a dictionary to define any new or unknown words. Then discuss how the words will relate to the unit with a partner.

| | | |
|---|---|---|
| acquire *(v.)* 🗝+ OPAL | incentive *(n.)* 🗝+ | permanent *(adj.)* 🗝+ |
| approach *(v.)* 🗝+ | income *(n.)* 🗝+ | reluctant *(adj.)* 🗝+ |
| contact *(v.)* 🗝+ | institution *(n.)* 🗝+ | utilize *(v.)* 🗝+ OPAL |
| enable *(v.)* 🗝+ OPAL | particular *(adj.)* 🗝+ OPAL | |

🗝+ Oxford 5000™ words                               OPAL Oxford Phrasal Academic Lexicon

**iQ PRACTICE** Go online to listen and practice your pronunciation.
*Practice › Unit 6 › Activity 7*

# WORK WITH THE READING

**A. INVESTIGATE** Read the blog post and gather information about whether or not school prepares you for work.

Home                                                            🔍   Sign in 👤

# Making My First Post-College Career Decision
### by Devin Reams

Tuesday, April 7                                              💬 comments 16

## Going Corporate[1]

1   As college graduation **approaches** and I prepare to enter the working world, I've had a hard time deciding what I should do with my life. On the one hand, I wonder: am I an entrepreneur—the sort of innovative person who could start and grow my own business? Then at other times I think: would it be better to accept a position in a large corporation and climb the ranks[2]? As I get ready to make the transition from student to full-time employee, I find myself thinking about these questions quite often. The good news is, I think I've finally got some answers.

## From Internship to Full-Time Job

2   I've always been interested in accounting and technology, and for the past year, I've been interning at a large telecommunications company. It's been a great way for me to get some work experience and to see if this **particular** field is right for me. My internship has shown me that telecommunications isn't really the kind of work that I want to do long-term. Nevertheless, I've learned a lot about communicating, collaborating, and dealing with office politics[3] in the workplace.

[1] **going corporate:** planning to join a large company as an employee
[2] **climb the ranks:** to move upward in a company through promotions
[3] **office politics:** competition among people in the workplace

I know that I'll be able to use these skills in whatever job I do.

3    When I began my final year in college last fall, I started perusing the job postings, looking for a full-time (paying) position in accounting. At the time, I noticed job ads for all of the public accounting firms, and though I thought they were interesting, I ignored them. I assumed they were for the December graduates[4]. Was I ever mistaken! It turns out that they were postings for regular May graduates like me! When I realized my error, I quickly put together a résumé and **contacted** professors for recommendations. I eventually interviewed with several companies, and within a week, I'd gotten a job. I felt relieved; I had taken care of my future. It was November, and I wouldn't even be starting until the following July.

## Learning Is Key

4    Though I interviewed with different companies, I decided to accept a position with a large accounting firm, primarily because I'd already interned in the corporate world[5] and wanted to gain more experience working for a large **institution**. Also, compared with the telecommunications company I'd been at, accounting firms' employees tend to work fewer hours for more pay.

5    Why did I feel the need to get a job so quickly? Maybe I was anxious about earning an **income** and supporting myself after graduation, but I prefer to think I accepted the position because of what I could learn. At this point in my life, I believe that working for a large accounting firm will **enable** me to meet different people and **utilize** the skills I've **acquired** in school and during my internship. I also think it will provide me with the experience I need to grow in this field. However, once the job becomes predictable—once I stop learning and being challenged—then there won't be any **incentive** for me to continue with this company. At that point, I'll have to make some decisions about what I want to do next.

## Creating Opportunities

6    Ultimately, I see myself doing one of two things in life: becoming an executive[6] somewhere or starting something successful on my own. Do I have lofty[7] goals? Sure I do. Do I know how, when, or where I will achieve them? Not at all. For this reason, I'd rather start out at a big company and see where it leads me. Eventually, I will either develop something on my own or continue to learn and do well as an employee. In any case, I know that I'll be given many new opportunities in my job with the accounting firm, and I'll do my best to take advantage of those.

7    With all that said, I'm only 20 years old: I have time to make decisions. At this point, I'm **reluctant** to make a **permanent** career choice, and in reality, I may never make such a choice. In the end, I might become a corporate executive somewhere *and* start my own company. Whatever happens, I'm sure I'll do fine. Anyway, it's impossible to predict the future, and so for now, I just want to see how it goes with my first job out of college.

---

[4] **December graduates:** In the U.S., most students graduate in May or June, but some finish early or take an extra term and graduate in December.

[5] **the corporate world:** related to working for a large company

[6] **executive:** a senior manager in a company

[7] **lofty:** large and important

VOCABULARY
SKILL REVIEW

In Unit 5, you learned how to use collocations with prepositions to express cause and effect. Use collocations from Unit 5 to write sentences with the following words from Activity B: *incentive* and *income*.

**B. VOCABULARY** Complete the sentences with the vocabulary from Reading 2.

| | | |
|---|---|---|
| acquire (*v.*) | incentive (*n.*) | permanent (*adj.*) |
| approach (*v.*) | income (*n.*) | reluctant (*adj.*) |
| contact (*v.*) | institution (*n.*) | utilize (*v.*) |
| enable (*v.*) | particular (*adj.*) | |

1. She spends almost a third of her monthly _____ on clothes for work.

2. We'll get a $1,000 bonus if we finish the project early. That's a(n) _____ to work harder!

3. The best way to _____ Mr. Perez is by email. He checks his messages often.

4. Getting a college degree will _____ you to get a better job.

5. Tom wants to major in business, but he doesn't know what _____ type of business he is most interested in.

6. Even though Laura is unhappy, she's _____ to quit her current job until she gets a new one.

7. I had a temporary job for a year, then the company offered me a _____ position because they were so impressed with my work.

8. Ann wants a job where she'll be able to _____ her Spanish language skills.

9. As I _____ my high school graduation, there is a part of me that isn't ready to finish school.

10. Simon works for a large financial _____ in London. The company has offices worldwide.

11. The training program helps people _____ new workplace skills and get better jobs.

**iQ** PRACTICE  Go online for more practice with the vocabulary.
*Practice ⟩ Unit 6 ⟩ Activity 8*

**C. IDENTIFY** Each of these headings refers to the main idea of a paragraph in the blog. Write the correct paragraph number next to each heading. (There is one extra heading.)

____ a. A chance to grow and learn

____ b. Get that job!

____ c. Future career goals

____ d. What I like about accounting and technology

____ e. What being an intern taught me

____ f. No rush to decide

_1__ g. Graduation nerves: What do I do next?

____ h. Accounting: The right choice for me

**D. COMPOSE** Use the actions in the box to complete blogger Devin Reams's timeline below. Then write a paragraph using the ideas from the timeline to show what happened and will happen to him.

| graduate from college | start a job |
| put together résumé | reconsider employment options |
| start interning | take advantage of opportunities in job |
| get a job | |

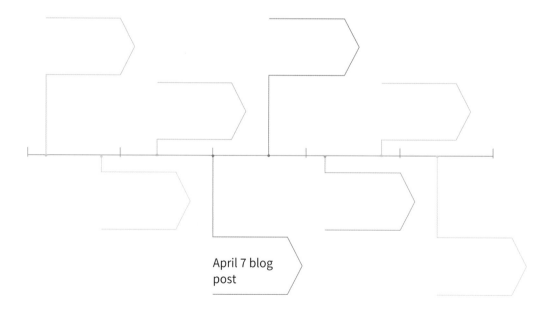

April 7 blog post

**E. CATEGORIZE** Read the statements. Write *T* (true) or *F* (false) for each statement and the paragraph number where the answer is found. Then correct each false statement to make it true according to the blog post.

____ 1. The blogger Devin Reams is interested in a career in telecommunications. (paragraph ____)

____ 2. He feels that his experience as an intern was useful. (paragraph ____)

____ 3. He plans to start working full-time in December when he graduates. (paragraph ____)

____ 4. He believes that telecommunications firms pay higher salaries than accounting firms. (paragraph ____)

____ 5. When his job is no longer challenging, he'll probably quit it and look for a new one. (paragraph ____)

____ 6. He can imagine himself in a management position at some point in the future. (paragraph ____)

____ 7. Having a steady job is Reams's goal. (paragraph ____)

____ 8. He is optimistic about the future. (paragraph ____)

**F. APPLY** The blogger Devin Reams writes about having made several decisions. Using what he writes or implies, complete the chart with each choice he made and a reason for that choice.

| Decision | Choice | Reason |
|---|---|---|
| What kind of internship did he take? | telecommunications company | to see whether he liked the field and to get experience working in a large corporation |
| When did he apply for a full-time job? | | |
| What kind of job did he accept? | | |
| What will he do when his new job becomes predictable? | | |
| When will he start his own company? | | |

**G. DISCUSS** Answer the questions with a partner.

1. What do you think of the career choices blogger Devin Reams in Reading 2 has made so far and his plans for the future? Respond to his post and explain your opinion.

2. Reams describes his career goals. What are yours? Talk about at least one goal. Explain what it is and how and when you plan to achieve it.

# WORK WITH THE VIDEO

**A. PREVIEW** Do you think it is important to have a job you love? Why or why not? What could you do to find your perfect job?

### VIDEO VOCABULARY

**art gallery (n.)** a building where paintings and other works of art are shown to the public

**cover letter (n.)** a letter introducing yourself to a potential employer

**nerve-racking (adj.)** making you feel very nervous and worried

**thoroughly (adv.)** completely and with great attention to detail

**iQ RESOURCES** Go online to watch the video about a recent college graduate. *Resources > Video > Unit 8 > Unit Video*

**B. COMPOSE** Watch the video two or three times. What is Roxana doing to find a job? Take notes in first part of the chart.

| | Roxana's job search |
|---|---|
| Notes from the video | |
| My ideas | |

**C. EXTEND** What do you think are the two most important things Roxana has done to find a job? What are other actions Roxanna could take? Write your ideas in the chart above. Discuss your ideas with a partner.

# WRITE WHAT YOU THINK

**SYNTHESIZE** Think about Reading 1, Reading 2, and the unit video as you discuss these questions. Then choose one question and write a paragraph of 5–7 sentences in response.

1. Is it important for a person to get a full-time job immediately after finishing school?

2. The blogger Devin Reams in Reading 2 feels no pressure to choose a permanent job. Considering the ideas presented in Reading 1, what do you think are some of the advantages and disadvantages of this attitude?

3. Why might a young person want to become an entrepreneur rather than work for a company?

## VOCABULARY SKILL  Word forms

analyze

analyst

Learning all forms of a word and how they are used helps you build your vocabulary. This skill will also give you more flexibility in your writing and speaking.

Notice how different forms of the same word are used in different contexts.

**analyze** (*v.*) to examine the nature or structure of something, especially by separating it into its parts
    Please **analyze** the information in the report closely.

**analyst** (*n.*) a person who examines facts in order to give an opinion about them
    Martin is a financial **analyst** for a large corporation.

**analytical** (*adj.*) using a logical method in order to understand something
    The course helps students to develop **analytical** skills.

**analytically** (*adv.*) doing something by using a logical method
    Many recent graduates are unprepared to think **analytically**.

Dictionaries will list all the word forms and their definitions. When you look up a word, you will usually need to read several entries to find all the word forms.

All dictionary entries adapted from the *Oxford American Dictionary for learners of English* © Oxford University Press 2011.

**TIP FOR SUCCESS**

When you learn the meaning and spelling changes for different word forms, also pay attention to how the pronunciation is different (e.g., *acquire/acquisition*).

**A. CATEGORIZE** These words come from Readings 1 and 2. Complete the chart. Use your dictionary to help you. (An *X* indicates that a word form doesn't exist or you don't need to know it at this time.)

| Verb | Noun | Adjective | Adverb |
|------|------|-----------|--------|
| 1. acquire | *acquisition* | ✗ | ✗ |
| 2. | adjustment | | ✗ |
| 3. ✗ | | ambiguous | |
| 4. anticipate | | anticipated | ✗ |
| 5. | collaboration | | |

| | | | |
|---|---|---|---|
| 6. ✗ | constant | | |
| 7. | interpretation | interpretive | ✗ |
| 8. ✗ | particulars | | |
| 9. ✗ | permanence | | |
| 10. ✗ | | reluctant | |

**B. APPLY** Complete each pair of sentences with the correct forms of a word from the chart in Activity A.

1. a. Starting my job was a big _____, but I'm finally used to it.

   b. Your office chair can go higher or lower. The seat is _____.

2. a. Abdullah works in sales and is _____ on the phone with clients.

   b. New employees need _____ instruction. Learning about a new job takes time.

3. a. Are you only visiting, or have you moved here _____?

   b. When I started, I was part time. Now I'm a _____ employee.

4. a. May was _____ to ask her teacher for help, but she finally did.

   b. Adam asked his boss for a raise, and she _____ agreed.

5. a. Her answer was _____. What exactly did she mean?

   b. The message is worded _____. I'm not sure what it means.

6. a. The staff will _____ on the new marketing plan.

   b. There needs to be close _____ between teachers and parents for students to do well in school.

7. a. Tonight's soccer match has been highly _____ all year.

   b. They got 1,000 replies. They didn't _____ that!

8. a. Let's talk generally about our business trip now. We can discuss the _____ (where we'll stay, what we'll do, etc.) later.

   b. Keep your schedule open, _____ the hours from 10 to noon.

**C. COMPOSE** Choose two words from the chart in Activity A. Write one sentence for each form of the word. Then share your sentences with a partner.

**iQ PRACTICE** Go online for more practice with word forms.
*Practice > Unit 6 > Activity 9*

# WRITING

**OBJECTIVE ▶**  At the end of this unit, you will write a summary of Reading 1. This summary will include specific information from the reading stated in your own words.

## GRAMMAR  Reported speech with the present tense and shifting tenses

You can use **reported speech** to report what someone says, writes, thinks, or feels. In academic writing, it is common to report information with the present tense when the information involves current opinions or ongoing situations.

### Reported statements with *that* clauses

- Identify the person who made the statement using a present tense reporting clause.

- Put the information that you are reporting in a *that* clause. (The word *that* is often omitted.)

| **Original:** | Jim Sweeny: You should make a list of questions. |
|---|---|
| **Reported:** | Jim Sweeny says (that) students should make a list of questions.* |

reporting clause          noun clause

You can also report statements with verbs like *tell* or *explain*, or verbs that express thoughts or feelings such as *feel*, *think*, and *believe*. Notice that *tell* is followed by a noun or pronoun.

Jim Sweeny tells students (that) they should make a list of questions.

Jim Sweeny thinks (that) students should make a list of questions.

### Reported questions with *wh-* clauses

You usually use a *wh-* clause to report a question. Although these clauses begin with question words (*who*, *what*, etc.), they use statement word order.

| **Original:** | Many students: What should you wear to an interview? |
|---|---|
| **Reported:** | Many students wonder what they should wear to an interview**. |

reporting clause          noun clause

You can also report that someone *answered* a question about something. In this case, the *wh-* clause doesn't report exactly what someone said but says what question was answered. Reporting verbs include *explain*, *describe*, and *tell*.

| **Original answer:** | News article: You should wear a suit to an interview**. |
|---|---|
| **Reported answer:** | The article explains what you should wear to an interview. |
| | The article tells you what you should wear to an interview. |

*In reported speech, pronouns and possessives often have to change to keep the original meaning.
**You** should make a list of questions.  →  *The article says (that)* **students** *should make a list of questions.*

**Answers the question *What should you wear to an interview?*

## Reported speech with shifting tenses

When a past tense reporting verb is used, there is often a shift in tense in the verb(s) in the noun clause.

Some common shifts are present to past tense, present perfect (progressive) and past tense to past perfect (progressive), and *will* to *would*.

| | |
|---|---|
| **Original:** | As I prepare to enter the working world, I've **had** a hard time deciding what to do. |
| **Reported:** | He said that as he prepared to enter the working world, he'**d had** a hard time deciding what to do. |
| **Original:** | I **started** perusing the job postings. |
| **Reported:** | He reported that he **had started** perusing the job postings. |
| **Original:** | I **will develop** something on my own or continue to learn and do well as an employee. |
| **Reported:** | He added that he **would develop** something on his own or continue to learn and do well as an employee. |

**iQ** RESOURCES Go online to watch the Grammar Skill Video.
*Resources > Video > Unit 6 > Grammar Skill Video*

**TIP FOR SUCCESS**

A reporting clause can contain a general subject, such as *many people say* or *some people think*.

**A. IDENTIFY** Check (✓) the sentences that use reported speech. Then circle the reporting clause and underline the noun clause in the sentences you checked.

☐ 1. Many recent graduates say that they have difficulty adjusting to life on the job.

☐ 2. Joseph Lewis notes that in school you advance each year, but at work the same isn't true.

☐ 3. In the workplace, employees must regularly interact with others and are often dependent on their coworkers for their success.

☐ 4. Many people wonder how we can better prepare young adults for the workplace.

☐ 5. One recent report tells educators that less time should be spent on testing in school.

☐ 6. In the article, some recent graduates explain what current students can do to prepare.

☐ 7. Volunteering part time at a company, hospital, or government organization can help one gain experience and learn skills needed to succeed in the real world.

☐ 8. Other graduates feel there should be more focus on developing writing and public speaking skills.

**B. IDENTIFY** Circle the answer that best completes each statement.

1. Michael is always studying. I wonder ____.

    a. what his major is    b. what is his major    c. what major he is

2. My brother says ____ to major in journalism.

    a. that he was wanting    b. that wants    c. he wants

3. The article ____ students how to dress for a job interview.

    a. tells that    b. tells    c. tells to

4. Take this quiz. It will tell you ____ for you.

    a. which best job is    b. which is best job    c. which job is best

5. A lot of students believe ____ include more teamwork activities in class.

    a. teachers they should    b. that teachers should    c. teachers that should

6. The website explains ____ apply for an internship at the company.

    a. how    b. you how    c. how you

**C. APPLY** Read each sentence. Report the information, using the verb in parentheses and a noun clause. Change pronouns where appropriate.

1. Jim Sweeny to students: There are things you can do to prepare for an interview. (tell)

    *Jim Sweeny tells students (that) there are things they can do*
    *to prepare for an interview.*

2. News article: Many recent graduates aren't ready for the workplace. (say)

    _____

    _____

3. Many students: Learning a foreign language is challenging. (believe)

    _____

    _____

4. Tara: How can I get a good job? (wonder)

    _____

5. Many students: What should we do after graduation? (want to know)

    _____

6. The school handbook: Students must take four years of English and three years of math to graduate. (tell)

_____

_____

**D. APPLY** Read each sentence about blogger Devin Reams. Report the information using the verb in parentheses and a noun clause. Shift the tense of the bold verbs and change pronouns where appropriate.

1. As I **get** ready to make the transition to full-time employee, I **find** myself thinking about these questions. (say)

   _He said that as he got ready to make the transition to full-time_

   _employee, he found himself thinking about these questions._

2. I'**ve been interning** at a large telecommunications company. (report)

   _____

3. I **started** perusing the job postings, looking for a full-time position in accounting. (explain)

   _____

   _____

4. I **decided** to accept a position with a large accounting firm. (tell his readers)

   _____

   _____

5. I **know** I'll be given many new opportunities in my job with an accounting firm. (add)

   _____

   _____

6. Why **do** I **have** lofty goals? (ask)

   _____

7. How, when, or where **will** I achieve them? (wonder)

   _____

8. Whatever **happens**, I'm sure I'll do fine. (conclude)

   _____

**iQ PRACTICE** Go online for more practice with reported speech with the present tense and shifting tenses. *Practice > Unit 6 > Activities 10–11*

A **summary** is a shorter version of the original text. When you write a summary, you tell the reader the main ideas using some words from the text and some of your own words.

### Before you write a summary

1. Read the entire text and ask yourself what the author's **purpose** is.

2. Reread the introductory paragraph(s) and find the **thesis statement**.

3. Reread the rest of the text. In each paragraph, highlight, underline, or circle the **main idea** and **key points**. You can also annotate the important information.

### When you write a summary

1. Begin by stating the **title** of the text, the **author's full name** (if it's given), and his or her **purpose** for writing.

2. Use the text you highlighted or annotated to explain the author's **thesis** and **main ideas**.

3. Follow these guidelines.

   • Keep the summary short (about one-third to one-fourth as long as the original).

   • Include only the original text's main ideas. Do not include details, examples, information that is not in the original, or your own opinion.

   • Write the summary mostly in your own words, but do not change the author's ideas. This is called *paraphrasing*.

**A. IDENTIFY** Read the article about preparing for a job interview. Then answer the questions that follow. Refer to the first set of steps in the Writing Skill box.

# Preparing for Your First Job Interview
by Jim Sweeny

You've just graduated from school. Now comes the scary part: interviewing for your first job. For many recent graduates, this is an anxiety-provoking time. However, there are some simple ways to prepare for this challenging experience.

First, you should make a list of the questions you might be asked. In many job interviews, you have to answer questions about your academic experience and how it has prepared you for the job. For example, you might be asked to discuss how your participation in student government or sports has given you experience working on a team. You will, of course, also be asked how your experience and talents fit with the company's goals.

Once you've got your questions, you should then think about possible answers and practice responding to them. Employers will expect you to talk in detail about your experience and use examples. Make sure that your answers describe particular situations you faced, the actions you took, and the results you achieved. Once you've got your responses, try practicing on your friends or family members. This will make you feel comfortable speaking in front of a person.

Finally, don't get discouraged if you aren't hired the first, second, or third time you interview. Think of every interview as practice for the most important one: the interview that will get you a job.

1. What is the author's purpose for writing the text?
   a. He's describing his first job interview experience.
   b. He's comparing and contrasting two interviewing styles.
   c. He's explaining how to get ready for a job interview.

2. What is the thesis statement? Underline it.

3. What two main ideas did you mark that support the thesis statement?

4. In the last paragraph, how does the author conclude the article?
   a. He restates the main points.
   b. He makes a final suggestion.
   c. He makes a prediction about the future.

**B. WRITING MODEL** Read the model summaries of the article on page 176. Complete the checklist below. Then discuss the questions that follow with a partner.

### Summary 1

In the essay "Preparing for Your First Job Interview," author Jim Sweeny gives advice to recent graduates who are interviewing for their first job. Specifically, he says that there are simple things they can do to prepare for the interview. First, Sweeny tells students that they should make a list of questions they might be asked. These questions are usually about how a person's school experience relates to the job. Then Sweeny says that students should prepare answers to the questions and practice responding to them, and he explains a way to do this. In conclusion, he tells students not to get discouraged by the interviewing process.

### Summary 2

In this essay, the author gives advice to recent graduates who are interviewing for their first job. He says that looking for a first job is stressful, but there are ways to prepare for an interview. Sweeny says that students should be prepared to answer questions about their school experience and how it relates to the job they are applying for. In fact, the questions I was asked at my first interview were about my school activities. In conclusion, he tells students not to get discouraged by the interviewing process.

| The summary . . . | Summary 1 | Summary 2 |
| --- | --- | --- |
| 1. states the original text's title. | ☐ | ☐ |
| 2. states the author's full name (if given). | ☐ | ☐ |
| 3. states the author's purpose for writing. | ☐ | ☐ |
| 4. identifies the thesis statement. | ☐ | ☐ |
| 5. identifies all of the text's main ideas. | ☐ | ☐ |
| 6. does not include details, examples, information not in the text, or the writer's opinion. | ☐ | ☐ |
| 7. is mostly written in the student's own words. | ☐ | ☐ |
| 8. is clear and easy to follow. | ☐ | ☐ |

1.  Which summary is better? Why?

2.  What three things can be done to the poor summary to improve it?

**C. WRITING MODEL** Read the model summary of Reading 2. Then follow the steps below.

Yes ✓

No ✗

Maybe ?

In the blog post "Making My First Post-College Career Decision," a graduating student discussed his transition from student to employee. The student explained what career path he had chosen and why. He said he'd interned in a large telecommunications company and gained workplace experience but had learned it wasn't the kind of work he wanted to do. In his senior year, he interviewed for jobs in accounting and accepted one in a large accounting firm. Many graduating students don't find a job that easily. He asked why he'd needed to get a job so quickly and answered that he believed he'd accepted the job, so he could utilize the skills he had acquired in school and in his internship and get experience in the field. Employees in accounting firms work fewer hours. He added, however, that when he stopped learning and being challenged in the job, he would need to make another decision. He saw himself becoming an executive or starting his own business. He wondered if he had lofty goals and said he did. It doesn't seem likely he'll succeed. He concluded that he would take advantage of the opportunities his new accounting job provided but that he was young and had time to make decisions about his future. He believed he would do fine and was ready for the transition.

1. Underline the purpose twice.

2. Put the thesis statement in brackets.

3. Circle the reporting verbs.

4. Underline the shifts in tense.

5. Cross out three sentences that don't belong: one detail, one idea not in the original text, and one opinion.

**D. IDENTIFY** Complete the checklist for the summary in Activity C.

| The summary . . . | |
| --- | --- |
| 1. states the original text's title. | ☐ |
| 2. states the author's full name (if given). | ☐ |
| 3. states the author's purpose for writing. | ☐ |
| 4. identifies the thesis statement. | ☐ |
| 5. identifies all of the text's main ideas. | ☐ |
| 6. does not include details, examples, information not in the text, or the writer's opinion. | ☐ |
| 7. is mostly written in the student's own words. | ☐ |
| 8. is clear and easy to follow. | ☐ |

**iQ** PRACTICE  Go online for more practice with writing a summary.
*Practice > Unit 6 > Activity 12*

# UNIT ASSIGNMENT
## OBJECTIVE ▶

**Write a summary**

In this assignment, you are going to write a summary of Reading 1. As you prepare your summary, think about the Unit Question, "Does school prepare you for work?" Use information from Reading 1 and your work in this unit to support your summary. Refer to the Self-Assessment checklist on page 180.

**iQ** PRACTICE  Go online to the Writing Tutor to read a model summary.
*Practice ▶ Unit 6 ▶ Activity 13*

# PLAN AND WRITE

**A. BRAINSTORM** Follow these steps to help you organize your ideas.

1. Reread Reading 1. Look at any annotating or highlighting that you did. Cross out details, examples, information not in the reading, or any text that expresses your own opinion.

2. Review the outline you completed on page 161. Decide if you need to add or change anything to make it more accurate.

**WRITING TIP**
Use the full name of the author and anyone mentioned in the text the first time you cite the person. After that, use the person's last name.

**B. PLAN** Follow these steps to plan your summary.

1. Identify the title of the text and the author's full name (if given).

2. Identify the author's purpose.

3. Rewrite the thesis statement using your own words.

4. Identify the main ideas. Rewrite them using mostly your own words.

5. Using mostly your own words, state how the author concludes the article.

**iQ** RESOURCES  Go online to download and complete the outline for your summary. *Resources ▶ Writing Tools ▶ Unit 6 ▶ Outline*

**C. WRITE** Use your planning notes to write your summary.

1. Write your summary of Reading 1. Remember to summarize important points by paraphrasing the author's purpose, thesis statement, main ideas, and conclusions. Use reported speech to report the ideas of the author and others.

2. Look at the Self-Assessment checklist on page 180 to guide your writing.

**iQ** PRACTICE  Go online to the Writing Tutor to write your assignment.
*Practice ▶ Unit 6 ▶ Activity 14*

# REVISE AND EDIT

**iQ** RESOURCES  Go online to download the peer review worksheet.
*Resources > Writing Tools > Unit 6 > Peer Review Worksheet*

**A. PEER REVIEW** Read your partner's summary. Then use the peer review worksheet. Discuss the review with your partner.

**B. REWRITE** Based on your partner's review, revise and rewrite your summary.

**C. EDIT** Complete the Self-Assessment checklist as you prepare to write the final draft of your summary. Be prepared to hand in your work or discuss it in class.

| SELF-ASSESSMENT | Yes | No |
|---|---|---|
| Does the summary state the text's title, author's name, and author's purpose? | ☐ | ☐ |
| Does the summary clearly identify the thesis statement and all the main ideas? | ☐ | ☐ |
| Does it include only the main ideas and important information from the text? | ☐ | ☐ |
| Is it mostly written in your own words? | ☐ | ☐ |
| Is reported speech used correctly? | ☐ | ☐ |
| Does the summary include vocabulary from the unit? | ☐ | ☐ |
| Did you check the summary for punctuation, spelling, and grammar? | ☐ | ☐ |

**D. REFLECT** Discuss these questions with a partner or group.

1. What is something new you learned in this unit?

2. Look back at the Unit Question—Does school prepare you for work? Is your answer different now than when you started the unit? If yes, how is it different? Why?

**iQ** PRACTICE  Go online to the discussion board to discuss the questions.
*Practice > Unit 6 > Activity 15*

# TRACK YOUR SUCCESS

**iQ** PRACTICE  Go online to check the words and phrases you have learned in this unit. *Practice > Unit 6 > Activity 16*

Check (✓) the skills and strategies you learned. If you need more work on a skill, refer to the page(s) in parentheses.

CRITICAL THINKING  ☐ I can justify my opinions. (p. 159)

READING  ☐ I can create and use an outline. (p. 160)

VOCABULARY  ☐ I can recognize the different forms of a word. (p. 169)

GRAMMAR  ☐ I can use reported speech with the present tense and shifting tenses. (pp. 171–172)

WRITING  ☐ I can write a summary. (p. 175)

OBJECTIVE ▶  ☐ I can gather information and ideas to summarize a text.

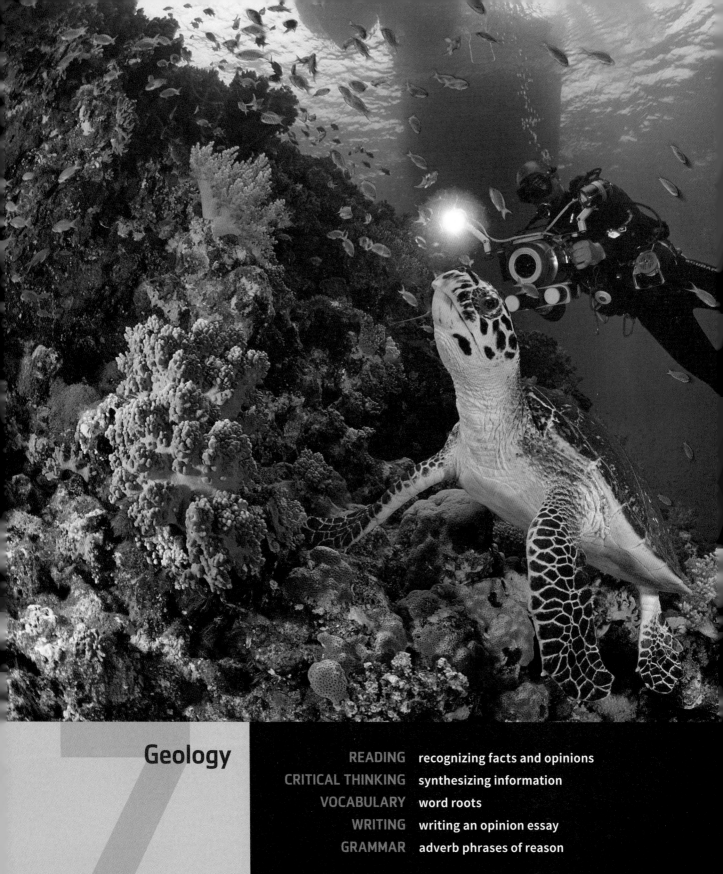

## Geology

| | |
|---|---|
| READING | recognizing facts and opinions |
| CRITICAL THINKING | synthesizing information |
| VOCABULARY | word roots |
| WRITING | writing an opinion essay |
| GRAMMAR | adverb phrases of reason |

# Is discovery always a good thing?

**A.** Discuss these questions with your classmates.

1. What discoveries have you heard about in recent years? Which discovery did you find the most exciting?

2. Do you think money should be spent on exploration, or is it better spent on other things?

3. Look at the photo. What can be discovered by deep-sea exploration? Do you think it is important to make new discoveries?

**B.** Listen to *The Q Classroom* online. Then answer these questions.

1. Sophy and Yuna disagree about the Unit Question. What opinions do they express? What's your opinion?

2. Marcus doesn't think we should spend money on discovery in space or the deep ocean. What does he think we should spend money on? What's your opinion?

**iQ** PRACTICE Go to the online discussion board to discuss the Unit Question with your classmates. *Practice > Unit 7 > Activity 1*

**UNIT OBJECTIVE**

Read two news magazine articles. Gather information and ideas to write an opinion essay about a specific discovery or type of exploration.

## READING 1

# Ocean Discoveries

You are going to read a news magazine article about two ocean discoveries. Use the article to gather information and ideas for your Unit Assignment.

## PREVIEW THE READING

**A. PREVIEW**  Read the title. Look at the headings and the pictures.

1. What are the two ocean discoveries?

_____

2. What do you expect to learn about the two discoveries?

_____

**B. QUICK WRITE**  What can we gain from ocean discoveries? What are the downsides of ocean discoveries? Write for 5–10 minutes in response. Remember to use this section for your Unit Assignment.

**C. VOCABULARY**  Check (✓) the words you know. Use a dictionary to define any new or unknown words. Then discuss with a partner how the words will relate to the unit.

| | |
|---|---|
| accommodate *(v.)* 🔑+ | propose *(v.)* 🔑+ OPAL |
| disperse *(v.)* | resilient *(adj.)* |
| empirical *(adj.)* 🔑+ OPAL | reveal *(v.)* 🔑+ OPAL |
| evidence *(n.)* 🔑+ OPAL | significant *(adj.)* 🔑+ OPAL |
| expedition *(n.)* 🔑+ | sophisticated *(adj.)* 🔑+ |
| habitat *(n.)* 🔑+ | sufficient *(adj.)* 🔑+ OPAL |

🔑+ Oxford 5000™ words          **OPAL** Oxford Phrasal Academic Lexicon

**iQ PRACTICE**  Go online to listen and practice your pronunciation.
*Practice > Unit 7 > Activity 2*

# WORK WITH THE READING

 **A. INVESTIGATE** Read the article and gather information about the two ocean discoveries.

# OCEAN DISCOVERIES

1    We think of Earth as largely explored. Most people would say that there can't be many more discoveries to be made. However, about 70 percent of Earth's surface is covered by water, and it may be surprising to hear that less than 5 percent of the world's oceans have been explored. New species of organisms are being discovered in the oceans every year, particularly in the deep ocean. There is still much to discover about the geographical features of many areas of the oceans as well. Because they have developed new technologies, scientists are now better able to explore the oceans. These technologies, including improved DNA sequencing, better satellite[1] data, and more **sophisticated** underwater vehicles, have resulted in exciting new discoveries with implications for all of us. Here are two such discoveries:

## A CORAL REEF

2    Imagine the excitement of finding a previously unknown coral reef. This is exactly what happened in the summer of 2018. A deep-sea **expedition** discovered a large coral reef in the Atlantic Ocean. Scientists on the research vessel *Atlantis* discovered the deep-sea stony coral about 257 kilometers (160 mi.) from shore near the southeastern part of the U.S. Using the human-operated vehicle (HOV) *Alvin*, the crew came upon the unexpected sight on the sea bottom at about 0.8 kilometers (0.5 mi.) below the ocean surface. Growing on the skeletal[2] remains of dead coral was a huge population of *Lophelia pertusa,* a branching cold-water white coral. These corals have probably been growing in the area for millennia, speculates lead scientist Erik Cordes, an associate professor of biology at Temple University in Philadelphia. The corals were found northwest of coral-covered mounds[3] discovered earlier in the summer when the NOAA ship *Okeanos Explorer* was mapping the ocean floor.

Those mounds are 80 to 90 meters (262–295 ft.) high. Together, the areas explored by the two research vessels covered about 137 kilometers (85 mi.) of living coral (Cordes, 2018).

3    The scientists on the *Atlantis* who explored the deep-sea **habitat** where the coral was found plan to spend the next few years examining the specimens[4] they collected there. What are the implications of this find? The scientists hope to better predict how the organisms that live there—

[1] **satellite:** an electronic device that is sent into space and moves around the Earth or another planet. It is used for communicating by radio, television, etc., and for providing information.

[2] **skeletal:** connected with the skeleton (the structure of bones that supports the body of a person or an animal)

[3] **mound:** large pile of earth or stones; a small hill

[4] **specimen:** a small amount of something that shows what the rest of it is like

many of them fragile[5]—might be impacted by human activity. Existing far from shore and at such a depth makes the coral reef unique. Recounting the scientists' excitement upon finding a pristine[6] coral reef, Cordes said, "There aren't many of those left on Earth, and we just found a big one. This is a really big finding. I'm thrilled." Adding to their excitement is the fact that extensive connected reefs like this one are typically more resilient in the face of environmental change. And because these coral reefs create habitats for diverse communities of invertebrates[7] and fish, and help recycle nutrients from organic matter through mixing and upwelling, they might help improve the health of not only the East Coast ecosystem but also the larger Atlantic ecosystem. Should *we* be excited, too?

# A NEW CONTINENT

4    Given the vastness of the Atlantic Ocean alone, perhaps discovering a new stretch of coral is not so surprising after all. But discovering a whole new continent? Scientists have **proposed** a new continent in the southwest Pacific Ocean: a landmass two-thirds the size of Australia. This landmass, named *Zealandia*, is thought to have separated from Australia and Antarctica about 80 million years ago as the super-continent known as Gondwana broke up. It has gone through dramatic changes since then and is today about 94 percent submerged[8] almost a mile deep. Today, only New Zealand and New Caledonia remain above the surface of the ocean.

5    Researchers have published **evidence** in the journal *GSA Today* that the 4.9-million-square-kilometer (1.9-million-sq-mi.) mass is one contiguous[9] piece of the continental crust that is distinct from the Australian continent. Nick Mortimer of the GNS Science Research Institute in Dunedin, New Zealand, was the lead author of the paper titled "Zealandia: Earth's Hidden Continent." The paper, published in the spring of 2017, claims that new discoveries and evidence, gathered through **empirical** observation and description, are **sufficient** to prove that Zealandia is a continent (Mortimer et al., 2017).

6    In the summer of that same year, an international research team of 32 scientists spent nine weeks aboard the research vessel *JOIDES Resolution* in the first extensive survey of Zealandia. They took sediment core samples at different depths. Co-chief scientist Gerald Dickens of Rice University in Houston, Texas, said, "More than 8,000 specimens were studied, and several hundred fossil[10] species were identified." (Byrd, 2017). He said that expedition scientists made **significant** new fossil discoveries. These discoveries provided additional evidence of the geographical history of Zealandia. The samples proved that Zealandia was not always as deep

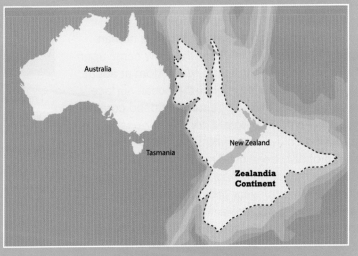

as it is today and **revealed** that the geography and climate of Zealandia were very different in the past.

7    There is disagreement among scientists on the definition of *continent* and whether a landmass meets the criteria to be recognized as a continent. Mortimer and his co-authors argue, "Currently used conventions and definitions of *continental crust*, *continents*, and *microcontinents* require no modification to **accommodate** Zealandia." It remains to be seen if Zealandia appears on future maps as a new continent.

8    What is the significance of finding a new continent? Some scientists believe such a discovery has implications for our understanding of how plants and animals have **dispersed** and evolved. Additionally, they suggest that the core specimens can help us know how our global climate system works. Furthermore, because it has been surveyed extensively, Zealandia can serve as a test for computer models that scientists use to predict changes in our climate. All of these insights have the potential to impact life on Earth in the future.

9    These two discoveries exemplify the potential for additional new discoveries in Earth's vast oceans. Clearly, the scientists involved in exploring both the deep-sea coral in the Atlantic and the large landmass in the Pacific are thrilled by their finds and the opportunity to learn more. Should we be, too? Will the coral reef remain pristine now that it has been discovered? Would it be better if it had remained hidden? Does it matter if Zealandia is a continent or not? Does studying it further really have the potential to impact climate? Is this essential work that should continue? These are important questions about the ocean discoveries. The key is in our motivation to continue (or not) to explore our world.

**References**

Byrd, Deborah. (2017). Scientists reveal secrets of lost continent Zealandia. *EarthSky*. Retrieved from http://Earthsky.org/Earth/lost-continent-zealandia-drilling-expedition-2017

Cordes, Erik. (2018). Mission Summary: What We Have Learned from DEEP SEARCH Expedition AT-41

Mortimer, Nick et al. (2017). Zealandia: Earth's Hidden Continent. *GSA Today* 27 (3)

**B. VOCABULARY** Here are some words from Reading 1. Read the sentences. Then write each bold word next to the correct definition. You may need to change verbs to their base form.

1. The **expedition** had the purpose of studying the effect of ice loss on polar bears.

2. Some plants spread when their seeds are **dispersed** by the wind.

3. Mapping equipment has become much more **sophisticated**, so scientists can determine ice loss in the Arctic with greater accuracy.

4. A lot of data and many facts contributed to the **evidence** the scientists presented in their report on the Arctic.

5. Arctic ice loss is reducing the **habitat** of polar bears.

6. Scientists are concerned that there is not **sufficient** food to sustain the polar bear population in the Arctic.

7. Because he is young and **resilient**, he recovered quickly from this illness.

8. There has been a **significant** drop in the population of polar bears, causing fears that they will become extinct.

9. They conducted experiments and used that **empirical** data to demonstrate their point.

10. The graph clearly showed what the study data **revealed**: that there are now many fewer polar bears.

11. Scientist have **proposed**—and hope to receive approval on—a plan to lessen the effect of climate change on the Arctic region.

12. Any plan for further Arctic exploration must **accommodate** the facts presented in the study.

a. _____ *(adj.)* to spread or to make something spread over a wide area

b. _____ *(n.)* the place where a particular type of animal or plant is normally found

c. _____ *(v.)* to consider something, such as somebody's opinion or a fact, and be influenced by it when you are deciding what to do or explaining something

d. _____ *(adj.)* (of a machine, system, etc.) clever and complicated in the way that it works or is presented

e. _____ *(n.)* an organized journey with a particular purpose, especially to find out about a place that is not well known

f. _____ *(v.)* to show something that previously could not be seen

g. _____ *(n.)* the facts, signs, or objects that make you believe that something is true

h. _____ *(adj.)* able to feel better quickly after something unpleasant such as a shock, injury, etc.

**VOCABULARY SKILL REVIEW**
In Unit 6, you learned to recognize different word forms to expand your vocabulary. Use a dictionary to find different forms of the vocabulary words *accommodate, propose, resilient,* and *significant.*

i. _____ *(adj.)* enough for a particular purpose; as much as you need

j. _____ *(v.)* to suggest a plan, an idea, etc., for people to think about and decide on

k. _____ *(adj.)* based on experiments or experience rather than ideas or theories

l. _____ *(adj.)* large or important enough to have an effect or to be noticed

**iQ** PRACTICE  Go online for more practice with vocabulary.
*Practice › Unit 7 › Activity 3*

**C. RESTATE** Answer the questions.

1. What technologies make it possible to explore the oceans?

   _____

2. Where was the coral reef found?

   _____

3. What makes the coral reef unique?

   _____

4. Why are the scientist so excited about the coral reef?

   _____

5. What are the implications of this discovery?

   _____

6. What did the scientists find in the sediment core samples they took in Zealandia?

   _____

7. What did their evidence prove about Zealandia?

   _____

8. Why does Nick Mortimer think Zealandia should be considered a continent?

   _____

9. What do scientists think is significant about finding a new continent in the Pacific?

   _____

**D. CATEGORIZE** Read the statements. Write *T* (true) or *F* (false) and the paragraph number where the answer is found. Then correct each false statement to make it true according to the article.

_____ 1. Seventy percent of the Earth's oceans have been explored. (paragraph ____)

_____ 2. The coral reef is in shallow, warm water. (paragraph ____)

_____ 3. The coral reef has both new and very old growth. (paragraph ____)

_____ 4. There are mounds because the living coral grows on top of dead coral. (paragraph ____)

_____ 5. The coral is more resilient in the face of environmental change because it is deep. (paragraph ____)

_____ 6. Zealandia is larger than Australia. (paragraph ____)

___ 7. Zealandia is different than it was when it separated from Australia and Antarctica 80 million years ago. (paragraph ___)

___ 8. Zealandia is made up of pieces of continental crust. (paragraph ___)

___ 9. An international research team spent nine weeks in the summer of 2017 surveying Zealandia. (paragraph ___)

___ 10. Scientists agree on what a continent is. (paragraph ___)

E. **CATEGORIZE** Complete the chart with information from the reading. Compare charts with a partner. Then discuss the implications and significance of each discovery with your partner. Do you agree? Can you add ideas to those in the reading?

| | Deep sea coral reef | Zealandia |
|---|---|---|
| Location | | Pacific Ocean near Australia |
| Expedition/Study | 1. NOAA expedition<br>2. Deep-sea expedition | 1.<br>2. |
| Vessel | 1.<br>2. | 1. N/A<br>2. Research vessel *JOIDES Resolution* |
| Method | | New discoveries and evidence through empirical observation and description<br><br>Core sediment samples at different depths |
| Lead scientist | | Nick Mortimer<br>Gerald Dickens |
| Implications/Significance of discovery | Pristine coral reef<br><br>Scientists hope to better predict how the fragile organisms might be impacted by humans | |
| Your ideas | | |

F. **SYNTHESIZE** Look back at your Quick Write on page 184. What can we gain from ocean discoveries? What are the downsides? Add any new ideas or information you learned from the reading.

**iQ** PRACTICE Go online for additional reading and comprehension.
*Practice > Unit 7 > Activity 4*

# WRITE WHAT YOU THINK

**A. DISCUSS** Discuss the questions in a group. Think about the Unit Question, "Is discovery always a good thing?"

1. Which of the two discoveries seems more important? Why?

2. Ocean research is typically time-consuming and costly. Are these discoveries worth the time and money spent?

3. If you could go on an expedition, where would you go? What would you want to explore? Why?

**B. SYNTHESIZE** Choose one of the questions from Activity A and write a paragraph of 5–7 sentences in response. Look back at your Quick Write on page 184 as you think about what you learned.

## READING SKILL  Recognizing facts and opinions

**Facts and opinions** are used as support of ideas. When reading a text, it is important to distinguish facts from opinions. Facts are pieces of information that are generally accepted as true. Factual statements can be proved or disproved. For example, they may provide data, including numerical data (statistics), or give explanations. Common expressions that signal facts include *evidence shows that, prove,* and *show.* When facts are attributed to an expert, a neutral verb such as *say* or *tell* is common, and the facts are stated directly.

In contrast, opinions offer personal ideas or judgments. Opinions can be strong support of claims in a text when they are used with or based on factual data and represent knowledge gained through study. Opinions can be those of the author or of experts cited in the text. Using the opinions of experts strengthens claims an author makes. When using the opinions of experts, credentials (academic institution and location) are provided to demonstrate their credibility to the reader. Opinions are often introduced with verbs such as *argue, claim, believe, suggest,* and *speculate,* and hedges using modals, adverbials, or expressions of possibility and probability.

Recognizing facts and opinions and how they are used together in a text to support claims can help you analyze the reliability and effectiveness of the information provided.

> **Fact:** Gerald Dickens said, "More than 8,000 specimens were studied." (provides numerical data)
>
> **Opinion:** He continued, saying, "We feel we've gathered enough information to change *continental* to the noun *continent*." (gives a judgment based on data and knowledge gained through study)

**IDENTIFY** Read the statements from Reading 1. Write *F* (fact) or *O* (opinion). Underline the words that signal facts or opinions. Justify your answers to a partner.

**A Coral Reef**

_____ 1. These corals have probably been growing in the area for millennia, speculates lead scientist Erik Cordes.

_____ 2. Recounting the scientists' excitement upon finding a pristine coral reef, Cordes said, "There aren't many of those [pristine coral reefs] left on Earth, and we just found a big one. This is a really big finding. I'm thrilled."

_____ 3. Adding to their excitement is the fact that extensive connected reefs like this one are typically more resilient in the face of environmental change . . .

_____ 4. [The newly discovered coral reef] might help improve the health of not only the East Coast ecosystem but also the larger Atlantic ecosystem.

**A New Continent**

_____ 5. This landmass, named *Zealandia*, is thought to have separated from Australia and Antarctica about 80 million years ago as the super-continent known as Gondwana broke up.

_____ 6. Researchers have published evidence in the journal *GSA Today* that the 4.9-million-square-kilometer (1.9-million-sq-mi.) mass is one contiguous piece of the continental crust that is distinct from the Australian continent.

_____ 7. The paper . . . claims that new discoveries and evidence, gathered through empirical observation and description, are sufficient to prove that Zealandia is a continent.

_____ 8. Co-chief scientist Gerald Dickens of Rice University in Houston, Texas, said, "More than 8,000 specimens were studied, and several hundred fossil species were identified."

_____ 9. The samples proved that Zealandia was not always as deep as it is today and revealed that the geography and climate of Zealandia were very different in the past.

_____ 10. Some scientists believe such a discovery has implications for our understanding of how plants and animals have dispersed and evolved.

_____ 11. Additionally, they suggest that the core specimens can help us know how our global climate system works.

**iQ** PRACTICE  Go online for more practice recognizing facts and opinions.
*Practice > Unit 7 > Activity 5*

Alaska's Pebble Mine: Minerals vs. Nature

OBJECTIVE ▶

You are going to read an article by Svati Kirsten Narula for the news magazine *The Atlantic*. The article is about the proposed Pebble Mine in Alaska's Bristol Bay region. There is a controversy about whether extracting minerals will destroy the natural beauty and resources of the area. Use the article to gather information and ideas for your Unit Assignment.

## PREVIEW THE READING

**A. PREVIEW** Read the title and first paragraph. Why do you think some people do not want the Pebble Mine project? Why do you think other people are in favor of it? Discuss your opinion with your classmates.

**B. QUICK WRITE** Is the discovery and extraction of minerals a good thing? Write for 5–10 minutes in response. Be sure to use this section for your Unit Assignment.

**C. VOCABULARY** Check (✓) the words you know. Then work with a partner to locate each word in the reading. Use clues to help define the words you don't know. Check your definitions in the dictionary.

| | | |
|---|---|---|
| abundant *(adj.)* | dread *(v.)* | preliminary *(adj.)* 𝄞+ |
| alliance *(n.)* 𝄞+ | ecological *(adj.)* 𝄞+ OPAL | reserves *(n.)* 𝄞+ |
| ample *(adj.)* | intervene *(v.)* 𝄞+ OPAL | sustainable *(adj.)* 𝄞+ |
| controversial *(adj.)* 𝄞+ | overwhelmingly *(adv.)* | unduly *(adv.)* |

𝄞+ Oxford 5000™ words                                         OPAL Oxford Phrasal Academic Lexicon

**iQ** PRACTICE  Go online to listen and practice your pronunciation.
*Practice ⟩ Unit 7 ⟩ Activity 6*

The salmon fishery in Bristol Bay, Alaska

# WORK WITH THE READING

 **A. INVESTIGATE** Read the article and gather information about whether discovery is always a good thing.

# Alaska's Pebble Mine:
## Minerals vs. Nature by Svati Kirsten Narula

1   Alaska's Bristol Bay region is located on the Bering Sea in the state's southwest corner. It is rich with large **reserves** of natural resources. One of those resources, the world's largest sockeye-salmon fishery, generates an estimated $1.5 billion annually. The thousands of acres of surrounding wetlands, ponds, and lakes are treasured because there isn't much untouched land left in America. Bristol Bay is also home to a large population of Alaska Natives, whose cultures and lifestyles revolve around the region's "wildness" and especially its salmon. Those are the living, breathing resources of Bristol Bay. And then there are the inorganic resources—oil and gas and mineral deposits. These are not yet fully explored, but they represent much more wealth than Alaska is receiving now.

2   A deposit of gold, molybdenum[1], and copper has been discovered in Bristol Bay. In fact, it is the largest known untapped copper deposit in the world. It's known as the Pebble Prospect. A Canadian company called *Northern Dynasty Minerals* started exploring the area in 2000. The corporation's plans to build the "Pebble Mine" have yet to progress much beyond the idea stage.

3   The Pebble Mine hasn't been built yet because the process of getting state and federal permits for a project of this size is long. The project is also highly **controversial**. The mine pits[2] two of Alaska's biggest industries, fishing and mining, against each other in a classic resource war. Both are extractive[3], but only fishing is **sustainable**. Weighing gold against salmon is weighing money against nature.

4   According to some, deciding whether to mine ought to be left to Alaskans. They will feel the effects either way. The Pebble Partnership promises to create jobs and bring in revenue. The state residents should know best whether this would do more long-term good than the protection of salmon stocks and preservation of untouched land. Polls have shown that the majority of Alaskans oppose the mine.

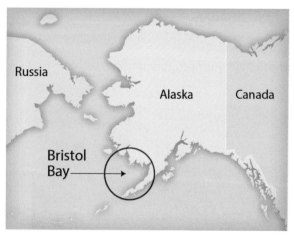

---

[1] **molybdenum:** a silver-grey metal that breaks easily
[2] **pit against:** to test someone in a struggle against someone else
[3] **extractive:** relating to the process of removing or obtaining something

5    However, in 2010, concerned Alaskans decided that the federal government needed to **intervene**. An unlikely **alliance** of commercial fishermen, native tribes, and concerned citizens joined together. They decided that their best hope for stopping the Pebble Mine was to get the federal government to step in. The alliance petitioned the U.S. Environmental Protection Agency (EPA) to conduct a **preliminary** investigation. It would look at the potential **ecological** impact of a large-scale mining operation in Bristol Bay. The agency could shut down the Pebble Mine project by determining that it would have "unacceptable" negative effects on the Bristol Bay watershed[4].

6    In the spring of 2013, the EPA released a draft of its watershed assessment. It indicated that the mine would have an **overwhelmingly** negative impact on the Bristol Bay watershed. EPA Administrator Gina McCarthy said in a statement, "Extensive scientific study has given us **ample** reason to believe that the Pebble Mine would likely have significant and negative impacts on the Bristol Bay watershed and its **abundant** salmon fisheries. This process is not something the agency does very often, but Bristol Bay is an extraordinary and unique resource."

7    It isn't surprising that companies have been fighting to mine the rich deposits of gold and copper in Bristol Bay for more than a decade. But the most recent development in the Pebble Mine story delivered a small shock. On February 28, 2014, the agency did what environmentalists hoped and what the Pebble Partnership **dreaded** it would. It temporarily prevented the U.S. Army Corps of Engineers from issuing any mining permits in Bristol Bay. That effectively halts the development process. However, this action is not a final decision.

8    Northern Dynasty CEO Tom Collier said his company is not going to give up on its plan. According to the Associated Press, Collier said the EPA's actions to date "have gone well outside of its normal practice, have been biased throughout, and have been **unduly** influenced by environmental advocacy organizations." He also said that he remains "confident" about the future of the mine, and that his company will continue to try and gain the EPA's approval to move forward. If anything, this is the beginning, not the end, of the Pebble Mine controversy.

9    According to nature writer and longtime Alaska resident Bill Sherwonit, "Ultimately, for Alaskans, the issue will boil down to this: do the benefits of tapping into one of the planet's richest mineral lodes outweigh the risks to one of the world's last, great fisheries?"

The Bristol Bay shore near Naknek, Alaska

[4] **watershed:** the region or area drained by a river, stream, etc.

**B. VOCABULARY** Complete the sentences with the vocabulary from Reading 2. You may need to change the form of some of the words.

| | | |
|---|---|---|
| abundant *(adj.)* | dread *(v.)* | preliminary *(adj.)* |
| alliance *(n.)* | ecological *(adj.)* | reserves *(n.)* |
| ample *(adj.)* | intervene *(v.)* | sustainable *(adj.)* |
| controversial *(adj.)* | overwhelmingly *(adv.)* | unduly *(adv.)* |

1. The two groups formed a(n) _____ to fight against building a new highway.

2. This is a very _____ topic, and it's unlikely they can come to an agreement about what to do.

3. The oil _____ on Earth are not sufficient to meet future demand.

4. They were asked to _____ in the conflict to prevent matters from getting worse.

5. The levels of pollution in the area are _____ high. It's now difficult to see clearly through all the smog.

6. That type of farming destroys the land, so it is not _____.

7. We don't make much money, but it is _____ because it covers our expenses and then some.

8. There was _____ evidence to confirm that she had discovered a new source of energy. No one could doubt her.

9. The news they received was _____ bad. There wasn't any hope.

10. Because I didn't study for the test, I _____ finding out my score.

11. The extensive damage from the fire was a(n) _____ disaster, destroying the forest and killing wildlife.

12. The _____ results from the first study show that the mine will damage the area.

**iQ PRACTICE** Go online for more practice with the vocabulary.
*Practice > Unit 7 > Activity 7*

**C. IDENTIFY** Circle the answer that best completes each statement.

1. The purpose of the article is ____.

   a. to argue for building the Pebble Mine

   b. to encourage people to visit Bristol Bay

   c. to explain the controversy about extracting minerals in Bristol Bay

2. Paragraphs 4 and 5 are about ____.

   a. why the Pebble Mine should not be built in Bristol Bay

   b. who should decide about allowing mining of the resources in Bristol Bay

   c. what the results of a study of the Bristol Bay watershed are

3. The EPA study is discussed in paragraphs 6 and 7 to ____.

   a. inform the reader of the results of the study

   b. bias the reader against building the mine

   c. explain the reason for doing a study

4. In paragraph 8, the CEO of Northern Dynasty Minerals ____.

   a. expresses facts about the future of the mine

   b. gives his opinion of the future of the mine

   c. explains why he doesn't like the EPA

5. In paragraph 9, longtime Alaska resident Bill Sherwonit is quoted to ____.

   a. convince the reader that mining in Bristol Bay is a bad idea

   b. pose a factual question about the future of Bristol Bay

   c. give an opinion that Alaskans will have to make a hard decision

**D. IDENTIFY** Read each statement. Write *Y* (yes) if it can be inferred from the reading or *N* (no) if it is not a correct inference. Write the paragraph number where the answer is found.

____ 1. Bristol Bay is important to the people of Alaska. (paragraph ____)

____ 2. Native people in Bristol Bay live in modern cities. (paragraph ____)

____ 3. The alliance doesn't want the mine to be built. (paragraph ____)

____ 4. The groups in the alliance have common goals. (paragraph ____)

____ 5. The study found a slight, negative impact on the watershed. (paragraph ____)

____ 6. The company that wants to build the mine agrees that the EPA should have expressed an opinion. (paragraph ____)

____ 7. Environmentalists are happy with the study results. (paragraph ____)

____ 8. The controversy will be resolved soon. (paragraph ____)

**E. EXPLAIN** Answer these questions.

1. What are the resources of Bristol Bay? _____

_____

_____

2. Which resources are sustainable? _____

_____

3. When did Northern Dynasty start exploring Bristol Bay?

_____

4. Why hasn't the Pebble Mine been built? _____

_____

5. What are the positive aspects of building the Pebble Mine?

_____

6. What are the negative aspects of building the Pebble Mine?

_____

7. Who asked the federal government to intervene? _____

_____

_____

8. What did they ask for? _____

_____

9. What were the findings of the study conducted by the EPA?

_____

_____

10. What happened in February 2014 as a result of the study?

_____

11. What will the company trying to build the Pebble Mine do about the results?

_____

# WORK WITH THE VIDEO

**A. PREVIEW** Would you want a wind farm near where you live? Why or why not?

## VIDEO VOCABULARY

**inefficient (adj.)** not doing a job well

**legitimate (adj.)** fair and acceptable

**effective (adj.)** producing a successful result

**ambition (n.)** something you want to do or achieve very much

**dominant (adj.)** more important than other things

**dominate (v.)** to be the most noticeable feature

iQ RESOURCES  Go online to watch the video about the wind power debate.
*Resources > Video > Unit 7 > Unit Video*

**B. COMPOSE** Watch the video two or three times. Take notes in the chart.

|  | Against wind farms | For wind farms |
|---|---|---|
| Notes from the video |  |  |
| My ideas |  |  |

**C. EXTEND** What is your opinion of wind farms? What are some other arguments for them? Against them? Discuss your ideas with a partner.

# WRITE WHAT YOU THINK

**A. SYNTHESIZE** Think about Reading 1, Reading 2, and the unit video as you discuss these questions. Then choose one question and write a paragraph of 5–7 sentences in response.

1. Reading 2 explains the controversy about mining in Bristol Bay. Do you think the article is biased toward one side? If so, which side and why?

2. Consider this statement: "All the major discoveries on Earth have already been made—new discoveries just fill in the details." How true do you think the statement is?

3. Are we right to keep investigating the few wild places left on Earth in the name of discovery? Explain your ideas with support from the readings and any knowledge you have of similar situations.

 ## CRITICAL THINKING STRATEGY

### Synthesizing information

The questions in Write What You Think ask you to support your ideas with information from the texts and from your own knowledge. *Synthesizing* means putting together information from different sources to support your thesis. When synthesizing, it is necessary to explain how the different sources of information are connected and how they support your idea. Synthesizing is a necessary skill for academic writing. For example:

| | |
|---|---|
| If we want to protect our environment and Earth's resources, it is clear that we need to support scientific exploration. | My idea |
| Two examples of how science is providing us with the information we need to make good decisions are a recent deep-sea expedition and an ecological investigation into a proposed project. | Explanation |
| Scientists who discovered the deep-sea coral reef are examining the specimens they collected in order to determine the impact of human activity on the coral. | Source information— Reading 1 "Ocean Discoveries" |
| Concerned residents of Alaska's Bristol Bay region asked the U.S. Environmental Protection Agency to conduct an investigation into the ecological impact of the mining operation on the area. | Source information— Reading 2 "Alaska's Pebble Mine: Minerals vs. Nature" |

**iQ PRACTICE** Go online to watch the Critical Thinking Video and check your comprehension. *Practice > Unit 7 > Activity 8*

**B. APPLY** Choose one or more of the questions and write a paragraph of 3–5 sentences in response. Use source information from Readings 1 and 2 and your own ideas. Provide an explanation to connect your idea and the source information.

1. How is the exploration of a coral reef similar to that of oil, gas, and mineral deposits? How is it different?

   _The exploration of a coral reef is both similar to and different from that of_
   _oil, gas, and mineral deposits. Both types of explorations deal with natural_
   _resources that can be exploited for profit. However, Reading 1 indicates_
   _that the coral reef that had been discovered is located far from humans,_
   _while Reading 2 shows that the oil, gas, and mineral deposits in the_
   _Bristol Bay region are very close to where people are living._

2. How do the disputes over Zealandia and the Pebble Mine impact us?

3. What is special about pristine areas such as the coral reef that Erik Cordes's crew found and Alaska's Bristol Bay? How might human activity affect them?

4. Discovery often leads to the choice of making money or preserving nature. What factors are these decisions based on?

## VOCABULARY SKILL Word roots

Many words, particularly in academic English, come from Latin or Greek roots. A **root** is the part of a word that contains the basic meaning. Roots can be combined with prefixes and suffixes to form words and word families. The Latin root -**dict**-, for example, means *say* or *speak*. It is used to form words such as:

> **contradict** *(v.)* to say that something that someone else has said is wrong
> I'm tired of Roger. He keeps **contradicting** everything I say.
>
> **diction** *(n.)* the way that someone says words
> That newsreader needs to improve his **diction**. I can't understand a word on his new program.
>
> **predict** *(v.)* to say something will happen in the future
> It is difficult to **predict** the weather.

Knowing the basic meaning of common roots, prefixes, and suffixes will help you understand the meaning of many unfamiliar words.

All dictionary entries adapted from the *Oxford American Dictionary for learners of English* © Oxford University Press 2011.

**A. IDENTIFY** Work with a partner. Study the word roots and examples in the chart. Add two other examples from the box. Then circle the correct basic meaning. Use your dictionary if necessary.

| | | | |
|---|---|---|---|
| ~~antibiotics~~ | fragile | portable | transport |
| ~~biography~~ | inscribe | preservation | unconscious |
| conscious | inspect | reserves | video |
| fraction | manuscript | speculate | vision |

| Word root | Basic meaning | Examples |
|---|---|---|
| 1. -bio- | (life)/ death | **bio**logy, **bio**diversity, *antibiotics, biography* |
| 2. -fract-, -frag- | fix / break | **frac**ture, **frag**ment |
| 3. -port- | carry / drop | sup**port**, re**port** |
| 4. -sci- | forget / know | **sci**ence, **sci**entist |
| 5. -scrib-, -script- | hear / write | de**scrib**e, de**scrip**tion |
| 6. -serv- | give / keep | con**serv**e |
| 7. -spec-, -spect- | look / say | **spec**imen, **spec**ies |
| 8. -vid-, -vis- | listen / see | e**vid**ence, **vis**it |

**B. COMPOSE** Choose five words from Activity A that are less familiar to you. Write sentences that illustrate their meanings.

1. *Because she had an infection, she had to take antibiotics.*
2. _____
3. _____
4. _____
5. _____
6. _____

**iQ PRACTICE** Go online for more practice with word roots.
*Practice > Unit 7 > Activity 9*

# WRITING

**OBJECTIVE ▶**

At the end of this unit, you will write an opinion essay about a specific discovery or type of exploration. This essay will include specific information from the readings, the unit video, and your own ideas.

## WRITING SKILL  Writing an opinion essay

The purpose of writing an **opinion essay** is to give a personal response to a topic. The essay expresses how you feel about an issue. It may try to convince your readers that your view of a topic is the correct one or one that they should take seriously.

An effective opinion essay should follow these guidelines.

- In your introduction, express your opinion clearly in a thesis statement.
- In your body paragraphs, provide specific reasons for your opinion— one main reason in each body paragraph. Support your reasons with facts, examples, and logical arguments.
- In your conclusion, summarize your opinion.

**WRITING TIP**

In an opinion essay, avoid generalizations and other unsupported statements. They weaken your position because they are often easy to challenge.

**A. WRITING MODEL**  Read the model opinion essay. Underline the thesis statement and circle the three main reasons for the author's opinion.

### Is Deep-Sea Exploration Worth the Money?

1    In difficult economic times, the amount of money spent on exploration and discovery is always reduced. This has happened several times over the last 50 years with both space and deep-sea exploration. People are generally more enthusiastic about space, but I feel the oceans hold the solutions to some of the biggest problems of the twenty-first century. We must continue to invest in exploration of the deep sea so that we can take advantage of its benefits.

2    The deep sea contains resources that could bring improvements in the field of medicine. Antibiotics are becoming less effective in the treatment of illnesses, and scientists think that plant life in the deep oceans may provide a solution. They hope to develop new medicines that will make it possible to fight disease for years to come. Some substances produced from deep-sea species are already being used in improved medical testing procedures. Recognizing the importance of this research, the 2008 Nobel Committee awarded the Nobel Prize for Chemistry to scientists in this area.

3    At a time when existing forms of fuel are limited, the deep ocean could provide new sources of fuel. For more than 50 years, oil companies have been drilling in areas like the North Sea. Realizing that these offshore resources will not last forever, oil companies are now considering other sources, including the huge amounts of oil beneath the ocean

bed. However, extracting it safely will require major advancements in technology. Another possible deep-sea fuel source is methane. Having discovered that methane exists on the ocean floor in the form of ice crystals, scientists believe this could be a fuel source for the future.

4  Finally, using the deep sea for the disposal of nuclear waste is a controversial issue that needs to be explored further. Some organizations have proposed dropping nuclear waste into the deepest parts of the ocean and sealing it into the ocean floor. Many scientists claim that this process would involve less danger to the environment than current storage methods. While I find this idea disturbing, I accept that most people do not want to live near nuclear waste, so I think the proposal needs to be investigated.

5  These are just three of the ways in which learning about the deep ocean may change our lives for the better. In my view, such advances in our knowledge justify the expense of carrying out deep-sea research. The demand for land is only continuing to grow. The time has come when the 70 percent of our planet covered by water is just too big to ignore.

**ACADEMIC LANGUAGE**

The phrase *the ways in which* is commonly used in academic writing.

_____ | **OPAL**

Oxford Phrasal Academic Lexicon

**TIP FOR SUCCESS**

Remember: When you summarize, you combine or shorten language using some words from the text and some of your own words.

**B. CATEGORIZE** Complete the outline of the essay by briefly summarizing the information you have read.

I.  Thesis statement: _____

_____

II.  Reason 1: <u>The deep sea could bring improvements in medicine.</u>

   A.  Support 1: _____

   B.  Support 2: <u>Scientists who research this area won a Nobel Prize.</u>

III.  Reason 2: _____

   A.  Support 1: _____

   B.  Support 2: _____

IV.  Reason 3: _____

   A.  Support 1: _____

   B.  Support 2: <u>Deep-ocean disposal could be safer than current methods.</u>

V.  Concluding idea: _____

_____

**C. CREATE** Choose three topics from the box. Then write your opinion and three reasons to support your opinion.

archeological exploration     minerals
Arctic exploration     preservation of resources
~~finding a park~~     new species of animal
genetically modified food     space exploration

1. Opinion: _Finding a park within a city is an important discovery._

   Reason 1: _Being in a park is good for my health._

   Reason 2: _A park extends my living space._

   Reason 3: _Being in a park gives me choices._

2. Opinion: _____

   Reason 1: _____

   Reason 2: _____

   Reason 3: _____

3. Opinion: _____

   Reason 1: _____

   Reason 2: _____

   Reason 3: _____

4. Opinion: _____

   Reason 1: _____

   Reason 2: _____

   Reason 3: _____

**D. WRITING MODEL** Read the model opinion essay. Then answer the questions that follow.

## Exploring the Concrete Jungle

1   "Concrete jungle" is a common expression used to speak about cities, especially those in the United States that do not have much "green space." Finding a public park or garden in the midst of all the concrete can be a truly wonderful discovery.

2   I feel better when I can spend time outdoors around trees and grass, not to mention birds and butterflies. The presence of other living things is calming and revitalizing, and I can clear my mind of all the stress of the day. In fact, the University of Exeter Medical School has shown that there is an increase in mental health for people who move to greener cities. In addition, just getting to a park makes me get up and get moving, so I get some exercise even before I arrive at my destination. Once at the park, I usually keep moving, whether at a brisk walk or a leisurely stroll, so I continue to benefit physically.

3   A second reason for searching out a park is that it extends my living space. I live in a small apartment with very little room. I can use a park for activities that I cannot do at home, such as exercising and walking. At home, I am likely to knock something off a table or hit my foot on a piece of furniture. Another extension of my living space comes from my very limited ability to keep plants alive. By visiting a public garden, I can enjoy flowers and plants without worrying about overwatering them or not having enough sunlight for them.

4   Furthermore, I have choices in a park. I can stay by myself, strike up a conversation with someone, or engage in a game of soccer, depending on what I want to do that day. I have no obligation to buy something, as I do in a coffee shop or café, and no pressure to spend money, like I have in a shopping mall. While some parks are closed at night, others are not, so I can enjoy what they have to offer at many times of the day or night.

5   I am lucky to live in a city that has a lot of public parks, which improve my health, extend my living space, and give me choices. Because I appreciate having plants, animals, and other people around me, I look for green areas wherever I go. How about you? Have you discovered any parks or gardens around you?

1.   What is the thesis statement? Underline it, and circle the reasons that support it.

2.   For each reason, give two supporting details from the essay.

   Reason 1: _____

   _____

Reason 2: _____

_____

Reason 3: _____

_____

**iQ** PRACTICE  Go online for more practice writing opinion essays.
*Practice > Unit 7 > Activity 10*

## GRAMMAR  Adverb phrases of reason

Adverb clauses of reason give information about why an action occurs. They usually begin with a subordinator such as *because* or *since*. When the subjects of both clauses are the same, an adverb clause can often be reduced (shortened) to an **adverb phrase**.

To reduce an adverb clause with a simple verb, omit the subject and change the verb to the present participle (verb + *-ing*).

> **Adverb clause:** **Since they realize** that offshore resources will not last forever, oil companies are now considering other sources.
>
> **Because they recognized** the importance of this research, the Nobel Committee awarded the Nobel Prize for Chemistry to scientists in this area.
>
> **Adverb phrase:** **Realizing** that offshore resources will not last forever, oil companies are now considering other sources.
>
> **Recognizing** the importance of this research, the Nobel Committee awarded the Nobel Prize for Chemistry to scientists in this area.

To reduce an adverb clause with a perfect verb, use *having* + the past participle of the verb.

> **Adverb clause:** **Because they had discovered** that methane exists on the ocean floor, scientists believed this could be a fuel source for the future.
>
> **Adverb phrase:** **Having discovered** that methane exists on the ocean floor, scientists believed this could be a fuel source for the future.

Adverb phrases of reason almost always come before the main clause.

**iQ** RESOURCES  Go online to watch the Grammar Skill Video.
*Resources > Video > Unit 7 > Grammar Skill Video*

**TIP FOR SUCCESS**

Using adverb phrases can help you express complex ideas in fewer words. Vary your writing by using both adverb clauses and adverb phrases.

**A. COMPOSE**  Reduce each adverb clause in bold to an adverb phrase.

1. **Because they want to develop the area,** energy companies came to Bristol Bay.

   Wanting to develop the area, _____

2. **Since they have lived there for centuries,** the Alaska Natives do not want Bristol Bay to be damaged.

_____

3. **Because they have developed new technologies,** scientists are now better able to explore the oceans.

_____

4. **Since they are above sea level,** New Zealand and New Caledonia are the only visible features of the landmass.

_____

5. **Because it has been surveyed extensively,** Zealandia can provide a test for computer models that scientists use to predict changes in our climate. All of this impacts life on Earth.

_____

B. **APPLY** Write the full adverb clause form of each adverb phrase. Look at the main clause to help you choose the correct verb form: present, past, or perfect.

1. Understanding the significance of calling Zealandia a continent, geologists are actively discussing the findings of the latest expedition.

   _Because they understand the significance of calling Zealandia a continent,_

2. Recognizing the importance of the discovery, newspapers published the story immediately.

   _____

3. Having heard about the discovery of the coral reef, other scientists are eager to learn more.

   _____

4. Hoping to stop the Pebble Mine, an alliance of commercial fishermen, native tribes, and concerned citizens asked the government to get involved.

   _____

5. Having determined that the mine would have a negative impact, the EPA temporarily stopped Northern Dynasty Minerals from building it.

   _____

**iQ PRACTICE** Go online for more practice with adverb phrases of reason and time. _Practice > Unit 7 > Activities 11–12_

## UNIT ASSIGNMENT

### OBJECTIVE ▶

**Write an opinion essay**

In this assignment, you are going to write a five-paragraph opinion essay about a specific discovery or type of exploration. As you prepare your essay, think about the Unit Question, "Is discovery always a good thing?" Use information from Reading 1, Reading 2, the unit video, and your work in this unit to support your essay. Refer to the Self-Assessment checklist on page 210.

**iQ** PRACTICE   Go online to the writing tutor to read a model opinion essay. *Practice > Unit 7 > Activity 13*

# PLAN AND WRITE

**A. BRAINSTORM** Follow these steps to help you organize your ideas.

1. Think of specific discoveries that you read about in this unit, other discoveries that interest you, or different types of exploration in general (such as space exploration or archeological exploration).

2. Work with a partner. Choose three discoveries or types of exploration and write them in the chart. Brainstorm the positive and negative aspects of each and add your ideas.

| Discoveries or types of exploration | Positive aspects | Negative aspects |
|---|---|---|
| 1. | | |
| 2. | | |
| 3. | | |

3. Compare the positive and negative aspects of each discovery or type of exploration. Choose one and decide whether you think it is a good thing or a bad thing.

**B. PLAN** Follow these steps to plan your essay.

1. Write a thesis statement that clearly expresses your opinion about whether the discovery or type of exploration is a good thing or a bad thing.

2. Choose your best ideas from Activity A. Include three specific reasons and two or three pieces of supporting information for each reason.

**iQ** RESOURCES  Go online to download and complete the outline for your opinion essay. *Resources > Writing Tools > Unit 7 > Outline*

**C. WRITE** Use your planning notes to write your essay.

1. Write your opinion essay. Remember to write an introduction with a thesis statement expressing your opinion, body paragraphs providing specific reasons, and a conclusion summarizing your opinion.

2. Look at the Self-Assessment checklist below to guide your writing.

**iQ** PRACTICE  Go online to the Writing Tutor to write your assignment. *Practice > Unit 7 > Activity 14*

# REVISE AND EDIT

**iQ** RESOURCES  Go online to download the peer review worksheet. *Resources > Unit 7 > Peer Review Worksheet*

**A. PEER REVIEW** Read your partner's essay. Then use the peer review worksheet. Discuss the review with your partner.

**B. REWRITE** Based on your partner's review, revise and rewrite your essay.

**C. EDIT** Complete the Self-Assessment checklist as you prepare to write the final draft of your essay. Be prepared to hand in your work or discuss it in class.

| SELF-ASSESSMENT | Yes | No |
|---|---|---|
| Does the essay clearly express how you feel about the topic? | ☐ | ☐ |
| Are the reasons supported with facts, examples, and logical arguments? | ☐ | ☐ |
| If adverb phrases of reason are included, are they used correctly? | ☐ | ☐ |
| Does the essay include vocabulary from the unit? | ☐ | ☐ |
| Did you check the essay for punctuation, spelling, and grammar? | ☐ | ☐ |

**D. REFLECT** Discuss these questions with a partner or group.

1. What is something new you learned in this unit?

2. Look back at the Unit Question—Is discovery always a good thing? Is your answer different now than when you started the unit? If yes, how is it different? Why?

**iQ** PRACTICE  Go to the online discussion board to discuss the questions. *Practice > Unit 7 > Activity 15*

# TRACK YOUR SUCCESS

**iQ** PRACTICE  Go online to check the words and phrases you have learned in this unit. *Practice > Unit 7 > Activity 16*

Check (✓) the skills and strategies you learned. If you need more work on a skill, refer to the page(s) in parentheses.

READING ☐ I can recognize facts and opinions. (p. 191)

CRITICAL THINKING ☐ I can synthesize information. (p. 200)

VOCABULARY ☐ I can recognize word roots and their meanings. (p. 201)

WRITING ☐ I can write an opinion essay. (p. 203)

GRAMMAR ☐ I can use adverb phrases of reason. (p. 207)

OBJECTIVE ▶ ☐ I can gather information and ideas to write an opinion essay about a specific discovery or type of exploration.

# Engineering

8

# Can failure lead to success?

**A.** Discuss these questions with your classmates.

1. Have you participated in a project where you learned a skill or put into practice a skill you learned? How important is learning by doing?

2. Give an example of a historical failure that taught us something.

3. What are the people in the photo doing? Who benefits from this type of project?

**B.** Listen to *The Q Classroom* online. Then answer these questions.

1. What examples of failure leading to success do the students give? What example can you think of?

2. Do you agree with Marcus that the desire to succeed will ultimately lead to success? Why or why not?

**iQ** PRACTICE   Go to the online discussion board to discuss the Unit Question with your classmates. *Practice › Unit 8 › Activity 1*

**UNIT OBJECTIVE**

Read an article from an engineering magazine and an article from an international newspaper. Gather information and ideas to write a persuasive essay about whether failure can lead to success.

## READING 1

# The Tacoma Narrows Bridge Collapse and the Lessons Learned

**OBJECTIVE ▶**

You are going to read an engineering magazine article about a bridge that failed and what engineers learned by studying it. Use the article to gather information and ideas for your Unit Assignment.

## PREVIEW THE READING

**A. PREVIEW** Read the title. Look at the images and chart.

1. What do you think you will learn about the Tacoma Narrows Bridge?

2. What do you think caused the bridge to fail?

**B. QUICK WRITE** Have you tried to do something and failed? What do we learn by failing? Is failure a good or bad thing? Write for 5–10 minutes in response. Remember to use this section for your Unit Assignment.

**C. VOCABULARY** Check (✓) the words you know. Use a dictionary to define any new or unknown words. Then discuss with a partner how the words will relate to the unit.

| | |
|---|---|
| **attach** *(v.)* 🔑+ | **prevail** *(v.)* 🔑+ |
| **convenience** *(n.)* 🔑+ | **ratio** *(n.)* 🔑+ OPAL |
| **cumulative** *(adj.)* OPAL | **stabilize** *(v.)* 🔑+ OPAL |
| **flexible** *(adj.)* 🔑+ OPAL | **susceptible** *(adj.)* |
| **fragile** *(adj.)* 🔑+ | **twist** *(v.)* 🔑+ |
| **induce** *(v.)* 🔑+ OPAL | **vibrate** *(v.)* |

🔑+ Oxford 5000™ words          OPAL Oxford Phrasal Academic Lexicon

**iQ PRACTICE** Go online to listen and practice your pronunciation.
*Practice > Unit 8 > Activity 2*

# WORK WITH THE READING

 **A. INVESTIGATE** Read the article and gather information about whether failure can lead to success.

# The Tacoma Narrows Bridge Collapse and the Lessons Learned

1    Suspension bridges are amazing structures. They appear **fragile** but are very strong. They are relatively light and **flexible**. This makes them ideal for long crossings, but **susceptible** to wind, causing them to **vibrate** and move, both vertically (up and down) and laterally (sideways). It was a mixture of these elements—lightness, flexibility, and wind—as well as a forgotten lesson learned, that led to one of the most famous bridge failures in history: the Tacoma Narrows Bridge collapse.

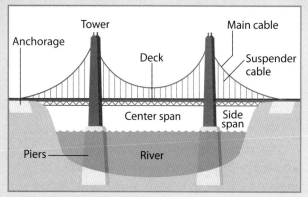

A suspension bridge

## The Tacoma Narrows Bridge

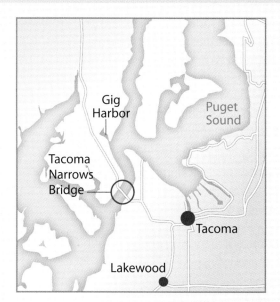

2    When completed in the summer of 1940, the Tacoma Narrows Bridge was the third longest suspension bridge in the world with a center span[1] of 2,800 feet and a total length of 5,979 feet. For comparison, typical center spans range from 2,000 to 7,000 feet, and the longest suspension bridge in the world today is the Akashi Kaikyo Bridge in Japan with a center span of 6,527 feet and a total length of 12,828 feet. Like other suspension bridges, the Tacoma Narrows Bridge had a roadway (called a *deck*) suspended by large cables. The cables were anchored[2] at each end of the bridge and passed over the top of tall towers built onto piers. The deck was **attached** with suspender cables, and its weight was supported primarily by the towers. However, unlike its predecessors, the Tacoma Narrows Bridge was just 39 feet wide, allowing for only two lanes of traffic.

3    After the bridge opened, many drivers drove it not for the **convenience** of crossing over Puget Sound but for the experience: when moderate winds blew, the bridge would sway from side to side and sometimes even undulate[3]. On windy days, the sensation was so pronounced that drivers reported that the car ahead of them would sometimes disappear and reappear several times as they crossed the bridge. People compared the bridge to a roller coaster, and it was given a nickname: Galloping Gertie.

---

[1] **span:** the part of a bridge or an arch between one vertical support and another

[2] **anchored:** fixed firmly in position so that it cannot move

[3] **undulate:** to go or move gently up and down like waves

4    Because of concerns about the movement, University of Washington engineering professor F. B. Farquharson and his engineering students were hired to try to **stabilize** the bridge. Ultimately, however, their efforts were unsuccessful. The bridge collapsed on November 7, 1940, just four months after it opened. Fortunately, there were no human fatalities. Only a dog that wouldn't leave a car died when the bridge fell. The last people on the bridge were *Tacoma News Tribune* photographer Howard Clifford and Farquharson. They ran off the bridge just as the center span finally broke off at 11:00 a.m. Dramatic video shows the bridge **twisting** violently in the wind and eventually falling into the water.

## Why the Bridge Failed

5    The bridge's failure led to a decades-long attempt to understand the effect of wind-**induced** motion on suspension bridges. At the time, engineers concluded that the **cumulative** effect of undampened[4] rhythmic forces produced the motion that ultimately caused the bridge to fail. For years that idea **prevailed**—specifically, that the collapse was related to resonance, a phenomenon that caused the wind to resonate[5] with the natural frequency of the bridge's structure, resulting in a steady increase in amplitude[6] until the bridge was destroyed. This explanation and the film of the collapse were widely used in physics classes to demonstrate resonance.

6    Today, most engineers disagree with that explanation. They believe that aerodynamic instability caused the bridge to fail. In studying the film and other evidence, they believe a cable slipped and the bridge's motion changed from vertical to twisting. The deck—too narrow, light, and shallow—continued to lift and twist. This in turn caused the wind to split around the bridge, which created a swirling[7] pattern that further lifted and twisted the deck. The bridge went into a self-induced vibration. The forces acting on the bridge were no longer caused by the wind but rather became self-generated: its twisting generated more twisting. Eventually, this motion resulted in the deck breaking and falling. This vibration, called *torsional flutter*, is the most probable explanation of the bridge's failure. In other words, the bridge was too flexible, both vertically and in torsion (twisting). Due to its width-to-length **ratio**, 1 to 72, the bridge was not resistant enough to twisting forces. Today, no suspension bridge has a ratio greater than 1 to 47.

## Lesson Learned

7    The story of the Tacoma Narrows Bridge can be seen as a lesson learned, forgotten, and then relearned. Engineers in the late 1800s appear to have known that suspension bridges that were too light and too flexible would fail, and so they built bridges heavier and stiffer[8], like the 1883 Brooklyn Bridge. But that lesson apparently was forgotten, as J.K. Finch suggested in his summary of suspension bridge failures published soon after the Tacoma Narrows Bridge collapse. The failure also shows that aerodynamic forces were not well understood. Today, wind-tunnel testing of bridge designs is commonplace.

8    In 1950, a new Tacoma Narrows Bridge was built, featuring a wider roadway, deeper and stiffer supports, and features to dampen the effect of the wind. That bridge, along with hundreds of other suspension bridges around the world, still stands today and is hopefully proof that lessons have been learned.

---

[4] **undampened:** excessive or continuing forces such as vibration, and therefore instability, in a mechanical device
[5] **resonate:** to move in response to something
[6] **amplitude:** the greatest distance that a wave, especially a sound or radio wave, vibrates
[7] **swirling:** moving around quickly in a circle; to make something do this
[8] **stiff:** firm and difficult to move

# The Tacoma Narrows Bridge & Contemporaries

|  | George Washington | Golden Gate | Brooklyn | Tacoma Narrows |
|---|---|---|---|---|
| Year completed | 1935 | 1937 | 1883 | 1940 |
| Cost | $59.5 million | $35 million | $15.5 million | $6.4 million |
| Length of center span | 3,500 ft | 4,200 ft | 1,595 ft | 2,800 ft |
| Width (of wind truss) | 106 ft | 90 ft | 90 ft | 39 ft |
| Ratio: width-to-length (of center span) | 1:33 | 1:47 | 1:19 | 1:72 |

1 foot = 0.3048 meters

**ACADEMIC LANGUAGE**

The phrase *can be seen (as)* is often used in academic writing to give an example.

**OPAL**
Oxford Phrasal Academic Lexicon

**B. VOCABULARY** Here are some words from Reading 1. Read the sentences. Then write the correct form of each bold word next to the correct definition.

1. We need a **flexible** material—something that bends but won't break.

2. There are double the number of men to women in that occupation, making the **ratio** 2 to 1.

3. Climate change is increased by the **cumulative** effect of many human activities.

4. When she knocked it over, the **fragile** statue broke into many pieces.

5. She caught her foot in the hole, fell down, and **twisted** her ankle.

6. They worked to **stabilize** the damaged building after the earthquake.

7. It is better to fall asleep naturally than to **induce** sleep with drugs.

8. The cable broke at the place where it was **attached** to the tower.

9. She was so convincing that her idea **prevailed** over all others.

10. Anything mechanical that moves will naturally **vibrate**, and it is important to control that movement.

11. He must be **susceptible** to colds since he is always sick.

12. We appreciate the **convenience** of living near a bridge into town.

a. _____ *(v.)* to become or to make something become firm, steady, and unlikely to change; to make something stable

b. _____ *(n.)* something that is useful and can make things easier or quicker to do, or more comfortable

c. _____ *(v.)* to fasten or join one thing to another

d. _____ *(adj.)* able to bend easily without breaking

e. _____ *(adj.)* (to somebody/something) very likely to be influenced, harmed, or affected by somebody/something

f. _____ *(v.)* (against/over something) (of ideas, opinions, etc.) to be accepted, especially after a struggle or an argument

g. _____ *(v.)* to move or make something move very quickly and with small movements

h. _____ *(n.)* (of A to B) the relationship between two groups, represented by two numbers showing how much larger one group is than the other

i. _____ *(v.)* to cause something

j _____ *(adj.)* having a result that increases in strength or importance each time more of something is added

k. _____ *(v.)* to bend or turn something into a shape or position that is not normal or natural; to be bent or turned in this way

l. _____ *(adj.)* easily broken or damaged

**iQ PRACTICE** Go online for more practice with vocabulary.
*Practice > Unit 8 > Activity 3*

## C. IDENTIFY Circle the answer that best completes each statement.

1. Suspension bridges are susceptible to the wind because they are ____.

   a. too long

   b. fragile

   c. light and flexible

2. People drove across the bridge because it was ____.

   a. fun when it was windy

   b. the only way to cross the Puget Sound

   c. the longest bridge in the world

3. Engineers were hired to stabilize the bridge to ____.

   a. prevent fatalities

   b. stop it from moving so much

   c. keep people from driving on it for fun

4. The Tacoma Narrows bridge failure was used in physics classes in order to ____.

   a. demonstrate resonance

   b. explain bridge failures

   c. shock students

5. Suspension bridges today are built with a width-to-length ratio no greater than 1 to 47 so that they are ____.

   a. stronger

   b. less flexible

   c. lighter

6. The best explanation of "torsional flutter" is ____.

   a. split winds in a swirling pattern

   b. lifting and twisting

   c. self-induced twisting motion

7. J.K. Finch's summary showed that engineers ____.

   a. didn't know the reasons for the failure of early bridges

   b. had forgotten by the 1930s the lessons learned

   c. didn't learn from early bridge failures for a hundred years

8. The purpose of the article is ____.

   a. to inform readers about a suspension bridge

   b. to exemplify how failures teach lessons

   c. to entertain us

**D. CATEGORIZE** Read the statements. Write *T* (true) or *F* (false) and the paragraph number where the answer is found. Then correct each false statement to make it true according to the article.

____ 1. Suspension bridges are fragile. (paragraph ____)

____ 2. The Tacoma Narrows Bridge was the longest suspension bridge at the time it was built. (paragraph ____)

____ 3. The cause of the bridge failure was resonance. (paragraph ____)

____ 4. When a cable slipped, the bridge immediately fell. (paragraph ____)

____ 5. The Brooklyn Bridge is an example of the lesson engineers forgot. (paragraph ____)

**E. EXPLAIN** Answer the questions. Use examples from the readings.

1.  Why do suspension bridges move?

    _____

2.  Why was the Tacoma Narrows Bridge nicknamed Galloping Gertie?

    _____

3.  Who died in the collapse of the bridge?

    _____

4.  What are two theories of why the bridge failed?

    _____

5.  Why did the Tacoma Narrows Bridge twist?

    _____

6.  What was the lesson that engineers of suspension bridges forgot?

    _____

7.  Why was the Brooklyn Bridge built heavier and stiffer?

    _____

 **CRITICAL THINKING STRATEGY**

### Hypothesizing

To **hypothesize** is to suggest a way of explaining something when you do
not definitely know the reason. Scientists hypothesize when they take all the
information they know and try to come up with new ideas or explanations.
For example, the engineers who studied the collapse of the Tacoma Narrows
Bridge had different hypotheses about the root cause of the bridge's failure.
Look at the chart.

| What happened | Explanation | Hypothesis |
|---|---|---|
| The motion changed from vertical to torsional. | The motion was caused by resonance. | Resonance |
| The twisting motion became greater and greater. | The motion was due to aerodynamic instability, resulting in self-induced vibration. | Torsional flutter |

**iQ** PRACTICE  Go online to watch the Critical Thinking Skill Video and
check your comprehension. *Practice › Unit 8 › Activity 4*

**F. CATEGORIZE** Read the causes and explanations for the Tacoma Narrows Bridge failure. Check (✓) the correct column for each statement based on which hypothesis it best fits. Check (✓) *Both* if it is a cause in both hypotheses.

| Cause/Explanation | Resonance | Torsional flutter | Both |
|---|---|---|---|
| 1. Undampened rhythmic force (paragraph 5) | ✓ | | |
| 2. Wind resonating at the natural frequency of the bridge structure (paragraph 5) | ✓ | | |
| 3. Steady increase in amplitude (paragraph 5) | | | |
| 4. Self-induced vibration (paragraph 6) | | | |
| 5. Twisting generating more twisting (paragraph 6) | | ✓ | |
| 6. Deck too narrow, light, and shallow (paragraph 6) | | | |
| 7. Winds split around the bridge in a swirling pattern (paragraph 6) | | | |
| 8. Bridge too flexible (paragraph 6) | | | |

**G. ANALYZE** For each event, write a hypothesis for why the event occurs. When you finish, check your ideas against the answers on page 222.

1. Why can we see through glass? _____

   _____

2. Why does ice float? _____

   _____

3. Why do apples turn brown when they are cut into pieces? _____

   _____

4. Why do cats sleep so much? _____

   _____

5. Why do balloons stick to a wall if you rub them in your hair? _____

   _____

**H. SYNTHESIZE** Look back at your Quick Write on page 214. Is failure a good thing or a bad thing? What do we learn by failing? Add any new ideas or information you learned from the reading.

iQ PRACTICE Go online for additional reading and comprehension.
*Practice > Unit 8 > Activity 5*

# WRITE WHAT YOU THINK

**A. DISCUSS** Discuss the questions in a group. Think about the Unit Question, "Can failure lead to success?"

1. How is studying failure a good way to learn?

2. Is it important to find a cause for every failure?

3. In what ways is studying success a better way to learn?

**B. SYNTHESIZE** Choose one of the questions from Activity A and write a paragraph of 5–7 sentences in response. Look back at your Quick Write on page 214 as you think about what you learned.

---

**Activity G Answers:**

1. Photons, or particles of light, pass through glass, making it transparent, because the atoms in glass need energy to absorb the photons. The energy that the photons carry is not enough to cause the atoms to absorb them.

2. Ice floats because when liquid water changes to solid water, or ice, the hydrogen in the water molecules attract each other and form a crystal structure. This causes the molecules to move more slowly and spread out. Since the same weight of ice takes up more space, it is less dense and so it floats.

3. Apples have an enzyme that turns brown when it mixes with oxygen from the air.

4. In the wild, cats must hunt for their food, which takes a lot of energy. To preserve energy, cats sleep about 16 hours per day. Even when they don't have to hunt for food, cats still sleep that much.

5. By rubbing balloons in your hair, you are adding negative charges from your hair to the balloons. The balloons are then attracted to the wall, which is more positive than they are.

---

When you are reading a text, it is important to distinguish the author's opinion from any counterarguments. A **counterargument** is an idea that opposes the author's point of view. It is often introduced by a clause that identifies the source or a clause with a general subject, such as *many experts say* or *some people think*.

> **Counterargument:** <u>Engineers used to think</u> that the Tacoma Narrows Bridge collapsed because of resonance.

A counterargument is generally followed by a **refutation** from the author. A refutation tries to show that the counterargument is weak or incorrect. The refutation is often introduced by an expression that shows disagreement, such as *on the contrary, however,* or *but in fact*.

> **Refutation:** <u>However</u>, engineers now disagree with the explanation. Most today believe that aerodynamic instability caused the bridge to fail.

**C. IDENTIFY** Match the counterarguments with the correct refutations. Then underline the clauses and expressions that introduce them.

**Counterarguments**

1. The original engineer argued that the weight of the deck would be heavy enough to dampen excessive motion. ____

2. The design was chosen because people thought it would save money. ____

3. Initially, engineers contended that the failure was due to the bridge resonating at the same frequency as the wind. ____

4. The engineering professor and his students believed they had found solutions to save the bridge. ____

5. The engineers believed that the design of the bridge—longer, more flexible, and narrow—was sound. ____

6. Some claimed that the Tacoma Narrows Bridge would never be rebuilt. ____

**Refutations**

a. In reality, the cost of rebuilding made the bridge much more expensive.

b. However, aerodynamic instability was shown to be the more likely cause when wind tunnel studies were conducted.

c. On the contrary, a new, safer bridge was built in the same place.

d. But, in fact, the deck was too light and moved both laterally and vertically in the wind.

e. Despite their efforts, the bridge collapsed.

f. In fact, they appear to have forgotten lessons from early suspension bridge failures with this design.

**iQ PRACTICE** Go online for more practice with identifying counterarguments and refutations. *Practice > Unit 8 > Activity 6*

## READING 2

# How to Design a Student Project That Benefits the Developing World

**OBJECTIVE ▶**

You are going to read an article by Keith Pullen, a writer for the international newspaper *The Guardian.* Pullen, a professor of energy systems at City University, London, looks at student engineering projects. Use the article to gather information and ideas for your Unit Assignment.

## PREVIEW THE READING

**A. PREVIEW** Read the first two paragraphs. Check (✓) everything you found.

- ☐ 1. examples of fields of engineering
- ☐ 2. a definition of engineering
- ☐ 3. a purpose for engineering
- ☐ 4. examples of current engineering projects
- ☐ 5. a concern of professional engineers
- ☐ 6. a concern of engineering students
- ☐ 7. a way for engineering schools to show connection to the world

**B. QUICK WRITE** The title of the article begins with "How to" not "Why." Why do you think universities want student projects to benefit a real-world community and not be just assignments? Write for 5–10 minutes in response. Remember to use this section for your Unit Assignment.

**C. VOCABULARY** Check (✓) the words you know. Use a dictionary to define any unknown words. Then discuss how the words will relate to the unit.

| | | |
|---|---|---|
| alleviation *(n.)* | incur *(v.)* ₽+ | relevance *(n.)* ₽+ OPAL |
| charity *(n.)* ₽+ | locale *(n.)* | respective *(adj.)* ₽+ |
| criteria *(n.)* ₽+ OPAL | methodology *(n.)* ₽+ OPAL | substantial *(adj.)* ₽+ OPAL |
| faculty *(n.)* ₽+ | output *(n.)* ₽+ OPAL | vague *(adj.)* ₽+ |

₽+ Oxford 5000™ words          OPAL Oxford Phrasal Academic Lexicon

**iQ PRACTICE** Go online to listen and practice your pronunciation. *Practice > Unit 8 > Activity 7*

# WORK WITH THE READING

 **A. INVESTIGATE** Read the article and gather information about how student projects can benefit real world communities.

# HOW TO DESIGN A STUDENT PROJECT THAT BENEFITS THE DEVELOPING WORLD

*by Keith Pullen*

*Can university projects provide valuable experience for students and sustainable solutions for poor communities? Keith Pullen, a professor of energy systems at City University, London, explains how his engineering department meets both objectives.*

1    Engineering is the science, skill, and profession of applying scientific, economic, social, and practical knowledge in order to design and build structures, machines, devices, systems, and processes. This is true in all fields of engineering: mechanical, marine, chemical, materials, mining, civil, electrical and electronic, biomedical, or aeronautical engineering. The study and practice of engineering is about positively impacting the quality of life enjoyed by society as a whole.

2    Frequently, students arrive at university armed with good qualifications. However, they are **vague** about the kind and quality of impact they can make on society when they leave three to four years later. One of the ways in which engineering education programs demonstrate **relevance** to society is in addressing pressing concerns, such as poverty **alleviation** and sustainable development in emerging nations.

3    This comes into even sharper focus in light of the need for a fresh approach to technology transfer. The approach must factor in the needs of the people on the ground[1]. It should be one that builds the capacity of local technicians in maintenance and mechanics, nurtures local entrepreneurship, and above all, harnesses the creativity of innovative students.

4    Developing Technologies (DT) is a **charity** that was established in the Department of Mechanical Engineering at Imperial College, London. It is now based at the School of Engineering and Mathematical Sciences at City University, London. It operates at both institutions.

[1] **on the ground:** in the place where something is happening and among the people who are in the situation

5　It uses the project work of BEng and MEng[2] mechanical engineering students to provide affordable technical support to organizations working in developing countries. The overall objective is poverty relief in the communities where the charity has established a presence through its contacts in the NGO[3] community.

6　To ensure that DT's engineering programs set out to develop usable technologies, DT combines engineering and technical education with the needs of rural communities. DT works in countries such as Nigeria, Sierra Leone, Tanzania, and Ghana. A recent example was the work we did with the self-help community organization Rural Water Aid (RWA) in Sierra Leone. Its aim was to develop a low-cost percussion drill. A heavy drill bit is repeatedly raised and dropped to bore the well so that RWA can supply water to local villages.

7　We appraise the projects we undertake against a number of **criteria**. They are prioritized for selection. It is essential that the projects meet the following conditions:

- ✿ They are appropriate with regard to the environment, local culture, situations, and benefit/costs ratios.
- ✿ They are appropriate and affordable for students: they include suitable academic content, reliable access to necessary information, knowledge, resources, and achievable **output**.
- ✿ They have high potential for overseas implementation and dissemination[4] with good partner support.
- ✿ They meet a wider demand beyond the specific partner application, with potential to have a significant impact on poverty relief.

8　Conducting field trips is an essential aspect of DT. These trips are organized in collaboration with Engineers Without Borders. Typically, students learn about the project they are working on while at the university. They study the culture, physical environment, and technical requirements related to the project. They learn how these may be applied to the developing country's needs. Then, by way of internships and short training sessions, they travel to the rural **locale** to apply their technical solutions during the summer holidays.

9　It is important to create an enabling learning environment for our students. However, the cost of the technologies we develop are also key to having real impact. Our approach and **methodology** is to be both affordable and sustainable. Much of the work in developing the technology is done within the **respective** engineering schools and **faculties** in the UK. Therefore, we **incur** no additional overhead costs. Thus, there isn't much expense to the recipients or end-users of the technology concerned. The charities on the ground assist DT in meeting costs in the countries concerned.

10　The final piece of the project puzzle is to ensure that there is a capacity-building component in DT projects. Local people develop mechanical skills (building and repairing low-technology vehicles, for example). They are also enabled to grow their own micro businesses and gain greater self-reliance. DT projects have the most **substantial** impact in relation to cost.

11　Overall, Developing Technologies has demonstrated the ability to parlay the enthusiasm of engineering students on respective courses into practical technologies[5]. These technologies help to reduce poverty. DT has also imparted soft skills to participating students. Students gain skills such as team-working, communication, and social awareness. They learn to work in multidisciplinary settings.

---

[2] **BEng and MEng:** bachelor's of engineering and master's of engineering
[3] **NGO (non-governmental organization):** a charity, association, etc., that is independent of government and business
[4] **dissemination:** the act of spreading information or knowledge so that it reaches many people
[5] **parlay something into something:** to use or develop something to make it more successful or worth more

**B. VOCABULARY** Complete the sentences with vocabulary from Reading 2. You may need to change the form of some of the words.

| | | |
|---|---|---|
| alleviation (n.) | incur (v.) | relevance (n.) |
| charity (n.) | locale (n.) | respective (adj.) |
| criteria (n.) | methodology (n.) | substantial (adj.) |
| faculty (n.) | output (n.) | vague (adj.) |

1. The _____ I give money to helps people build new homes.

2. That organization's goal is the _____ of suffering for people who have lost their homes.

3. There can be _____ damage to houses in an earthquake or flood.

4. We looked for a convenient and safe _____ in which to establish our new business.

5. Members of _____ from various departments attended the university meeting.

6. I saved money to pay for my classes. I didn't want to _____ debt when I went to school.

7. Do you know what _____ that scientist followed when she did her experiment?

8. I would like to find a career that has _____ to the city I'm living in. I want to do something that makes a difference in my neighborhood.

9. I have a(n) _____ idea of what the requirements of the mechanical engineering course are, but I'm not exactly sure.

10. The professors returned to their _____ departments at the end of the faculty meeting.

11. What _____ were used to judge the essays in the contest?

12. The factory monitors its _____ to make sure that production doesn't slow down.

**iQ** PRACTICE Go online for more practice with the vocabulary.
*Practice > Unit 8 > Activity 8*

**C. IDENTIFY** Check (✓) the main idea of the article.

☐ 1. Universities should require students to do projects that benefit others.

☐ 2. Engineering programs can simultaneously give students real-life experience and address real-world concerns.

☐ 3. Students have to follow certain guidelines when doing engineering projects.

**D. IDENTIFY** Circle the answer that best completes each statement.

1. Student projects can benefit both the students and their university by ____.

   a. providing a job for the students at the university

   b. providing experience for the students and demonstrating the university's value to society

   c. demonstrating the qualifications of the students and providing work for the university

2. A good student project ____, according to the article.

   a. lets local people develop skills, helps local businesses, and works with students' ideas

   b. requires mechanical engineering skills, builds maintenance skills, and creates local entrepreneurship

   c. builds capacity of entrepreneurs, employs local students, and maintains innovative technicians

3. Developing Technologies ____.

   a. works with engineering students at two universities

   b. works with NGOs

   c. both a and b

4. The students who work on the projects ____.

   a. do all their work at the university and don't go to the actual locale

   b. go to the locale before they start work on the project

   c. go to the locale after they design the project

5. The people in the areas served by the student projects do not pay much, if anything, for the projects because ____.

   a. the universities and their partners pay most of the costs

   b. the students pay for the cost of the project, including costs in the countries concerned

   c. the government pays for everything

**E. IDENTIFY** Check (✓) the statement that the author would agree with. If the author would not agree, change the statement. Indicate the paragraph number where you found your answers.

☐ 1. Students come to the university with good ideas about how they can affect society when they graduate. (paragraph ___)

☐ 2. If a student project has no practical use for a given community, we won't do the project. (paragraph ___)

☐ 3. Students need guidance at the university, but they are on their own when they get to the field. (paragraph ___)

☐ 4. The universities have to hire specialists to work with the students. (paragraph ___)

☐ 5. The cost isn't important as long as the students learn something. (paragraph ___)

☐ 6. Local participants in the country where the project is done should also benefit from the project. (paragraph ___)

☐ 7. The students learn only engineering skills through their projects. (paragraph ___)

☐ 8. Students have a chance to work on a real project, make mistakes, correct the mistakes, and learn from them before they get a job as an engineer. (paragraph ___)

**F. EXPLAIN** Answer these questions. Then discuss them with a partner.

1. Why do you think the student projects have to have "achievable output"?

_____

_____

2. Why do you think Developing Technologies was set up as a charity?

_____

_____

3. Why is it important to have partners "on the ground" for the student projects?

_____

_____

# WORK WITH THE VIDEO

**A. PREVIEW** Do you think nuclear power is a viable energy source? Or is it too dangerous? Why?

## VIDEO VOCABULARY

**radiation (n.)** powerful and very dangerous rays sent out from radioactive substances

**evacuate (v.)** to move people from a place of danger to a safer place

**exposed (adj.)** without protection from something harmful

**defect (n.)** a fault in something or in the way it has been made which means that it is not perfect

**viable (adj.)** that can be done; that will be successful

**iQ RESOURCES** Go online to watch the video about the Chernobyl nuclear power station, site of the world's first major nuclear power plant accident.
*Resources > Video > Unit 8 > Unit Video*

**B. COMPOSE** Watch the video two or three times. Take notes in the chart.

|  | What happened | Explanation |
|---|---|---|
| Notes from the video |  |  |

**C. EXTEND** Do you think we should continue to use nuclear power? Why or why not? Discuss your ideas with a partner.

# WRITE WHAT YOU THINK

**SYNTHESIZE** Think about Reading 1, Reading 2, and the unit video as you discuss these questions. Then choose one question and write a paragraph of 5–7 sentences in response.

1. What were the failures and lessons learned in the readings and the video?

2. How is one situation from the readings and the video different from the other two?

3. We will always make mistakes. How can we lessen the impact of our mistakes?

There are several common collocation patterns with prepositions that are important to recognize and learn.

### Verb + preposition

Typically, students **learn about** the project they are working on while at the university.

### Verb + object + preposition

University projects **provide experience for** students.

Rural Water Aid **supplied water to** local villages.

### Adjective + preposition

Students are **vague about** the kind and quality of impact they can make.

The projects are **affordable for** students.

### Noun + preposition

There is a **need for** a fresh approach to technology transfer.

They have high **potential for** overseas implementation.

Engineering education programs demonstrate **relevance to** society in addressing pressing concerns.

Many verbs, adjectives, and nouns are followed by only one specific preposition.

Others can be followed by various prepositions with different uses or meanings.

**iQ RESOURCES** Go online to watch the Vocabulary Skill Video.
*Resources > Video > Unit 8 > Vocabulary Skill Video*

**TIP FOR SUCCESS**

When you write down a new word while reading, check the word to see if there is a preposition you should also write down. Dictionaries often list common collocations.

**A. APPLY** Read each paragraph and the sentences that follow. Complete the collocations with the correct preposition.

Developing Technologies uses the project work of BEng and MEng mechanical engineering students to provide support to organizations that work in developing countries. The overall objective is poverty relief in the communities where the charity has established a presence. Developing Technologies has built a relationship with various NGOs over many years.

1. The new professor **provides support** _____ the students that **work** _____ his lab.

2. He has used **the work** _____ the students to motivate new students to join the program.

3. He **builds relationships** _____ the students through the whole process.

We appraise the projects against a number of criteria. They are prioritized for selection. It is essential that the projects meet the following conditions:

- They are appropriate with regard to the environment, local culture, situations and benefit/costs ratios.

- They are appropriate and affordable for students: they include suitable academic content, reliable access to necessary information, knowledge, resources and achievable output.

- They have high potential for overseas implementation and dissemination with good partner support.

- They meet a wider demand beyond the specific partner application, with potential to have a significant impact on poverty relief.

4. Our professor gives assignments that are **appropriate** _____ our level of understanding.

5. She has had **an impact** _____ our work inside and outside the classroom.

6. Our assignments are appropriate **with regard** _____ the skills we will need when we graduate.

7. We feel we have the **potential** _____ go on to have exciting careers.

B. **COMPOSE** Write five sentences with collocations from Activity A or the Vocabulary Skill box.

1. _____

2. _____

3. _____

4. _____

5. _____

**iQ** PRACTICE  Go online for more practice with collocations with prepositions. *Practice > Unit 8 > Activity 9*

# WRITING

**OBJECTIVE ▶**

At the end of this unit, you will write a persuasive essay about whether failure can lead to success. This essay will include specific information from the readings, the unit video, and your own ideas.

## WRITING SKILL  Writing a persuasive essay

In a **persuasive essay**, the writer presents an issue, takes a position on the issue, and develops an argument to convince the reader that this position is correct. Persuasive essays often require research: you must collect evidence that relates to the topic, such as facts, statistics, and quotations from expert sources.

Consider this question: *Are real-world projects beneficial to students?* As the writer, you can argue that real-world projects are beneficial or are not beneficial. Either way, your position should be expressed clearly in a thesis statement in your introduction. Then you must persuade the reader that this position is right. Your body paragraphs should:

- clearly present the main arguments that support your thesis statement
- include facts, evidence, and examples that support each main argument
- present one or more counterarguments to show that you have considered opposing opinions
- acknowledge counterarguments if appropriate and respond to them with refutations

Finally, your conclusion should summarize all the arguments you have stated. It may also give a warning, prediction, or suggestion about what should happen next.

See the Reading Skill on page 223 for information on counterarguments and refutations.

**A. WRITING MODEL** Read the model persuasive essay. Circle the thesis statement. Underline the main ideas in paragraphs 2, 3, and 4.

### How can real-world projects benefit students?

1     Andrea made a critical error in her design of a water filtration system. However, before the design was used, her team members and their faculty advisor caught the error. Everyone learned from the experience, and Andrea was able to redesign the system before the team actually built it. This demonstrates how requiring students to do real-world projects benefits the students.

2　　One main reason to require real-world projects is to prepare students for real life. We do that by assigning them projects that reflect professional projects. In fact, in the case of the Department of Mechanical Engineering at Imperial College, London, the student projects become professional projects, with the help of the faculty and NGO partners. Thus, the students gain experience not only in the design of their projects but also in the implementation of and follow-up to the projects. They face some of the same challenges that professional engineers do, both in engineering and in social interactions on their team, and they have a professional project to put on their résumé.

3　　Furthermore, the amount of learning may be greater if the students have to deal with real-world problems. They have to work with the world as it is, not as it could be in an ideal site. For example, designing and setting up a website can be a preliminary project for an aspiring coder. However, doing the same thing for a client, even if the designer doesn't get paid for the work, can introduce the coder to many different ideas, problems, and restrictions from the client himself or herself, such as the need to have users fill out forms securely. Whereas not paying strict attention to security on a "dummy" student project may not have serious ramifications, not paying attention on a real-world project can result in grave consequences.

4　　There are those who will argue that not having all the complications of a real-world project provides for better attention to the material to be learned. Not having to deal with clients, climates, and other external factors allows students to focus on the engineering principles, or principles from other disciplines, that are being put into practice. While this may be true for beginning-level students, those students in the final years of their studies should be exposed to all the complexity of a real situation. This exposure comes while they have the support of faculty and other professionals whose position it is to guide them through the complications that arise. When the students get their first jobs in the field, they may not have the same kind of support and may, therefore, be more likely to make serious mistakes. Having real-world experience equips them with strategies to lessen the likelihood of making these mistakes.

5　　Having students work on real-world projects is beneficial to students as well as to the recipients of the projects. The time and effort spent on such projects yields professional-level experience, deeper learning, and a safer environment in which to develop necessary skills for the profession. We live in a complex, competitive world, and having to design and implement a real-world project while still at a university will better prepare us for our careers.

**WRITING TIP**

The combination of counterargument and refutation is a powerful technique. It shows that you have considered other opinions and creates an opportunity to say what is wrong with them. This can be more persuasive than concentrating entirely on your own point of view.

**B. IDENTIFY** Reread the essay on pages 233–234. Then circle the correct answer.

1. The example of Andrea in the introduction ___.

   a. shows the author's view

   b. is a counterargument

   c. provides background information

2. The thesis statement is ___.

   a. at the beginning of the introduction

   b. at the end of the introduction

   c. in the first body paragraph

3. Consider this sentence from paragraph 2: "One main reason to require real-world projects is to prepare students for real life." This is ___.

   a. the main idea of the paragraph

   b. a fact that supports the main idea

   c. a counterargument

4. Consider this sentence from paragraph 3: "They have to work with the world as it is, not as it could be in an ideal site." This is ___.

   a. the main idea of the paragraph

   b. a fact that supports the main idea

   c. a counterargument

5. Consider this sentence from paragraph 4: "There are those who will argue that not having all the complications of a real-world project provides for better attention to the material to be learned." This is ___.

   a. a fact that supports the thesis statement

   b. a counterargument

   c. a refutation

6. Which of the following does the author probably agree with?

   a. Every student project should benefit someone in the real world.

   b. No student project should have to benefit someone in the real world.

   c. Students in the early years of the university shouldn't have to do real-world projects.

7. In the conclusion, the author ___.

   a. makes a prediction

   b. gives a recommendation

   c. issues a warning

**C. COMPOSE** Read the thesis statement and first body paragraph of a persuasive essay. Write possible arguments, counterarguments, and refutations for the essay.

**Thesis statement:** The study and practice of engineering is about positively impacting the quality of life enjoyed by society as a whole.

**Body paragraph 1**

One way that engineering education programs can demonstrate relevance to society is by addressing pressing concerns, such as poverty alleviation and sustainable development in emerging nations. Specifically, they can engage students in meaningful student projects. A good student project should be one that harnesses the creativity of innovative students. In addition, it should build the capacity of local technicians in maintenance and mechanics and nurture local entrepreneurship. While it is important to create an enabling learning environment for our students and help the local people, the cost of the technologies we develop is also key to having real impact.

1. Argument: They can engage students in meaningful student projects.

   Counterargument: _Students should enter the university with their own values, so engineering schools should not concern themselves with teaching such ideas._

   Refutation: _While students have their own values, many universities embrace the importance of learning for the good of society and expect their students to hold a similar value._

2. Argument: A good student project should be one that harnesses the creativity of innovative students.

   Counterargument: _____

   Refutation: In order to motivate innovative students, allowing them to use their creativity must be considered a highly important piece of the project.

3. Argument: A good student project should build the capacity of local technicians in maintenance and mechanics.

   Counterargument: Some feel that a good student project should focus on building the skills of the student, not on those of local technicians.

   Refutation: _____

4. Argument: _____

   Counterargument: Many argue that the cost of a student project shouldn't be a point of consideration.

   Refutation: _____

5. Argument: _____

   Counterargument: _____

   Refutation: _____

**iQ** PRACTICE   Go online for more practice writing a persuasive essay.
*Practice > Unit 8 > Activity 10*

## GRAMMAR  Adverb clauses of concession

In an argument, you can use certain adverb clauses to acknowledge an idea and show that it is less important than the idea in the main clause. This is called *concession*. Concession clauses convey the idea "That's true, but…" Some subordinators that show concession are *although, even though, though, while,* and *despite the fact that.*

> **Although the Tacoma Narrow Bridge collapse was a disaster**, the lessons learned contributed to the success of future suspension bridge projects, including the rebuilding of the Tacoma Narrows Bridge.
>
> (Argument = The lessons learned when the Tacoma Narrows Bridge collapsed helped engineers with future suspension bridge projects.)
>
> **While this may be true for beginning-level students,** those students in the final years of their studies should be exposed to all the complexity of a real situation.
>
> (Argument = Students in the final years of their studies should participate in real-life projects.)

Consider these two ideas about student projects.

> Understanding theory is important for students.
> Understanding theory takes time away from projects.

Depending on your point of view, one idea is your argument, and the other is the counterargument that you want to refute.

>       concession clause               main clause
> Even though it takes time away from projects, understanding theory is
> important for students.

(Argument: Students can't ignore theory.)

>       concession clause               main clause
> Even though it is important for students, understanding theory takes time away
> from projects.

(Argument: Students need time to work on their projects.)

**A. APPLY** Use the subordinators in parentheses to combine the sentences. First, write a sentence that supports idea *a*. Then write a sentence that supports idea *b*. When combining sentences, replace the subject in one of the clauses with a pronoun.

1. a. A bridge failure is a tragedy.

   b. A bridge failure teaches valuable lessons.

   (while) _While it is a tragedy, a bridge failure teaches valuable lessons._

   (though) _Though it teaches valuable lessons, a bridge failure is a tragedy._

2. a. Studying engineering failures teaches valuable lessons.

   b. Studying engineering failures should not be the only approach.

   (despite the fact that) _____

   _____

   (even though) _____

   _____

3. a. Students need to participate in real-life projects.

   b. Students need to study past engineering projects.

   (although) _____

   _____

   (while) _____

   _____

**B. COMPOSE** Think of your own ideas. Then discuss them with a partner. Identify the argument and counterargument in each sentence.

1. Even though the original hypothesis about the Tacoma Narrows bridge was wrong, ____.

2. Although ____, engineers should always study past projects.

3. Despite the fact that ____, the students were happy they had participated in the project.

4. Though real-life projects are great experiences for students, ____.

5. While I enjoyed the lectures in that class, ____.

**iQ** PRACTICE   Go online for more practice with adverb clauses of concession. *Practice > Unit 8 > Activities 11–12*

**UNIT ASSIGNMENT**  Write a persuasive essay

**OBJECTIVE ▶**

In this assignment, you are going to write a five-paragraph persuasive essay about whether failure can lead to success. As you prepare to write, think about the Unit Question, "Can failure lead to success?" Use information from Reading 1, Reading 2, the unit video, and your work in this unit to support your paragraph. Refer to the Self-Assessment checklist on page 241.

**iQ** PRACTICE   Go online to the Writing Tutor to read a model persuasive essay. *Practice › Unit 8 › Activity 13*

# PLAN AND WRITE

**A. BRAINSTORM** Follow these steps to help you organize your ideas.

1. Work in groups. Discuss the questions based on your experience.

   • What are some different ways to learn?

   • How do you learn best?

   • What are some examples of experiential learning?

   • What are some examples of student projects?

   • Is project-based learning better in some fields than others?

   • Can we learn from past failures? What about successes?

   • What are some ways you have put lessons learned from failures into practice?

   • What is the best way to put lessons learned into practice?

2. Can failure lead to success? Choose your topic and complete the T-chart with your ideas.

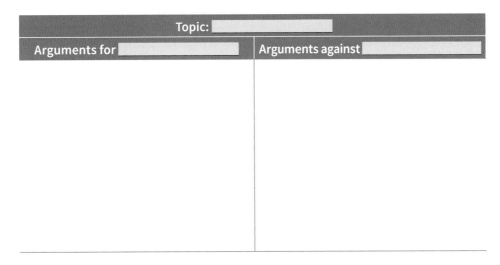

| Topic: | |
|---|---|
| **Arguments for** | **Arguments against** |
| | |

**B. PLAN** Follow these steps to plan your essay. Review the *Arguments for* in question 2 in Activity A. Then complete the chart below. Choose three arguments to persuade your reader that yours is the best way to put lessons learned into practice. Review the *Arguments against* and think of possible counterarguments. Then respond to them with refutations.

| Arguments for | Counterarguments | Refutations |
|---|---|---|
| 1. | | |
| 2. | | |
| 3. | | |

**iQ** RESOURCES  Go online to download and complete the outline for your persuasive essay. *Resources › Writing Tools › Unit 8 › Outline*

**C. WRITE** Use your planning notes to write your essay.

1. Write your persuasive essay. Remember to use arguments, counterarguments, and refutations to persuade your audience.

2. Look at the Self-Assessment checklist on page 241 to guide your writing.

**iQ** PRACTICE  Go online to the Writing Tutor to write your assignment. *Practice › Unit 8 › Activity 14*

**WRITING TIP**

You may wish to research quotations to provide facts and opinions that support your ideas. It is important to give the sources for any ideas that you use in your own writing, whether you paraphrase or quote the original words.

# REVISE AND EDIT

**iQ** RESOURCES  Go online to download the peer review worksheet.
*Resources* › *Writing Tools* › *Unit 8* › *Peer Review Worksheet*

**A. PEER REVIEW**  Read your partner's essay. Then use the peer review worksheet. Discuss the review with your partner.

**B. REWRITE**  Based on your partner's review, revise and rewrite your essay.

**C. EDIT**  Complete the Self-Assessment checklist as you prepare to write the final draft of your essay. Be prepared to hand in your work or discuss it in class.

| SELF-ASSESSMENT | Yes | No |
|---|---|---|
| Is there a thesis statement that clearly expresses the position? | ☐ | ☐ |
| Does the essay build a convincing argument using facts, evidence, and examples? | ☐ | ☐ |
| Are counterarguments and refutations appropriate and introduced clearly? | ☐ | ☐ |
| Is there a conclusion that summarizes the arguments? | ☐ | ☐ |
| Are adverb clauses of concession used appropriately? | ☐ | ☐ |
| Are collocations with prepositions used correctly? | ☐ | ☐ |
| Does the essay include vocabulary from the unit? | ☐ | ☐ |
| Did you check the essay for punctuation, spelling, and grammar? | ☐ | ☐ |

**D. REFLECT**  Discuss these questions with a partner or group.

1. What is something new you learned in this unit?

2. Look back at the Unit Question—Can failure lead to success? Is your answer different now than when you started the unit? If yes, how is it different? Why?

**iQ** PRACTICE  Go to the online discussion board to discuss the questions.
*Practice* › *Unit 8* › *Activity 15*

# TRACK YOUR SUCCESS

**iQ** PRACTICE   Go online to check the words and phrases you have learned in this unit. *Practice > Unit 8 > Activity 16*

Check (✓) the skills and strategies you learned. If you need more work on a skill, refer to the page(s) in parentheses.

| | |
|---|---|
| CRITICAL THINKING | ☐ I can hypothesize. (p. 220) |
| READING | ☐ I can identify counterarguments and refutations. (p. 223) |
| VOCABULARY | ☐ I can recognize and use collocations with prepositions. (p. 231) |
| WRITING | ☐ I can write a persuasive essay. (p. 233) |
| GRAMMAR | ☐ I can recognize and use adverb clauses of concession. (p. 237) |
| OBJECTIVE ▶ | ☐ I can gather information and ideas to write a persuasive essay about whether failure can lead to success. |

# VOCABULARY LIST AND CEFR CORRELATION

⚡+ The **Oxford 5000™** is an expanded core word list for advanced learners of English. The words have been chosen based on their frequency in the Oxford English Corpus and relevance to learners of English. As well as the Oxford 3000™ core word list, the Oxford 5000 includes an additional 2,000 words that are aligned to the CEFR, guiding advanced learners at B2-C1 level on the most useful high-level words to learn to expand their vocabulary.

OPAL The **Oxford Phrasal Academic Lexicon** is an essential guide to the most important words and phrases to know for academic English. The word lists are based on the Oxford Corpus of Academic English and the British Academic Spoken English corpus.

The **Common European Framework of Reference for Language (CEFR)** provides a basic description of what language learners have to do to use language effectively. The system contains 6 reference levels: A1, A2, B1, B2, C1, C2.

## UNIT 1

achievement *(n.)* ⚡+ OPAL B1
acknowledged for *(adj. phr.)* B2
adversity *(n.)* C1
advocate *(n.)* ⚡+ C1
aspire to *(v. phr.)* ⚡+ C1
authenticity *(n.)* C1
cause *(n.)* ⚡+ OPAL A2
confront *(v.)* ⚡+ C1
constrained *(adj.)* OPAL C1
diverse *(adj.)* ⚡+ OPAL B2
embody *(v.)* ⚡+ OPAL C1
empower *(v.)* ⚡+ OPAL C1
exponential *(adj.)* C2
funding *(n.)* ⚡+ OPAL B2
humanitarian *(adj.)* ⚡+ C1
humility *(n.)* C2
inclined *(adj.)* ⚡+ C1
inherently *(adv.)* C1
perceive *(v.)* ⚡+ OPAL B2
personify *(v.)* C2
phenomenon *(n.)* ⚡+ OPAL B2
pursue *(adj.)* ⚡+ B2
resolve *(n.)* ⚡+ OPAL B2
version *(n.)* ⚡+ OPAL B1

## UNIT 2

activation *(n.)* ⚡+ C1
align *(v.)* ⚡+ C1

allure *(n.)* C2
assume *(v.)* ⚡+ OPAL B2
broadly speaking *(adv. phr.)* B2
counter *(v.)* ⚡+ C1
crave *(v.)* C2
disclose *(v.)* ⚡+ C1
distinct *(adj.)* ⚡+ OPAL B2
endorse *(v.)* ⚡+ C1
escalate *(v.)* ⚡+ C1
essentially *(adv.)* ⚡+ OPAL B2
exaggerated *(adj.)* ⚡+ C1
functional *(adj.)* ⚡+ OPAL C1
impulsive *(adj.)* C1
insight *(n.)* ⚡+ OPAL B2
manipulate *(v.)* ⚡+ C1
metric *(n.)* C2
obsession *(n.)* ⚡+ C1
put a premium on *(v. phr.)* C2
resistance *(n.)* ⚡+ OPAL C1
tactic *(n.)* ⚡+ C1
tolerant *(adj.)* C1
transparency *(n.)* ⚡+ C1

## UNIT 3

anxiety *(n.)* ⚡+ OPAL B2
attribute *(v.)* ⚡+ OPAL C1
barrier *(n.)* ⚡+ OPAL B2
coping *(n.)* ⚡+ B2

courage *(n.)* ⚡+ B2
empathy *(n.)* C1
encounter *(v.)* ⚡+ OPAL B2
extensive *(adj.)* ⚡+ OPAL B2
fit in *(v. phr.)* B2
foundation *(n.)* ⚡+ B2
hesitation *(n.)* C1
interaction *(n.)* ⚡+ OPAL B2
intervention *(n.)* ⚡+ OPAL C1
negotiate *(v.)* ⚡+ B2
petrified *(adj.)* C2
pitch in *(v. phr.)* C2
refrain *(n.)* C2
self-fulfillment *(n.)* C2
shame *(n.)* ⚡+ B2
tragic *(adj.)* ⚡+ B2
void *(n.)* C2
work ethic *(n. phr.)* C2
wounded *(adj.)* ⚡+ B2

## UNIT 4

absorb *(v.)* ⚡+ B2
alleviate *(v.)* C1
caution *(v.)* ⚡+ C1
dedicated *(adj.)* ⚡+ C1
developing *(adj.)* B1
drought *(n.)* ⚡+ B2
enterprise *(n.)* ⚡+ C1
existence *(n.)* ⚡+ OPAL B2

extract *(v.)* ⚷+ B2
framework *(n.)* ⚷+ OPAL B2
generate *(v.)* ⚷+ OPAL B2
grid *(n.)* ⚷+ C1
implication *(n.)* ⚷+ B2
innovative *(adj.)* ⚷+ B2
intuitively *(adv.)* C1
motion *(n.)* ⚷+ B2
organic *(adj.)* ⚷+ B2
porous *(adj.)* C2
potentially *(adv.)* ⚷+ OPAL B2
premise *(n.)* ⚷+ C1
replacement *(n.)* ⚷+ OPAL C1
resemble *(v.)* ⚷+ C1
shortage *(n.)* ⚷+ B2
yield *(n.)* ⚷+ OPAL C1

## UNIT 5

access *(n.)* ⚷+ OPAL B1
approach *(n.)* ⚷+ OPAL B2
benefit *(n.)* ⚷+ OPAL A2
beverage *(n.)* C1
challenge *(v.)* ⚷+ OPAL B2
complexity *(n.)* ⚷+ OPAL C1
eliminate *(v.)* ⚷+ OPAL B2
encourage *(v.)* ⚷+ OPAL B1
expert *(n.)* ⚷+ OPAL A2
finding *(n.)* ⚷+ OPAL B2
follow through with *(v. phr.)*
    C1
genetic *(adj.)* ⚷+ B2
ingest *(v.)* C2
initial *(adj.)* ⚷+ OPAL B2
link *(n.)* ⚷+ OPAL A2
metabolize *(v.)* C2
participate *(v.)* ⚷+ OPAL B1
physical *(adj.)* ⚷+ OPAL A2
physician *(n.)* ⚷+ C1
practical *(adj.)* ⚷+ OPAL B1
promising *(adj.)* ⚷+ B2
series *(n.)* ⚷+ OPAL A2

thus *(adv.)* ⚷+ OPAL B2
variation *(n.)* ⚷+ OPAL B2

## UNIT 6

acquire *(v.)* ⚷+ OPAL B2
adjust *(v.)* ⚷+ OPAL B2
ambiguous *(adj.)* C1
analyze *(v.)* ⚷+ B1
anticipate *(v.)* ⚷+ B2
approach *(v.)* ⚷+ B2
collaborative *(adj.)* C1
constant *(adj.)* ⚷+ OPAL B2
contact *(v.)* ⚷+ B1
enable *(v.)* ⚷+ OPAL B2
expertise *(n.)* ⚷+ OPAL B2
fixed *(adj.)* ⚷+ B1
incentive *(n.)* ⚷+ B2
income *(n.)* ⚷+ B2
institution *(n.)* ⚷+ B2
interpret *(v.)* ⚷+ OPAL B2
particular *(adj.)* ⚷+ OPAL A2
pattern *(n.)* ⚷+ OPAL A2
permanent *(adj.)* ⚷+ B2
predictable *(adj.)* ⚷+ B2
reluctant *(adj.)* ⚷+ C1
transition *(n.)* ⚷+ OPAL B2
utilize *(v.)* ⚷+ OPAL C1

## UNIT 7

abundant *(adj.)* C1
accommodate *(v.)* ⚷+ B2
alliance *(n.)* ⚷+ C1
ample *(adj.)* C1
controversial *(adj.)* ⚷+ B2
disperse *(v.)* C1
dread *(v.)* C1
ecological *(adj.)* ⚷+ OPAL C1
empirical *(adj.)* ⚷+ OPAL C1
evidence *(n.)* ⚷+ OPAL A2
expedition *(n.)* ⚷+ B1
habitat *(n.)* ⚷+ B2

intervene *(v.)* ⚷+ OPAL C1
overwhelmingly *(adv.)* C1
preliminary *(adj.)* ⚷+ C1
propose *(v.)* ⚷+ OPAL B2
reserves *(n.)* ⚷+ B2
resilient *(adj.)* C1
reveal *(v.)* ⚷+ OPAL B2
significant *(adj.)* ⚷+ OPAL B2
sophisticated *(adj.)* ⚷+ B2
sufficient *(adj.)* ⚷+ OPAL B2
sustainable *(adj.)* ⚷+ B2
unduly *(adv.)* C2

## UNIT 8

alleviation *(n.)* C2
attach *(v.)* ⚷+ B1
charity *(n.)* ⚷+ A2
convenience *(n.)* ⚷+ B2
criteria *(n.)* ⚷+ OPAL B2
cumulative *(adj.)* OPAL C2
faculty *(n.)* ⚷+ C1
flexible *(adj.)* ⚷+ OPAL B2
fragile *(adj.)* ⚷+ C1
incur *(v.)* ⚷+ C1
induce *(v.)* ⚷+ OPAL C1
locale *(n.)* C2
methodology *(n.)* ⚷+ OPAL C1
output *(n.)* ⚷+ OPAL B2
prevail *(v.)* ⚷+ C1
ratio *(n.)* ⚷+ OPAL C1
relevance *(n.)* ⚷+ OPAL C1
respective *(adj.)* ⚷+ C1
stabilize *(v.)* ⚷+ OPAL C1
substantial *(adj.)* ⚷+ OPAL C1
susceptible *(adj.)* C1
twist *(v.)* ⚷+ C1
vague *(adj.)* ⚷+ C1
vibrate *(v.)* C2

# AUTHORS AND CONSULTANTS

## AUTHORS

**Debra Daise** teaches at the University of North Carolina at Charlotte after many years of teaching in Colorado. She has long been interested in helping students develop a love for reading and writing.

**Charl Norloff** taught ESL at the University of Colorado for 30 years. Prior to that, she taught EFL in the Middle East. She has a special interest in teaching reading and writing to help students prepare for academic success.

## SERIES CONSULTANTS

**Lawrence J. Zwier** holds an M.A. in TESL from the University of Minnesota. He is currently the Associate Director for Curriculum Development at the English Language Center at Michigan State University in East Lansing. He has taught ESL/EFL in the United States, Saudi Arabia, Malaysia, Japan, and Singapore.

**Marguerite Ann Snow** holds a Ph.D. in Applied Linguistics from UCLA. She teaches in the TESOL M.A. program in the Charter College of Education at California State University, Los Angeles. She was a Fulbright scholar in Hong Kong and Cyprus. In 2006, she received the President's Distinguished Professor award at CSULA. She has trained ESL teachers in the United States and EFL teachers in more than 25 countries. She is the author/editor of numerous publications in the areas of content-based instruction, English for academic purposes, and standards for English teaching and learning. She is a co-editor of *Teaching English as a Second or Foreign Language* (4th ed.).

**CRITICAL THINKING CONSULTANT** **James Dunn** is a Junior Associate Professor at Tokai University and the Coordinator of the JALT Critical Thinking Special Interest Group. His research interests include Critical Thinking skills' impact on student brain function during English learning, as measured by EEG. His educational goals are to help students understand that they are capable of more than they might think and to expand their cultural competence with critical thinking and higher-order thinking skills.

**ASSESSMENT CONSULTANT** **Elaine Boyd** has worked in assessment for over 30 years for international testing organizations. She has designed and delivered courses in assessment literacy and is also the author of several EL exam coursebooks for leading publishers. She is an Associate Tutor (M.A. TESOL/Linguistics) at University College, London. Her research interests are classroom assessment, issues in managing feedback, and intercultural competences.

**VOCABULARY CONSULTANT** **Cheryl Boyd Zimmerman** is Professor Emeritus at California State University, Fullerton. She specialized in second-language vocabulary acquisition, an area in which she is widely published. She taught graduate courses on second-language acquisition, culture, vocabulary, and the fundamentals of TESOL, and has been a frequent invited speaker on topics related to vocabulary teaching and learning. She is the author of *Word Knowledge: A Vocabulary Teacher's Handbook* and Series Director of *Inside Reading, Inside Writing*, and *Inside Listening and Speaking* published by Oxford University Press.

**ONLINE INTEGRATION** **Chantal Hemmi** holds an Ed.D. TEFL and is a Japan-based teacher trainer and curriculum designer. Since leaving her position as Academic Director of the British Council in Tokyo, she has been teaching at the Center for Language Education and Research at Sophia University on an EAP/CLIL program offered for undergraduates. She delivers lectures and teacher trainings throughout Japan, Indonesia, and Malaysia.

**COMMUNICATIVE GRAMMAR CONSULTANT** **Nancy Schoenfeld** holds an M.A. in TESOL from Biola University in La Mirada, California, and has been an English language instructor since 2000. She has taught ESL in California and Hawaii, and EFL in Thailand and Kuwait. She has also trained teachers in the United States and Indonesia. Her interests include teaching vocabulary, extensive reading, and student motivation. She is currently an English Language Instructor at Kuwait University.